ESSAYS

AND

TREASURE TROVE

BY

FRANCES RIDLEY HAVERGAL

"Knowing her intense desire that Christ should be magnified, whether
by her life or in her death, may it be to His glory
that in these pages she, being dead,
'Yet speaketh ! ' "

Taken from the Edition of *The Complete Works of Frances Ridley Havergal.*

David L. Chalkley, Editor   Dr. Glen T. Wegge, Associate Editor

ISBN 978-1-937236-19-9   Library of Congress: 2011919008

Book cover by Sherry Goodwin and David Carter.

CONTENTS.

ANNOUNCING THE HAVERGAL EDITION
NOW IN PREPARATION FOR PUBLICATION

The edition of *The Complete Works of Frances Ridley Havergal* has five parts:

Volume I *Behold Your King:*
The Complete Poetical Works of Frances Ridley Havergal

Volume II *Whose I Am and Whom I Serve:*
Prose Works of Frances Ridley Havergal

Volume III *Loving Messages for the Little Ones:*
Works for Children by Frances Ridley Havergal

Volume IV *Love for Love: Frances Ridley Havergal:*
Memorials, Letters and Biographical Works

Volume V *Songs of Truth and Love:*
Music by Frances Ridley Havergal and William Henry Havergal

David L. Chalkley, Editor   Dr. Glen T. Wegge, Music Editor

The Music of Frances Ridley Havergal by Glen T. Wegge, Ph.D.

This Companion Volume to the Havergal edition is a valuable presentation of F.R.H.'s extant scores. Except for a very few of her hymntunes published in hymnbooks, most or nearly all of F.R.H.'s scores have been very little—if any at all—seen, or even known of, for nearly a century. What a valuable body of music has been unknown for so long and is now made available to many. Dr. Wegge completed his Ph.D. in Music Theory at Indiana University at Bloomington, and his diligence and thoroughness in this volume are obvious. First an analysis of F.R.H.'s compositions is given, an essay that both addresses the most advanced musicians and also reaches those who are untrained in music; then all the extant scores that have been found are newly typeset, with complete texts for each score and extensive indices at the end of the book. This volume presents F.R.H.'s music in newly typeset scores diligently prepared by Dr. Wegge, and Volume V of the Havergal edition presents the scores in facsimile, the original 19th century scores. (The essay—a dissertation—analysing her scores is given the same both in this Companion Volume and in Volume V of the Havergal edition.)

Dr. Wegge is also preparing all of these scores for publication in performance folio editions.

A.D. 62.

Paul^a and certain other prisoners unto one named Julius, a centurion of Augustus' band.

2 And entering into a ship of Adramyttium, we launched, meaning to sail by the coasts of Asia; one Aristarchus,^f a Macedonian of Thessalonica, being with us.

3 And the next day we touched at Sidon. And Julius courteously entreated^i Paul, and gave him liberty to go unto his friends to refresh himself.

4 And when we had launched from thence, we sailed under Cyprus, because the winds were contrary. See c. 24. 1. 7.

5 And when we had sailed over the sea of Cilicia, and Pamphylia, we came to Myra, a city of Lycia.

6 And there the centurion found a ship of Alexandria sailing into Italy; and he put us therein.

7 And when we had sailed slowly many days, and scarce were come over against Cnidus, the wind not suffering us, we sailed under β Crete, over against Salmone;

8 And, hardly passing it, came unto a place which is called The fair havens; nigh whereunto was the city of Lasea.

9 Now when much time was spent, and when sailing was now dangerous, because the γ fast was now already past, Paul admonished them,

10 And said unto them, Sirs, I per-

a ch.25.12,25.
b chap.23.11.
c He. 1. 14.
d De. 32. 9.
Ps. 135. 4.
Is. 44. 5.
Mal. 3. 17.
Jno.17. 9,10
1 Co. 6. 20.
1 Pe.2.9,10.
e Ps. 116. 16.
Is. 44. 21.
Da. 3. 17.
6. 16.
f John 12. 26.
Ro. 1. 9.
2 Ti. 1. 3.
g Ge.19.21,29
h Lu. 1. 45.
Ro. 4. 20,21.
2 Ti. 1. 12.
i chap.24. 23.
28.16.
k chap. 28. 1.
l Ps. 130. 6.
β or, Candy.
γ The Fast was on the tenth day of

23 For there stood by me this night^b the^j angel^c of God, whose^d I am, and whom^e I serve,

24 Saying, Fear not, Paul; thou must be brought before Cæsar: and, lo, God hath given thee^g all them that sail with thee.

25 Wherefore, sirs, be of good cheer; for I^h believe God, that it shall be even^v as it was told me.

26 Howbeit, we must be cast upon a certain island.^k

27 But when the fourteenth night was come, as we were driven up and down in Adria, about midnight the shipmen deemed that they drew near to some country;

28 And sounded, and found it twenty fathoms: and when they had gone a little further, they sounded again, and found it fifteen fathoms.

29 Then fearing lest they should have fallen upon rocks, they cast four anchors out of the stern, and wished^l for the day.

30 And as the shipmen were about to flee out of the ship, when they had let down the boat into the sea, under colour as though they would have cast anchors out of the foreship,

31 Paul said to the centurion and to the soldiers, Except these abide in the ship, ye cannot be saved.

32 Then the soldiers cut off the ropes of the boat, and let her fall off.

This is part of Acts 27 in F.R.H.'s Bagster study Bible. Verse 23 " . . . whose I am and whom I serve."

LIST OF ILLUSTRATIONS.

Love for Love.

1 JOHN 4:16.

KNOWING that the God on high,
    With a tender Father's grace,
Waits to hear your faintest cry,
    Waits to show a Father's face,—
Stay and think!—oh, should not you
Love this gracious Father too?

Knowing Christ was crucified,
　　Knowing that He loves you now
Just as much as when He died
　　With the thorns upon His brow,—
Stay and think!—oh, should not you
Love this blessèd Saviour too?

Knowing that a Spirit strives
　　With your weary, wandering heart,
Who can change the restless lives,
　　Pure and perfect peace impart,—
Stay and think!—oh, should not you
Love this loving Spirit too?

Frances Ridley Havergal February 12, 1879

Accepted.

'Accepted in the Beloved.'—EPHESIANS 1:6. 'Perfect in Christ Jesus.'—COLOSSIANS 1:28.
'Complete in Him.'—COLOSSIANS 2:10.

ACCEPTED, Perfect, and Complete,
For God's inheritance made meet!
How true, how glorious, and how sweet!

In the Belovèd—by the King
Accepted, though not anything
But forfeit lives had we to bring.

And Perfect in Christ Jesus made,
On Him our great transgressions laid,
We in His righteousness arrayed.

Complete in Him, our glorious Head,
With Jesus raisèd from the dead,
And by His mighty Spirit led!

O blessèd Lord, is this for me?
Then let my whole life henceforth be
One Alleluia-song to Thee!

F.R.H. September 3, 1870

Covenant Blessings.

'He hath made with me an everlasting covenant, ordered in all things, and sure.'
—2 Samuel 23:5.

Jehovah's Covenant shall endure,
All ordered, everlasting, sure!
O child of God, rejoice to trace
Thy portion in its glorious grace.

'Tis thine, for Christ is given to be
The Covenant of God to thee:
In Him, God's golden scroll of light,
The darkest truths are clear and bright.

O sorrowing sinner, well He knew,
Ere time began, what He would do!
Then rest thy hope within the veil;
His covenant mercies shall not fail.

O doubting one, the Eternal Three
Are pledged in faithfulness for thee;
Claim every promise, sweet and sure,
By covenant oath of God secure.

O waiting one, each moment's fall
Is marked by love that planned them all;
Thy times, all ordered by His hand,
In God's eternal covenant stand.

O feeble one, look up and see
Strong consolation sworn for thee;
Jehovah's glorious arm is shown,
His covenant strength is all thine own.

O mourning one, each stroke of love
A covenant blessing yet shall prove;
His covenant love shall be thy stay;
His covenant grace be as thy day.

O Love that chose, O Love that died,
O Love that sealed and sanctified!
All glory, glory, glory be,
O covenant Triune God, to Thee!

F.R.H. 1871

ONE HOUR WITH JESUS.

"What! could ye not watch with Me one hour?"

BY

FRANCES RIDLEY HAVERGAL.

LONDON:

S. W. PARTRIDGE & CO. PATERNOSTER ROW.

NISBET & CO., 21, BERNERS STREET.

BIRMINGHAM: C. CASWELL.

ONE PENNY.

The First Epistle general of JOHN.

CHAPTER I.

THAT which was from the [a] beginning, which we have heard, which we have seen [c] with our eyes, which we have looked upon, and our hands have [d] handled, of the Word of life;

2 (For the life was manifested, and we have seen *it*, and bear witness, and shew unto you that eternal life,[f] which was with the Father, and was manifested unto us;)

3 That which we have seen and heard declare we unto you, that ye also may have fellowship with us: and truly our fellowship[i] *is* with the Father, and with his Son Jesus Christ.

4 And these things write we unto you, that[n] your joy may be full.

5 This then is the message which we have heard of him, and declare unto you, that God is light,[r] and in him is no darkness at all.

6 If we say that we have fellowship with him, and walk in darkness, we lie, and do not the truth: [Jo. 9. 12. 4. 12. 46.]

7 But if we walk[t] in the light, as he is in the light, we have fellowship one with another, and the blood[z] of Jesus Christ his Son cleanseth us from all sin. [He. 13. 12.]

8 If we say that we have no sin,[v] we deceive ourselves, and the truth is not in us.

9 If we confess[z] our sins, he is faithful and just to forgive us *our* sins, and to cleanse[b] us from all unrighteousness. [Is. 6. 7.]

10 If we say that we have not sinned, we make him a liar, and his word is not in us.

CHAPTER II.

MY little children, these things write I unto you, that ye sin not. And if any man sin, we have an advocate[a] with the Father, Jesus Christ the righteous: [2 a. 3. 5?]

2 And he is the propitiation[d] for our sins; and not for our's only, but also for *the sins of* the whole world.

3 And hereby we do know that we know him, if we keep[k] his commandments.

4 He that saith, I know him, and keepeth not his commandments, is a liar, and the truth is not in him.

5 But whoso keepeth his word, in him verily is the love of God perfected: hereby know we that we are in him.

6 He that saith he abideth[m] in him, ought himself also so to walk,[n] even as he walked. [1 Pe. 2. 21. P. 16. 13.]

7 Brethren, I write no new commandment unto you, but an old commandment, which ye had from the beginning. The old commandment is the word which ye have heard from the beginning.

8 Again, a new[q] commandment I write unto you; which thing is true in him and in you, because the darkness[r] is past, and the true light now shineth.

9 He that saith he is in the light, and hateth his brother, is in darkness[s] even until now.

10 He that loveth his brother abideth in the light, and there is none[γ] occasion of stumbling in him.

11 But he that hateth his brother is in darkness, and walketh[u] in darkness, and knoweth not whither he goeth, because that darkness hath blinded his eyes.

12 I write unto you, little children, because your sins are forgiven you for his name's[y] sake. [Ph. 3. 9. Ep. 4. 32, 33.]

---

a Jno. 1. 1, &c.
b chap. 1. 1.
c 2 Pe. 1. 16.
d Lu. 24. 39.
e Jno. 14. 7, 9.
f Jno. 17. 3.
g Ep. 6. 10.
h John 15. 7.
i Re. 2. 7, &c.
k Ro. 12. 2.
l John 17. 21.
m Mat. 6. 24.
Ga. 1. 10.
Ja. 4. 4.
n John 15. 11.
o 2 Pe. 2. 10.
p Ps. 119. 37.
q Ps. 73. 6.
r John 1. 4, 9.
1 Ti. 6. 16.
s Ps. 39. 6.
1 Co. 7. 31.
t John 12. 35.
u He. 1. 2.
w Mat. 24. 24.
1 Ti. 4. 1.
x Ep. 1. 7.
He. 9. 14.
1 Pe. 1. 19.
Re. 1. 5.
y 1 Ki. 8. 46.
Job 25. 4.
Ec. 7. 20.
Ja. 3. 2.
z Job 33. 27, 28.
Ps. 32. 5.
Pr. 28. 13.
a 2 Ti. 2. 19.
b Ps. 51. 2.
1 Co. 6. 11.
c 2 Ti. 3. 9.
d 2 Co. 1. 21.
e 1 Co. 2. 15.
f Ro. 8. 34.
He. 7. 25.
g Ro. 3. 25.
h chap. 4. 3.
i John 15. 23.
k Lu. 6. 46.
John 14. 15, 23.
l 2 John 6.
m John 15. 4, 5.
n John 13. 15.
o John 17. 3.
p John 14. 26.
q John 13. 34.
r Ro. 13. 12.
β or, *it.*
s 2 Pe. 1. 9.
γ *scandal.*
δ or, *know ye.*
t Je. 13. 23.
Mat. 7. 16, 18.
u Pr. 4. 25.
John 12. 35.
v Ep. 2. 4, 5.
w John 1. 12.
Re. 21. 7.
x John 17. 25.
y Ps. 25. 11.
Lu. 24. 47.
z Ro. 8. 14, 18.

---

13 I write unto you, fathers, because ye have known him[b] *that is* from the beginning. I write unto you, young men, because ye have overcome the wicked one. I write unto you, little children, because ye have known the Father.[e]

14 I have written unto you, fathers, because ye have known him *that is* from the beginning. I have written unto you, young men, because ye are strong,[g] and the word of God abideth[h] in you, and ye have overcome[i] the wicked one.

15 Love[k] not the world, neither the things *that are* in the world. If[m] any man love the world, the love of the Father is not in him.

16 For all that *is* in the world, the lust[n] of the flesh,[o] and the lust of the[p] eyes, and the pride[q] of life, is not of the Father, but is of the world.

17 And[s] the world passeth away, and the lust thereof: but he that doeth the will of God abideth for ever.

18 Little children, it is the last[u] time: and as ye have heard[w] that antichrist shall come, even now are there many antichrists; whereby we know that it is the last time.

19 They went out from us, but they were not of us; for[a] if they had been of us, they would *no doubt* have continued with us: but *they went out,* that they might be made manifest[c] that they were not all of us.

20 But ye have an unction[d] from the Holy One, and ye know[e] all things.

21 I have not written unto you because ye know not the truth, but because ye know it, and that no lie is of the truth.

22 Who is a liar, but he that[h] denieth that Jesus is the Christ? He is antichrist, that denieth the Father and the Son.

23 Whosoever[i] denieth the Son, the same hath not the Father: [*but*] *he that acknowledgeth the Son, hath the Father also.*

24 Let[l] that therefore abide in you, which ye have heard from the beginning. If that which ye have heard from the beginning shall remain in you, ye also shall continue in the Son, and in the Father.

25 And this is the promise that he hath promised us, *even* eternal[o] life.

26 These *things* have I written unto you concerning them that seduce you.

27 But the anointing which ye have received of him abideth[q] in you, and ye need not that any man teach you: but as[r] the same anointing teacheth[β] you of all things, and is truth, and is no lie, and even as it hath taught you, ye shall abide in[β] him.

28 And now, little children, abide in[β] him; that, when he shall appear, we may have confidence, and not be ashamed before him at his coming.

29 If ye know that he is righteous, ye know that[t] every one that doeth righteousness is born of him.

CHAPTER III.

BEHOLD, what manner of love[v] the Father hath bestowed upon us, that we should be called the sons[w] of God: therefore the world[x] knoweth us not, because it knew him not.

2 Beloved, now are we the sons[a] of

173

One Hour with Jesus.

"What! could ye not watch with Me one hour?"

AN echo of this utterance of pathetic surprise, this wonderfully gentle reproof, seems to float around a matter of daily experience, and, with too many, of daily faithlessness. Our Divine Master has called us to no Gethsemane-watch of strange and mysterious darkness. It is while the brightness of day is breaking—perhaps even long after it has broken—that His call to communion with Himself reaches our not always willing ear. "Come with me!" (Song of Solomon 4:8). And the drowsy reply too often is, "Presently, Lord! not just this minute!"

And then, after "yet a little sleep, a little slumber, a little folding of the hands to sleep," the precious hour is past which "might have been" so full of blessing.

"What! could ye not watch with Me one hour?"

What is the practical answer of very many of His disciples?

"Oh, *yes!* very easily and readily, when the 'one hour' is at night, and we do not feel particularly inclined to go to bed, especially if we have a nice fire to 'watch' by. But oh, *no!* if the 'one hour' involves getting up at seven instead of eight, especially on a cold and gloomy morning. *That* is a very different matter!"

Were the question asked, "What one thing do you suppose has most hindered the largest number of Christians this day and this year in their spiritual life and growth?" I should reply unhesitatingly, "Probably the temptation not to rise in time to put on their armour as well as their dress before breakfast."

A mere ten minutes—is that enough preparation for our warfare and provision for our wants; for spreading all our needs and difficulties before the Lord; for telling Jesus all that is in our hearts; for bringing before Him all the details of our work; for searching to know His mind and His will; for storing His word in our hearts; for replenishing our seed-baskets, that we may have something to sow, and getting Him to sharpen our sickles that we may reap; for confession and supplication and intercession, and, above all, for *praise?*

Ten minutes or a quarter of an hour! Is that enough for the many things which He has to say unto us? for the quiet teachings of His Spirit, for the dawning of His light on the dark sayings of old, and the flashing of His glory and power on the words which are spirit and life? Is that enough to spend in converse with the Friend of friends? Does this look as if we really cared very much about Him? Even if it were enough for our small, cool affection, is it enough, think you, for His great love? enough to satisfy the Heart that is waiting to commune with ours? He loves us so much that He will have us with Him forever, and we love Him so little that we did not care to turn out of bed this morning in time to have even half-an-hour of real intercourse with Him. For it would have been "with Him." There was no doubt about His being at the tryst. He slumbered not; "He faileth not"—but we failed. What have we missed this morning! How do we know what He may have had to say to us? What have we missed all the mornings of this past year!

"But it comes to the same thing if I go up-stairs after breakfast!" *Does* it "come to the same thing"? You know perfectly, and by repeated experience, that it *does not.* Letters and newspapers have come; you stay to read them, you must just see what So-and-so says, and what the telegrams are; and then you must just attend to sundry little duties, and then somebody wants you, and then you really ought to go out, and so perhaps you never "go up-stairs" at all. Or, if you do, perhaps your room is not "done," or you are interrupted or called down. Satan is astonishingly ingenious in defeating these good after-breakfast intentions. And yet these external devices are not his strongest. Suppose you do get away after breakfast without external hindrance or interruption, he has other moves to make. Do you not find that the "things which are seen" have got the start of the "things which are not seen"? not necessarily sinful things, but simply the "*other* things entering in" which are "not the things which are Jesus Christ's," yet they choke the word, and hinder prayer. You have an unsettled feeling; you do not feel sure you will not be wanted or interrupted; it is an effort—pretty often an unsuccessful one—to forget the news, public or private, which has come by post; bits of breakfast table-talk come back to mind; voices or sounds in the now stirring household distract you; you ought, you know you ought, to be doing something else at that hour, unless, indeed, you are a drone in the home-hive, or willfully "out of work" as to the Lord's vineyard. And so it does *not* "come to the same thing" at all, but you go forth ungirded to the race, unarmed to the warfare. What marvel if faintness and failure are the order of the day!

I suppose there is not one of us who has not made "good resolutions" about this, and—broken them. And this is not very surprising, considering that "good resolutions" are never mentioned in the Bible as any item of armour or weapons for "the good fight of faith." So let us try something better.

First, *Purpose*. This is what we want; neither languid and lazy wishing, nor fitful and impulsive resolving, but calm and humble and steady purpose, like David's (Psalm 17:3), Daniel's (Daniel 1:8), and St. Paul's (2 Timothy 3:10). Without purpose, even prayer is paralyzed, and answer prevented. Now, have we any purpose in this matter? in other words, do we really *mean* to do what we say we wish to do? If not, let us ask at once that the grace of purpose may be wrought in us by the Spirit of all grace.

Secondly, *Prayer*. Having purposed by His grace, let us ask that our purpose may, also by His grace, be carried into effect. It will not do merely to lament and pray vaguely about it. To-morrow morning will not do; the thing must be done to-night. To-night, then, tell the gracious Master all about it, tell Him of the past disloyalty and sin in this matter, so that you may go to the coming battle strong in the strength of His pardoning love and His cleansing blood, and His tenderly powerful "Go, and sin no more." Do not make a good resolution about all the mornings of your life—His way is "morning by morning" (Isaiah 50:4), and His way is best. Ask Him to give you the grace of energy for this one coming morning, if you are spared to see it. Ask Him to give you a holy night, that you may remember Him upon your bed, and that even the half-conscious moments may be full of Him. Ask Him that when you awake you may be "still with Him," and that He would then enable you unreluctantly to rise, eager and glad to watch with Him "one hour," uninterrupted and quiet, "alone with Jesus."

Even Prayer and Purpose may be neutralized by want of—

Thirdly, *Self-denying Forethought*. We almost make the difficulty for ourselves when we forget that we can not burn a candle at both ends. If we *will* sit up at night, of course we make it harder in proportion to get up in the morning. "I would give anything to be able to get this precious 'one hour'!" says a lie-a-bed Christian, or one who really needs a long night's sleep. No! there is one thing you will not give for it, and that is an hour of your pleasant evenings. It is too much to expect you to leave the cosy fireside, or the delightful book, or the lively circle an hour earlier, so that you may go to bed in good time, and be more ready to rise in the morning. No; you could not really be expected to include *that* in the "anything" you are ready to give for the true "early communion" with your Lord. And yet only try it, and see if the blessing is not a hundredfold more than the little sacrifice.

Perhaps we hardly need say that the habit of reading any ordinary book after we go up-stairs, "only just a few pages, you know," is simply fatal to the sweet and sacred "one hour," whether that night or next morning. Oh, let your own room at any rate be sacred to the One Blessed Guest! Do not keep Him waiting, because you "wanted just to finish a chapter" of any book but His own. Finishing one chapter too often leads to beginning another, and to filling the mind with "other things." And then, "Dear me, I had no idea it was so late!" And, all the while, the King was waiting! What wonder that you find the audience chamber closed, when you at last put down your book!

Will not this be enough? Not quite. Not even Purpose and Prayer and Self-denying Forethought are enough without—

Fourthly, *Trust.* Here is the joint in the harness, the breaking-down point. Praying, and not trusting Him to answer; putting on other pieces of armour, and not covering them all with the shield of faith; asking Him to do something for us, and then not entrusting ourselves to Him to have it done for us. Distrusting one's self is one thing; distrusting Jesus is quite another. No matter at all, nay, so much the better that you feel, "I have failed morning after morning; I am at my wits' end; I can not summon resolution, when the moment comes, to jump up; it is no use making resolutions, I only break them again and again!" Only, do not stop there. "I *can't,* but Jesus *can!*" will settle this, and everything else.

"I *can't* make myself get up, therefore—*i.e.*, just *because* I can't—I will put it into my Lord's hands, and trust Him to make me get up. He will undertake for me even in this." One feels humbled and ashamed to be reduced to this, and rightly enough; it proves how despicably weak we are. The apparent smallness of the trial enhances the greatness of the failure. It adds new force to "Without Me ye can do nothing," when conscience whispers, "Exactly so! nothing! not even get out of bed at the right moment!"

But it is when we have come to this point, and see that all the strength of ourselves and our resolutions *is* utter weakness, that we see there is nothing for it but to say, "Jesus, I will trust *Thee!*" Say that to Him to-night with reference to this often lost battle. Trust, simply and really *trust,* Him to win it for you, and you will see that He will not disappoint your trust. He NEVER does! The secret of success is trust in Him who "faileth not," and learning this secret in this one thing, may and should lead you to trust, and therefore to succeed, in many another battle. For—

> "From victory to victory
> His army shall be led."

But what about His suffering ones, His physically weak ones, who can not or must not rise early? How glad we are that the true reason or motive is "opened unto the eyes of Him with whom we have to do," the High-Priest who is "touched with the feeling of our infirmities!" He knows these cases, and, "in some way or other, the Lord will provide"; His grace will be sufficient, and that which is spiritual loss, if arising from our own indolence, will be turned into spiritual gain if arising from His accepted chastening. I think our dear Master will see to it that these shall not be losers; He will give opportunity, and grace to take it; He can even give quietness and communion amid the mid-day surroundings. Still, unquestionably, special watchfulness and special grace are needed, when, through ill-health, the usual early hour can not be secured.

These may surely take all the comfort of His most gracious words, "The spirit indeed is willing, but the flesh is weak." They are never to be perverted into excuse for sinful indolence; and it is never to be allowed that our Lord could have spoken excusingly of that flesh figurative, which is to be crucified, mortified, reckoned dead, given no quarter whatever. But they are gracious indeed, as referring to this literal mortal flesh in which the life of Jesus is to be made manifest, the body of which He is the Saviour, the frame which He tenderly "remembereth." Many a mistake arises from confusing these two distinct meanings of the word.

Some who are not invalids, have yet great difficulties, owing to household arrangements over which they have no control. Since these thoughts were first printed, I have received so many touching letters from younger or dependent members of Christian households, that I can not refuse to insert a loving appeal to my senior friends not to hinder any under their roofs in this most important matter. A late or uncertain hour for evening prayers is a more serious hindrance to young or delicate persons, or those who have had a busy day, than they imagine. "They do not like me to leave the room before prayers; and afterwards I am so tired that I really *can't* enjoy my Bible as I wish." If "*they*" only knew how the stereotyped domestic arrangements are hindering the grace of God in the heart of daughter, visitor, governess, or servant, surely, oh, surely! it would not be thought too great a sacrifice to "have prayers a little earlier." At *least,* no hindrance by word, or even look, should be placed in the way of any one's slipping away earlier in the evening, for a little time alone with Him *before* they are "too tired," and returning when the bell rings for family worship. Then retiring *immediately* to rest, the inestimable "one hour" in the morning need not be lost through physical weariness which a little kind consideration might avoid. In this matter—

> Evil is wrought by want of thought,
> As well as want of heart.

Let us not forget, but remember in grateful contrast, how many there are who have to be hard at work before our earliest thoughts of rising; to whom "an hour earlier" would be a physical impossibility, the long day's work being followed by unpeaceful evenings in the noisy dwellings of noisy alleys. No quiet for them till long after we are in our quiet rooms; the short interval between the latest sounds of drunkenness and the inexorable factory-bell being perhaps still further shortened by a long distance to walk. And no quiet corner to retire to, no possibility of kneeling "*alone* with Jesus," at any time of day or night! Will not some who thus have to seek Him "in the press," rise up in judgment against us who may have an undisturbed hour alone with Him every morning, if we will?

The following testimony is from one of England's most successful and eminent men of business. He writes:—

"In the busy life I have lived, I owe much to the practice of very early rising to secure the 'hour with Jesus' which you recommend. Even now, I find very early rising essential to the maintenance of spiritual life and close communion with God; and being now somewhat weak physically, nothing but the *desire* for this communion is sufficient to enable me to rise.

"My wife rises about 6, remaining in her room till 8, or she would not, with her large household, be equal, spiritually, to her duties."

Is not this one of the many "new leaves" which onward-pressing pilgrims should desire to turn over with the New Year? And will it not be the truest means of ensuring a Happy New Year? Happier, brighter, holier, more useful and more victorious; more radiant with His Presence and more full of His Power than any previous one.

The time past of our lives may surely suffice us for the neglect of this entirely personal and entirely precious privilege. We have suffered loss enough;—shall we not henceforth, "from this time," seek the gain, the spiritual wealth which this "one hour" will assuredly bring? Cold mornings! well, the good Master who knoweth our frame and its natural shrinking from "His cold" knows all about them. But was there ever an added difficulty for which He could not and would not give added strength and "more grace"? So do not let us wait for the summer mornings which may never be ours to spend in earthly communion, nor even for the childish idea of making a special start on New Year's Day.

When we are "called" *to-morrow* morning, let it remind us of her who "called Mary her sister, saying, The Master is come, and calleth for thee." For

He will certainly be there, waiting for us. What will you do? We know what Mary did. "*As soon as* she heard that, she arose quickly, and came unto Him."

—————❧—————

One Hour with Jesus.

"*What! could ye not watch with Me one hour?*"

BY
Frances Ridley Havergal.

LONDON:
S. W. PARTRIDGE & CO. PATERNOSTER ROW.
NISBET & CO., 21, BERNERS STREET.
BIRMINGHAM: C. CASWELL.

ONE PENNY.

32 And there were also two other, malefactors,[p] led with him to be put to death.

33 And when they were come to the place, which is called βCalvary, there they crucified him, and the malefactors, one on the right hand, and the other on the left.

34 Then said Jesus, Father,[q] forgive them; for they know not what they do. And they parted his raiment, and cast lots.

35 And the people stood beholding. And the rulers also with them[r] derided *him*, saying, He saved others; let him save himself, if he be Christ, the chosen of God.

36 And the soldiers also mocked him, coming to him, and offering him vinegar,

37 And saying, If thou be the king of the Jews, save thyself.

38 And a superscription also was written over him, in letters of Greek, and Latin, and Hebrew, THIS IS THE KING OF THE JEWS.

39 And one[u] of the malefactors which were hanged railed on him, saying, If thou be Christ, save thyself and us.

40 But the other answering, rebuked him, saying, Dost not thou fear[v] God, seeing thou art in the same[x] condemnation?

41 And we indeed justly; for we receive the due reward of our deeds: but this man hath done nothing[y] amiss.

42 And he said unto Jesus, Lord, remember[a] me when thou comest into thy kingdom.

43 And Jesus said unto him, Verily[c] I say unto thee, To day shalt thou be with me in paradise.[d]

44 And it was about the sixth hour, and there was a darkness over all the δearth until the ninth hour.

45 And the sun was darkened, and the veil of the temple was rent in the midst.

46 And when Jesus had cried with a loud voice, he said, Father,[f] into thy hands I commend my spirit: and[g] having said thus, he gave up the ghost.

47 Now when the centurion saw what was done, he glorified God, saying, Certainly this was a righteous man.

48 And all the people that came together to that sight, beholding the things which were done, smote their breasts, and returned.

49 And all his acquaintance, and the

Part of Luke 23 in F.R.H.'s last Bagster study Bible that she read at the end of her life.

"All Things" was a small booklet published by James Nisbet & Co., one of three in the "Bright Thought Series." The other two were "Most Blessed For Ever" (a posthumous collection of pieces by F.R.H., compiled soon after her death sister Maria, no copy yet found in this research) and "Hinderers and Hindrances."

ADDRESS TO YOUNG WOMEN'S CHRISTIAN ASSOCIATION, AT PLYMOUTH, September 1878.

"ALL THINGS."

EVERY year, I might almost say every day that I live, I seem to see more clearly how all the rest and gladness and power of our Christian life hinges on one thing; and that is,—taking God at His word, believing that He really means exactly what He says, and accepting the very words in which He reveals His goodness and grace, without substituting others or altering the precise moods, and tenses which He has seen fit to use. Now scarcely any word is so often altered by His dear children, (let alone outsiders,) as the word "all." Satan can't bear it. He always meets it with a "Yea, hath God said *all?*" It is surprising what a number of substitutionary words he has ready to suggest—" some," "a few," " certain things," and perhaps his favourite is "all—except." Now to whom shall we listen to-day, as we think over a few of the passages where God says "All things"? Will you listen to His word, or will you accept the devil's "all—except"? This is what I want this afternoon,—that we should every one of us simply take God's words about "all things," and my prayer is that the Holy Spirit may apply at least some *one* of the passages to *every* heart, and let it ring on a powerful chime of encouragement or comfort as may be needed, through many days to come. I don't think it very much matters what I say about the texts, they themselves are the message.

In seeking out what God has said about "all things," the texts found seem to group themselves into four sets.

I.   All things are of God.
II. All things are by Jesus Christ.
III. All things are for your sakes.
IV. All things are yours.

I. "All things are *of God.*" (2 Corinthians 5:18.) Here we seem to have a grand foundation laid in the past, and a most beautiful and perfect daily building upon it in the present.

1. Look back for a moment at the foundation, it is very strengthening to do so. Recollect how the great plan of our salvation, yours and mine, was "of God." The great promise of eternal life was "of God," given by Him before the world began, when we were not there to receive it, and therefore given to Jesus to hold for us. Search out, (from memory, or with concordance,) what God did for us before the foundation of the world, how He chose us in Christ, wrote our names in the Lamb's book of life, provided our redemption, and prepared the kingdom for us—think of all this being "of God," and seal it with the words "I know that whatsoever God doeth, it shall be for ever: nothing can be put to it, nor anything taken from it" (Ecclesiastes 3:14). What He hath done cannot be reversed, what is of Him cannot come to naught. Now just let us take the strong consolation of this. For this is the foundation of Christ's promise, "My sheep shall never perish,"—for "salvation is of the Lord" (Jonah 2:9).

2. But many of us have learnt the blessedness of seeing that all this is "of God," who do not quite take the comfort of the daily building upon it.

Now here comes in the splendid fact of the literality of "all things," with no added "except." For see Romans 11:36, John 17:7, 1 Chronicles 29:14. Just look at it! Positively "all things!" All that surrounds our lives and position, all that affects our work, our health, all that moulds our characters, *all* that is, and all that comes to His children, is "of God" and cometh "of God" to us. Of course the objection arises,—But what of things which really don't seem to be "of God" at all? Some one has beautifully said that though a wrong or injurious word or action may not be God's will for the person who says or does it, by the time it reaches me it is God's will for me, and is "of God" to me. Take as instances 1 Kings 12; it seemed a sad and distressing thing that Rehoboam should so act as to divide the kingdom, but God says "this thing is from Me." He had His own purposes to fulfil by it. Then Genesis 45:8, and 50:20. Don't you think it would have been terribly hard for you, if you had been Joseph's sister, to believe beforehand that his being sold was "of God"? Yet, when God has once for all told us that "all things are of Him," why should we not believe at once, instead of feeling all the misery of first doubting and then being ever so sorry that we did doubt, when after a while we see that it was of God! Now to be practical: just use this thought. The very next time something turns up which seems all wrong and disappointing, say "all things are of God," therefore this thing is "of God." Of Whom? God, the *Father*,—of whom are all things (1 Corinthians 8:6). Some of us know the force of that word by possession, and some by loss. The Father that pitieth, knoweth, careth for you, loveth you— the God whom Jesus called "My Father and your Father!" He knows the sorrows, the way that you take, the works (for He hath prepared them for us, and has wrought them in us); He knows *all things*, and all these things are "of Him." Now if there were no more, is it not enough that "all things are *of God!*"

II. But *how* are all things of God? We can't grasp a mere passive being, we crave a personal agent. Here it is. "One Lord Jesus Christ, *by whom* are all things" (1 Corinthians 8:6, Hebrews 2:10). The Father has appointed and exalted Him to this. Did you ever think of the immense comfort it is to know that God has given Him to be (1) Head over all things to His church, that it is to you and me,—the things that we can't manage, can't bring about, can't control,— the persons or circumstances, which seem altogether beyond our reach to bend, Jesus is over them all, *given* to us to be not only *our* Head, but Head over all things! What rest it is to know this! Then all things are put under His (2) *feet*. No matter that we see not yet "Thou *hast* put," the two can't be separated: Satan is under His feet with a bruised head; the world is under His feet (wonderful footstool that!); and we, if in Christ, joined to Him, must have all these things under our feet too. Then God has given all things into His (3) *hand* (John 3:35). Jesus knows it, He knew it even before He went forth to the great conflict (John 13:3). All His *saints* are in Thy hand (Deuteronomy 33:3), our *works* (Ecclesiastes 9:1), and our *times* (Psalm 31:15).

Now with *our* Lord Jesus Christ given to be Head over all things, having all things put under His feet, and all things given into His hand, what in the world have we to fear! Somebody met this the other day with "nothing, except myself!" And God meets this "except" with another "all things." He tells us of the Saviour, the Lord Jesus Christ, being able to subdue *all things* unto Himself. Then He must be able to subdue myself unto Himself. "But I don't find that He has done so!" And why not? "Because of your unbelief." As God has appointed faith as the means and the measure of our reception of His promises, is it any wonder that, when we don't, and won't, and don't even *want* to, believe a given promise, we don't find it fulfilled? Of course not! Here we have come to a most practical and closely touching test of taking God at His word. I put it to you, dear friends, *solemnly*. God says Jesus is able to subdue *all things* unto Himself. At this moment the devil is whispering at the hearts of some of you,— "Yes, hath God said *all* things? it only means able to subdue all things *except*." And some of you are adding to the word, and saying,—Yes, except my will, or except my wandering thoughts, or except my sinful nature, or except my forgetfulness, or something! Face it! Which is it to be? God says "all things." Satan says "all things *except*." Believing God's bare word, no matter how unlikely it seems, you shall find strength, freedom, yes, such a blessing as only He can give. Believing Satan, you shall just go on without all this, you shall go on doubting His power, and calling your doubt humility; and more than this, you shall go on sinning against God, the great monster sin of unbelief. It is no light thing to come face to face with any one of God's promises, and to turn away from it with a devil-breathed "Except."

Shall I go on now to think of what Jesus actually is doing? The great covenant is ordered in all things by God, but the agent of that covenant is Jesus Christ. As He has already fulfilled its conditions, so He is now carrying out its provisions. God is supplying all our need by Jesus Christ, just as much as He created all things by Him. And as Jesus is now upholding all by the word of His power, so He is upholding us from moment to moment. Must be! for unless we were annihilated we must be among the "all things." But still He loves to be inquired of, and so we pray (Psalm 119:116). "Uphold me according to Thy word," and "hold Thou me up," and how do you sometimes finish it up? "Hold Thou me up, and I know I shall fall to-day, notwithstanding!" Have you not had *that* ending pretty often in your hearts? Only you did not put it in so many words. Now trust that glorious Arm, trust that mighty Hand, that *pierced* Hand, and say, looking up to Jesus, "and I *shall* be safe!" Leaning on that Arm, letting ourselves rest in the hollow of that Hand, we shall be at leisure, so to speak, to look around, and watch the goings of our King, and to see the wonderful things He is doing in the world, in His church, in our lives, and I am not afraid to add, even in our hearts. Then, inevitably, we shall burst out into praise, and say "He hath done all things well," (Mark 7:37), while we wonder every one at *all things* which Jesus does (Luke 9:43).

This leads us to what seems to me the central thought and greatest passage of all, Colossians 1:16–18. Here we see God's great object in doing all things by Jesus Christ, "that in all things He might have the preeminence." Now it is very easy to concede this as a grand general truth, and to see how it applies to creation, providence, and redemption. But remember that "all things" includes every little detail of our lives and service. Has Jesus Christ really and truly the preeminence in all things here? The word implies coming first and being first. Does He really come first in our plans? I don't mean ultimately and nominally; but, oh, you know the difference! is Jesus just really the first thought, the first consideration? Especially in routine work, things that come round every week, has He this *real* coming *first?* In our homes has *He* the preeminence? are they really ordered not merely as if Jesus were the chief guest, but ordered so because He *is* the chief and always abiding Guest? Has He the preeminence always? Has He now, at this very moment? Is Jesus, our own dear Lord, really preeminent? Did you come to meet Him? Are you looking for *His* message only? That in all things *He! Himself!* Who else is worthy? It is His right. Once touch on His name, and one has no words. One wants so very much that He should have it. He whom we *do* love, He who so loves us. Well, *has* He? Some thing or some one must have it, must come first. If He doesn't come first, something else does, and that won't do! No matter how dear a cause may be, that must not have it. There is wrong done to our Master if any cause, any denominational interest, any personal feeling, any prejudice, has for even one single five minutes the preeminence in our consideration or motive. Go deeper still, what if self has the preeminence! One almost writhes with shame that it should ever be so; yet probably many hearts go with mine in bitter self accusation that it has been so. Just to think that whenever either self or anything else comes first, Jesus does *not*, and we are at that moment in actual, even if unconscious or rather unrecognised, rebellion against God's great purpose that His dear Son should have the preeminence! Why, it is actually the sin of the fallen angels! And perhaps we have never seen it to be sin at all! Now let us bring it to the fountain opened, and now let us entreat Him so entirely to reign over us and in us, that henceforth in *all* things He may really have the preeminence!

III. "All things are for your sakes" (2 Corinthians 4:15). Connect this with Proverbs 16:4, "the Lord hath made all things for Himself," and we get a wonderful view of the love of God and unity of interest with Him. Another parallel pair is Romans 8:28 with Ephesians 1:11. No wonder that all things work together for good when He worketh all things after the counsel of His will! For the will is the very centre point of conscious being; and as the nature is, so is the will. Now if God's nature is revealed to be Love, His will must be all love too. So when we are told that He worketh all things after the counsel of His will, that is the same as saying He worketh according to His love,—"the great love wherewith He loveth us."

Can love work willingly anything but good to its object? So, too, if He has made all things for Himself, love is the link which leads to the more wonderful declaration, "all things are for your sakes." Look out on creation,—stars by night, all that light reveals by day,—not only that your Father made them all, but all for your sakes. Look at wonders of natural history, and science, some of us have keen enjoyment in these. Recollect not only that they are the wonderful works and laws and embodied thoughts of your Father, but all for your sakes. Look at the strange entangled mazes (as they seem to us, being the wrong side of the tapestry,) of His government of the world, His ways with man in history, His singular present overrulings and developings of things,—all for your sakes. Look nearer at the surroundings of our own lives, things great and small affecting us, all for your sakes. Again, are you prepared actually to believe this? Perhaps you can accept the great facts that God made the world and governs the world all for His children's sakes, and yet do not practically believe that the things quite close to you every day, *this* day, are all for your sakes. You don't like some of these things, yet they are for your sakes. They are so arranged as to turn out for the very *best* for you. We talk of killing two birds with one stone, and think it clever to manage it. Think of the incomprehensible wisdom which fits all things into your single life so that all shall work together for good, and then that these "all things" are also and at the same time fitted all round into the lives of all His children with which they come in contact. "Ordered in all things." Do you think you could improve upon this ordering? Would you like to have a try at it, just for yourself only, and just for one day? Ah, would you dare it? What a terrible mess we should make if He left us to it, or if He entrusted us to order a little bit of the lives of those dear ones about whom we are so trustless!

Well then, if you would not dare to take the reins, why not leave them where they are, in His own hand? Is it not *senseless*, when one comes to think of it, let alone wrong, to fidget and worry about any one thing at all, when He says His covenant is ordered in *all* things and sure, and that all things are for your sakes? We do specially want to remember here that all things means all things, because when the things present are sorrowful, and faith-testing, and painful, and perplexing, we begin again with that dreadful word "except." Are some of us face to face with some of these things now? What shall we then say to these things? What have others said? Take three instances. Genesis 42:36: Jacob said, "All these things are against me." *Were* they? How tremendously he was mistaken! But he had not the clear promises we have. Hezekiah (Isaiah 38:16) got a great deal farther. He said: "By these things men live, and in all these things is the life of my spirit." "These things" meant for him going down to the gates of the grave, and being well-nigh cut off with pining sickness. Yet that which was almost death to the body was life to the spirit. Have not some of us found it so? I have, and many others. I won't ask others to take our word about it, but I do ask them to take this inspired word about it, and to trust and not be afraid if such things come to you. It is worth suffering to prove it. But St. Paul got farther still (Romans 8:37): "In all these things we are more than conquerors," etc. *What* things? We can't write out quite such a serious list as he did of things which seem to be against us.

He not only makes all things work together for good, but does more: "performeth all things for me." And if we did but open our eyes and *notice*, we should see Him at work for us. Every day is full of miracles when the Holy Spirit really opens our eyes to see God working them, and I often think it is the very little things which most magnify His lovingkindness. We talk about the telescope of faith, but I think we want even more the microscope of watchful and grateful love. Apply this to the little bits of our daily lives, in the light of the

Spirit, and how wonderfully they come out! We see these little things in their
true greatness, and in the beauty of their fitness as parts of His own perfect plan
of our lives, which He is working out for us hour by hour. Don't wait for to-
morrow; take this day, the morning hours past, the evening ones to come; and
apply this microscope, and see if you don't find you are walking in the midst of
miracles of love, and that all things are for your sakes.

IV. But there is a step beyond even this: "All things are yours." Here it
seems as if we want increase of faith, not only as to willingness and energy, but
as to actual capacity to take it in. It seems more than we can *grasp*, we are nar-
row-necked bottles set under a very Niagara of grace and blessing. One really
can only look at what He says about it, and bow one's head and say, "what *shall*
I render?" And the only true answer is, "I will take the cup of salvation, and
call upon the name of the Lord" (Psalm 116:13). What does He say? (Proverbs 28:10) "The upright shall have good things *in possession*," not in possibility
or even in promise. Then we find one bearing witness to it and saying 2 Corinthians 6:10; then we have it in parable (Luke 15:31); then explicitly and in
detail (2 Peter 1:3); then we hear of some one who had claimed and received it
(1 Corinthians 1:5); then we find the splendid proof that God means what He
says about it (Romans 8:32); then we have it set forth so positively that there is
no room left, it would seem, for any Satanic "except" (2 Corinthians 9:8); and
then it is summed up in these grand words which we are now looking at (1 Corinthians 3:21). *Can* you take that in? See what God has given you! Have you
ever *really* said "thank you" for it? Oh give unto God the glory *due* unto His
name, and may He give us "that due sense of all His mercies, that our hearts
may be unfeignedly thankful." If life has given us all things, have we any business to live as spiritual paupers? Half the reason why we don't praise Him as we
ought is because we don't really believe what great things He has given us. Oh
"*consider* what great things He hath done for you" (1 Samuel 12:24). Let us ask
Him for much more of His Holy Spirit, that we may know the things that are
freely given to us of God (1 Corinthians 2:12). And then, in proportion as we
know these things, and most of all, in proportion as we know God's greatest gift,
Jesus Himself, we shall say, "Yea, doubtless, and I count all things but loss for
the excellency of the knowledge of Christ Jesus my Lord" (Philippians 3:8).

"All things are yours." "Perhaps so," says Satan, "but that means only spiritual things, and has nothing to do with these temporal things which are pressing
you!": Is *this* the special trouble of any here? Money matters do come awkward sometimes!

Again we are met with an "all things": "seek ye first the kingdom of God,
and His righteousness; and all these things shall be added unto you" (Matthew

6:33). All *these* things, food and clothing, etc. No doubt some of us could bear witness to how really *curiously* God has fulfilled this, adding to the first sought grace of His kingdom just the thing that we didn't quite see our way to, as to some needed supply of dress, change of air, or other of "these things." Why should one ever have an anxious thought in this direction, when He has downright forbidden it on the one hand, "take no thought," etc., and when He so tenderly says "your Father knoweth," on the other!

Great gifts and privileges are always linked with duties and precepts, so we will just glance at a few. Here are our marching orders.

All things are of God; therefore, "let all your things be done with charity" (1 Corinthians 16:14); and also, "all things without murmurings," etc. (Philippians 2:14.) "All things are by Jesus Christ"; therefore, let us seek to "adorn the doctrine of God our Saviour in all things" (Titus 2:10); "in all things showing thyself a pattern of good works" (ver. 7). All things are for your sakes, and all things are yours; therefore, let us be "giving thanks always for all things" (Ephesians 5:20). Thus we shall "grow up into Him in all things, which is the Head, even Christ" (Ephesians 4:15); "being obedient in all things" (2 Corinthians 2:9). Then we may tell Him all things (Mark 6:30), and rest in His omniscience and omnipotence, for "all things are naked and opened unto the eyes of Him with whom we have to do" (Hebrews 4:13), and with Him "all things are possible" (Matthew 19:26).

My wish for you is that in your hearts and homes, service and rest, God "in all things" may be glorified through Jesus Christ.

F. R. H.

"HIM WITH WHOM WE HAVE TO DO."

A BIBLE MOTTO

FOR

1880.

BY THE LATE
FRANCES RIDLEY HAVERGAL.

———

WITH PREFATORY NOTE BY THE REV. C. BULLOCK, B.D.

———

London:
"HAND & HEART" PUBLISHING OFFICE,
1, PATERNOSTER BUILDINGS, E.C.
BIRMINGHAM: CHARLES CASWELL.
PAISLEY: J. & R. PARLANE. BELFAST: W. E. MAYNE.

"Yet Speaketh."

[From memorial lines by "F. R. H." to her sainted Father, now so touchingly applicable to herself.]

"Yet speaketh!" In the memory of those
　　To whom SHE was indeed "a living song,"
The voice, that like fair morning light arose,
　　Rings on with holy influence deep and strong.

"Yet speaketh!" O our SISTER, now we hear
　　The far-off whisper of thy melody;
Thou art "yet speaking" on the heavenly hill,
　　Each word a note of joy—and shall we not "be still"?

This advertisement with the printing number for this essay/pamphlet was found in an advertisement page at the back of *Footprints and "Living Songs:" Frances Ridley Havergal* published by Home Words Publishing Office, I, Paternoster Buildings, E.C. (no date, possibly 1883):

Sixtieth Thousand, with Illustration, 1*d.*
"HIM WITH WHOM WE HAVE TO DO."
Written by F.R.H. shortly before her death, for the January Number of *The Day of Days*.

PREFATORY NOTE.

THE following paper was placed in my hands by our dear Friend very shortly before her translation to her Eternal Home. I suggested its suitability as a Watchword or Bible Motto for the coming New Year, and asked her to add a few words bearing directly on the flight of time, in order that I might so use it in one of the magazines which it is my privilege to edit. The manuscript was returned to her for this purpose only a week or two before the Master's Call reached her. The lines were not added, but the solemnity of almost "Last Words" attaches to this Watchword for the New Year.

As a simple, comprehensive, and sympathetic summary of Gospel truth, full of the heart-poetry which so remarkably characterized all her prose writings, these pages—a voice from "Within the Palace Gates"—will point many an anxious one to "Jesus only," and stimulate many a faithful worker in the Gospel field to follow her as she followed Christ—the Saviour and King, "with whom we have to do."

As "a work of faith and labour of love"—a New Year's offering to the King—the writer would suggest to any readers who have not already contributed to the "Frances Ridley Havergal Memorial Church Missionary Fund," that in this way they may show their sympathy with the loyal devotion to the "King's Marching Orders," which so markedly characterized her writings, and her life.

The Fund already exceeds £1300, and represents the grateful offerings of some thousands of generous contributors: but the need for native Bible Women and the translation of suitable portions of the "Royal Books" for circulation in India and other countries—the objects to which the Fund will be devoted—may well prompt further effort and self-denial.*

Especial interest attaches to the second proposed object, since a wide field of missionary work is opening out at the present time in the extended employment of the Christian press. The Christian Vernacular Society for India has just issued a circular stating that—"For lack of Christian literature in the mother tongues—the sixteen native languages spoken by the 240,000,000 of our fellow-subjects

---

*Contributions can be sent to the Hon. Secretary of the Fund, the Rev. Charles Bullock, Blackheath, London, S.E., or to the Hon. Treasurer, C. Douglas Fox, Esq., Blackheath, London, S.E.

in India—the work of the missionary and Zenana teacher is greatly crippled." As in England the printed book reaches those whom the pastor never or seldom can reach, so the translated volume or tract may at little cost be scattered broadcast in heathen lands, and prepare the way for the direct ministry of the Word by the missionary himself.

We trust—we fully believe—the Frances Ridley Havergal Memorial Missionary Fund will be eminently blessed of God; and that the seed of loving testimony in her translated books scattered on heathen soil will spring up and bear fruit "an hundred-fold," to the glory of the King whom she loved and served.

The voice from "Within the Palace Gates" is the most powerful plea that could reach us:—

> "Will ye not band together,
>   And, working hand in hand,
> Set up a 'flag for Jesus'
>   In that wide heathen land?
>
> In many an Indian city,
>   Oh, let our standard wave,
> Our gift of love and honour,
>   To Him who came to save."

Life Mosaic.

C. B. [1]

BLACKHEATH, S.E.
1879.

---

[1] Rev. Charles Bullock had been the curate (assistant pastor) under F.R.H.'s father, Rev. William Henry Havergal, and he knew Frances well most of her adult life. Rev. Bullock edited the periodicals *The Fireside*, *The Day of Days*, and *Home Words*, and published books, and he did much to make F.R.H.'s works known in her life and after her death.

" Him
With Whom we have to Do. "

"It is I."

" Precious in the sight of the Lord is the death of His saints."

I could not do without Thee!
　　For years are fleeting fast,
And soon in solemn loneliness
　　The river must be passed.
But Thou wilt never leave me:
　　And though the waves roll high,
I know Thou wilt be near me,
　　And whisper "It is I."

F. R. H.

"Him with Whom we Have to Do."

A BIBLE MOTTO FOR THE NEW YEAR.

"Him with whom we have to do."—Hebrews 4:13.

THERE are wonderful depths of comfort in these words. I cannot fathom them for you. I only want to guide you to look where the deep places are, asking the Holy Spirit to put a long sounding line into your hand, that you may prove for yourself how great is the depth.

These words seem to meet every sort of need of comfort. If it is perplexity, or oppressive puzzle what to do, when we cannot see through things,—or if it is being unable to explain yourself to others, and trials or complications arising out of this, just fall back upon "Him with whom you have to do," to whose eyes all things are naked and opened. He is your Guide—why need you puzzle? He is your Shield—why need you try so hard or wish so much to explain and vindicate yourself?

If it is sense of *sin* which does not let you be comfortable, turn at once to "Him with whom you have to do." Remember, it is not with Satan that you have to do, nor with your accusing conscience, but with Jesus. He will deal with all the rest; you only have to deal with Him. And He is your Great High Priest. He has made full Atonement for you; for the very sins that are weighing on you now. The blood of that Atonement, His own precious blood, cleanseth us from all sin. Cleanseth whom? People that have not sinned? People that don't want to be cleansed? Thank God for the word, "cleanseth *us*"—us who have sinned, and who want to be cleansed. And you have to do with Him who shed it for your cleansing, who His own self bare your sins in His own body on the tree.

If it is *temptation* that will not let you rest, come straight away out of the very thick of it; it may be with the fiery darts sticking in you. Come with all the haunting thoughts that you hate, just as you are, to "Him with whom you have to do." You would not or could not tell the temptations to any one else; but then you have not got to do with any one else in the matter, but *only* with Jesus. And He "suffered, being tempted." The very fact that you are distressed by the temptation proves that it *is* temptation, and that you have a singular claim on the sympathy of our tempted Lord, a claim which He most tenderly acknowledges. But use it instantly; don't creep, but *flee* unto Him to hide you from the assaults which you are too weak to meet.

If it is *bodily weakness, sickness, or pain,* how very sweet it is to know that we have to do with Jesus, Who is "touched with the feeling of our infirmities." (The word is the same that is elsewhere translated sickness, John 11:2–4.) Don't you sometimes find it very hard to make even your doctor understand *what* the pain is like? Words don't seem to convey it. And after you have explained the trying and wearying sensation as best you can, you are convinced those who have not felt it do not understand it. Now, think of Jesus not merely entering into the fact, but into the feeling of what you are going through. "Touched with the *feeling*"—how deep that goes! When we turn away to Him in our wordless weariness of pain which *only* He understands, we find out that we have to do with Him in quite a different sense to how we have to do with any one else. We could not do without Him, and thank God we shall never have to do without Him.

Why enumerate other shadows which this same soft light can enter and dispel? They may be cast by any imaginable or unimaginable shape of trouble or need; but the same light rises for them all, if we will only turn towards the brightness of its rising. For Jesus is He "with whom we have to do" in *every thing.* Nothing can be outside of this, unless we wilfully decline to have to do with Him in it, or unbelievingly choose to have to do with "lords many."

And we are answerable only to Him in everything; for this is included in having to do with Him. To our own Master we stand or fall; and that latter alternative is instantly put out of the question, the Apostle adding, "Yea, he shall be holden up, for God is able to make him stand," *i.e.,* he who is his "own Master's servant." To Him only we have to give account, if from Him we take our orders.

We have to do with Him *directly:* so directly that it is difficult at first to grasp the directness. There is absolutely nothing between the soul and Jesus, if we will but have it so. We have Himself as our Mediator with God, and the very characteristic of a mediator is, as Job says, "that he might lay his hand upon us both." So the hand of Jesus, who is Himself "the Man of Thy right Hand," is laid upon us with no intermediate link and no intervening distance. We do not need any paper and print, let alone any human voice, between us and Himself.

> "To Thee, O dear, dear Saviour,
> My spirit turns for rest."

That turning is instinctive and instantaneous when we have once learnt what it is to have direct and personal dealing with the Lord Jesus Christ. Life is altogether a different thing then, whether shady or sunshiny, and a stranger intermeddleth not with our hidden joy.

Perhaps it is just this that makes such a strangely felt difference between those who equally profess and call themselves Christians. Is Jesus to us "*Him with whom we have to do,*" or is He only Him whom we know about, and believe about, and with whose laws and ordinances we have to do? This makes all the difference: and every one who has this personal dealing with Him *knows* it, and cannot help knowing it.

Do not let this discourage any one who cannot yet say, "Him with whom I have to do." For He is more ready and willing thus to have to do with you, than you with Him. You may enter at once into this most sweet and solemn position. He is here already: He only waits for you to come into it. Only bring Him your sins and your sinful self, "waiting not to rid your soul of one dark blot." Nothing else separates between you and Him, and He will take your sins all away and receive you graciously; and then you too shall know the sacred and secret blessedness of having to do only with Jesus.

A New Year's Gift Indeed!

"Lord, increase our faith!"

INCREASE our Faith, Belovèd Lord:
    For Thou alone canst give
The faith that takes Thee at Thy word,
    The faith by which we live.

Increase our Faith! So weak are we
    That we both may and must
Commit our very faith to Thee,
    Entrust to Thee our trust.

Increase our Faith! On this broad shield
    "All" fiery darts be caught;
We must be victors in the field
    Where Thou for us hast fought.

Increase our Faith! for Thou hast prayed
    That it should never fail;
Our steadfast anchorage is made
    With Thee, within the veil.

Increase our Faith, that unto Thee
    More fruit may still abound:
That it may grow " exceedingly,"
    And to Thy praise be found.

Increase our Faith, O Saviour dear,
    By Thy sweet sovereign grace,
Till, changing faith for vision clear,
    We see Thee face to face.

F. R. H. in "Home Words."

———— ❧ ————

This letter was found among original Havergal papers and archives. (The date and name of the periodical were not given.)

MISSION-WEEK IN BIRMINGHAM IN DECEMBER.

Dear Sir,—Will your readers make earnest supplication during the next two months for a special and abundant blessing upon the great mission-week to be held in Birmingham and its suburbs from December 8 to 15. There is, perhaps, no place where the opposing forces of good and evil are brought into sharper contrast. This great Midland Metropolis being, on the one hand, a stronghold of scepticism, and, on the other, a stronghold of evangelicalism. There is so much mental activity and energy, that we cannot but feel that any outpouring of blessing here would be likely to radiate in wide and influential circles, that, if blessed, this town would indeed *be* a blessing.

The prosposed mission-week claims, therefore, strong sympathy and earnest prayer from all who desire the extension of our Master's kingdom. Every possible means will be used in the thirty parishes which have united in this scheme.

Twenty-two mission-preachers, including many of the most eminent and powerful evangelical clergy, are already engaged for the week. Arrangements are being made to reach all classes, from the highest to the lowest, and to "go out," and "compel them to come in." And the already over-worked clergy are prepared to strain every nerve to bring these golden opportunities to bear upon the hearts of thousands. But we can only lay the wood in order. Now, will not the Lord's people unite with us in intense and continued prayer, that He may send the fire of the Holy Spirit upon it?

Already the spirit of grace and of supplication appears to be poured out, both upon individual Christians in private, and upon special prayer-meetings commenced in anticipation. As an instance, I may mention that in this parish the vicar, the Rev. C. B. Snepp, preached two fervent and heart-rousing sermons on Sunday last, from the text, "There shall be showers of blessing," stirring up his people to plead this promise, and exhorting them all to seek that preparation of heart which the Lord alone can give. At the conclusion of the morning sermon, he called upon choir and congregation to rise and join him in singing the hymn, "Showers of blessing, gracious promise," from his own rich and beautiful hymnal, "Songs of Grace and Glory," and this breaking of the usual routine appeared to have a singularly touching and solemnizing effect, deepening the impression of the burning words preceding it. He then invited his congregation to meet on the following evening for special prayer. This meeting was crowded, and was characterized by great solemnity. There was true wrestling with God for his great promised gifts, especially for the outpouring of the Holy Spirit, to convince, convert, and revive, for the manifestation of the Lord Jesus to many, many hearts.

Is not all this an earnest of coming blessing? And may it not stimulate to still greater faith and prayer and expectation? We ask your readers to join in the prayer, that they may have the joy of joining in the praise, for which we trust there will, indeed, be new and glorious cause.—I remain, dear sir, yours faithfully,

Frances Ridley Havergal.

HINTS

FOR

LADY WORKERS AT MISSION SERVICES.

BY A LADY.

EDITED BY THE
REV. A. W. THOROLD.

———————

LONDON: WILLIAM MACINTOSH,

24, Paternoster-row.

[By a Lady, Frances Ridley Havergal.]

HINTS FOR LADY WORKERS AT MISSION SERVICES.

———

THOUGH the "Mission-week" movement is rapidly spreading, it is still entirely new work to many. Lady workers are frequently asking, "How can we help in a Mission service? What is there for us to do?" May I offer a few very simple hints to such?

As to the spiritual part of our share in the work, I do not venture to offer any, feeling convinced that the only availing counsel will be given by the great Counsellor. No cut-and-dried plan or rules will do; but doubtless He who sends us, as He Himself was sent, "to heal the broken-hearted," and "to set at liberty them that are bruised," will show us the right way, and give us the right word, if we only keep looking to Him for it.

But a few words to those who ask, "How do you set about it?"

We take it for granted that we have been systematically at work beforehand, canvassing our districts, using every means of arousing interest and expectation in all within our reach, uniting in prayer with others, and wrestling continually for the shower of blessing, the real outpouring of the Spirit, which is our heart's desire.

Now for the evening's work. We agree beforehand as to the division of labour, so that no time may be lost in hesitation, and no power be wasted by having too many in one department and too few in another. Two or three of us linger outside the church or schoolroom, before, during, and after the service. Many passers-by, having nothing particular to do, will yield, on the spur of the moment, to a kindly and pleasant invitation to enter. The offer of a hymn-book goes a long way, and the promise of "a seat near the door" is always an attraction. After service, we watch the countenances as they come out, and we are nearly sure to see some who evidently "rather wish they had ventured to stay" for the After-Meeting. Sometimes a word is enough to decide them to return at once, and still oftener to induce them to step aside, and listen, in the shadow of the porch, to words from which they would timidly shrink in the full glare of the gas-light. Many a young girl has thus been noted, gently drawn aside, pleaded with, brought back into the After-Meeting, and blessed.

One or two more workers will sit just inside the door, ready to welcome timid strangers, or to receive those brought in by the workers outside. They will be on the watch, too, for children and others, who will often just peep inside the door if the building is lighted up at an unusual day or hour. A quick eye and bright smile are needed here. When a pew-opener is most wanted, he is sometimes at the other end of the church; so a kindly face at the door, ready to put the stranger into a near and quiet seat, and supply a hymn-book, secures many a one doubtful about coming in at all, who would perhaps go out if not speedily attended to.

These little services are useful, moreover, as making a sort of introduction, and giving easy openings for speaking to the same persons after service. We have established a connecting link, and may often turn the scale by inviting them to remain for the After-Meeting.

When the sermon or address has begun, let us for the time resolutely put away all thoughts of others, and only listen for ourselves, seeking to gain refreshment, courage, and personal blessing. It is time utterly wasted, if we sit listening for others, and thinking about the effect upon them; this can do no possible good to them, while it loses a precious opportunity for our own souls.

The mode of conducting After-Meetings varies much. Some Mission Preachers have continuous prayer throughout; others have alternate prayer, hymns, and short addresses; others have intervals of perfect stillness, during which all unite in silent prayer; others have nothing but personal dealing, except a prayer at the opening and closing. Our share of work is, of course, moulded accordingly.

When it is likely that a larger number will remain than the Mission preacher and other clergy can speak with individually, it is well to plan definitely beforehand what each worker shall undertake: a transept, half an aisle, the back benches, etc. This saves waiting to see what others are going to do, and also saves unnecessary moving about; each one taking her appointed place before " the door is shut," that solemn and suggestive signal for the commencement of the After-Meeting.

The few minutes (generally filled up by a hymn) during which those who do not intend to remain are leaving the church or schoolroom, are most important, and call for quick observation, tact, and promptness. It is the very turning-point with many a soul, and is often a moment of special temptation—a last effort of the enemy to retain his captive. We mark a hesitating hand on a pew-door, or an irresolute step in the aisle, or a troubled glance round, or even a nervous hurry to get away; and with any of these, even a simple but earnest whisper,—" Oh, *do* stay!" if we can think of nothing else to say,—is often enough to decide them to remain. But an instant's delay on the part of the worker, and the opportunity is lost!

Will my friends forgive a suggestion here? Let all movement be as noiseless as possible, so that no one shall notice you except the person with whom you are actually dealing. A rustling dress, or creaking boots, may hinder one who is trying to pray, and be an actual distress to some who, nervous and trembling, will fancy that others will notice that the lady is speaking to them.

All needless noise is jarring, in the intense solemn stillness of an After-Meeting. Satan contrives to use such very little things as hindrances, that we may well be careful to deprive him of the opportunity when we can.

Unless under very exceptional circumstances, it will be better and wiser to let our personal work in an After-Meeting be only among our own sex, leaving the clergy and lay helpers to deal with the other.

When "the door is shut," we shall probably have noticed some one, perhaps a poor woman, evidently impressed. It is, perhaps, best to go very softly and kneel down with her. It is less conspicuous than standing, and she will feel more at her ease; and it is more suitable for the words of prayer, *for* her and *with* her, which we shall surely utter. We will not let her feel that our dealing with her is overheard. She is virtually alone with us and with the Saviour; and He is "passing by." And here we pause; the moment is too solemn; we could not tell another what to say; we could not tell before-hand what we ourselves shall say, but the Master will tell us, and will put His message in our mouth, and He will guide home the arrow of His love, though our bow be only drawn at a venture.

We pass on to others, but we keep an eye upon her, and return to her, perhaps stooping to whisper a text in passing, before once again kneeling with her. If at the close of the meeting she is still "sore distressed," it may be advisable either to lead her to the vestry, that the Mission-preacher, who has been a messenger of conviction, may now, if God will, be made a messenger of peace to her; or to ask him to come out and speak to her where she kneels. But in some cases, especially with young persons, it is wiser only to invite them to come again, and to keep the case entirely in our own hands, lest nervous excitement at being brought forward, or, on the other hand, a lurking liking to be made much of, should mar the work.

Sometimes, when great emotion is shown, and there is convenient opportunity for so doing, it is well to lead the distressed one quite apart from others, and leave her kneeling, quite "alone with Jesus," in some empty or unoccupied corner.

It is very desirable to ascertain the names of those with whom we speak, in order that we may follow them up, or report them to the clergyman, as the case may be; yet very undesirable to distract their minds, even for an instant, or alarm a very timid one, by the enquiry. Therefore, if we have any other means of ascertaining or identifying, we use that in preference to a point-blank question.

When there seems no special timidity, it may be as well to speak or pray (but always softly) with two or three together, if there are many to be reached. In any case, we should aim at letting none go away without a special word, or an *opportunity* of personal help. Sometimes the very ones whom we most shrink from approaching, not only need but desire it most. This occurs most frequently with those in our own social station, especially if we have a slight personal acquaintance. We are so tempted to feel this a barrier, and an insurmountable difficulty! Yet if we overcome it, we shall have no reason for regret, but only for rejoicing. Why should we so hesitate to speak for Jesus to a *lady*? It is far more likely that no one ever yet spoke lovingly and personally to *her*, than to the poor woman to whom it seemed so easy to speak. Yet her need is as great, and her anxiety may be as deep, though more concealed. Would she resent it? would she dislike it? Try, dear sister-workers, only *try*, and you will find many a joyful surprise, and many a sweet reward in this direction. Never will you have better opportunities for breaking the ice than during a Mission-week. Do not lose these opportunities.

Perhaps you say in your heart: "Oh, I could never go and speak to people!" Nevertheless, stay to the After-Meeting as a helper, for we need praying hearts as well as praying voices; and while others are working, give yourself unto prayer for the blessing. It may be that your Lord will send you a sudden impulse to look up, and you will see some sorrowing one kneeling near you, and then an impulse will come to wish to point her to the Saviour. If so, yield to the call; rise and go to her; and it may be that the Master will give you the honour of being His messenger, though you never intended to take it, and will give you the joy of harvest while you hardly dared to claim the privilege of sowing.

There is another pleasant work for those who are too young, either in years or in faith, to come forward as general workers. Let such remain, not only to pray, but to *sing*. Often, the singing of such a hymn as "Just as I am," or "Jesus, I will trust Thee," during an After-Meeting, has been peculiarly blessed. Yet those who are speaking to others ought not to be burdened with the feeling that they must take up the singing, and thus interrupt their work; while even if the choir remain and lead, it is far better if other voices are ready to follow and join. In this way our *young* ladies may use for God the voices which He has bestowed on them, by taking whatever share they can in thus "singing for Jesus," and it will be more valuable help than they perhaps imagine.

At the close of the meeting there will be fragments to gather up, and we should watch for these. Some anxious one has been over-looked, or has purposely kept out of observation, and now lingers just inside, or perhaps just outside, the door, anywhere in the shadow, waiting for a ray of hope or comfort. And even if it is altogether too late for prayer and conversation, a word, if it be indeed His word, may be enough to turn the darkness into light; or, at any rate, a clue may be gained, to be followed up next day. For, in every case, we shall try not to lose sight, during the Mission-week, of those with whom we have once spoken; we shall make them our special objects of prayerful effort, resting not till the Lord, at whose feet we lay them in faith, has indeed put forth His power, and made them "perfectly whole."

F. R. H.

THE APPROACHING

MISSION SERVICES.

BY A LADY.

EDITED BY THE
REV. A. W. THOROLD.

LONDON: WILLIAM MACINTOSH,

24, PATERNOSTER-ROW.

Maria V. G. Havergal in her volume of *Letters by the Late Frances Ridley Havergal* added this as an appendix, with this title:

THE APPROACHING MISSION SERVICES
BY F. R. H.

EDITED BY A.W. THOROLD, D.D., LORD BISHOP
OF ROCHESTER.

James Nisbet & Co. also re-issued this as a leaflet.

THE APPROACHING
MISSION SERVICES.

A WEEK of SPECIAL MISSION SERVICES is proposed. The movement, which has spread so rapidly in all parts of the kingdom, has reached your own doors. Energetic preparation is being made, earnest prayer is being offered, and warm expectation is already awake.

What is it all about? Why do people talk of "expectation"? Why should clergymen give themselves so much trouble? And how will it affect the readers of this paper?

We will answer the last question first, and say to every one who reads this: Perhaps it will affect *you* for ever and ever and ever! Perhaps, ere that week closes, you, who know and love the Lord Jesus, will be sealed anew with a fresh baptism of the Spirit, blessed with richer manifestations of Christ's presence and love, filled with deeper joy, and stirred up to holier zeal and more single-hearted devotedness than ever before. Perhaps, ere that week closes, you, who earnestly desire to be saved, and yet have never dared to lay hold of Christ's full and free salvation, will be rejoicing "with joy unspeakable and full of glory." Perhaps, ere that week closes, you who have "no hope, and are without God in the world," will be made "new creatures" altogether, will know the terrible danger in which you have been living, and the hitherto unguessed joy of having a "sure and certain hope," and an Everlasting Friend to love and lean upon. Such are the effects which we hope for, pray for, and expect.

It is a thrillingly grand and glorious thing to stand on the eve of such a season, looking forward to such blessings, and to an actual share in them. It is a thrillingly solemn and awful thing to remember that one may be taken and another left; that a day of doom may follow close upon a day of grace, and that if the blessing is despised or neglected by any heart, that heart may be left dry, dead, untouched, while showers of blessing fall on all around.

But WHAT IS A MISSION WEEK? It is a means of grace which, more than any other of late years, God appears to have used for the conversion of sinners, and the raising of His own people to a higher, holier, and happier life.

Many important towns have followed this plan. The whole week is set apart for one object. Special services, not long, but intensely fervent, are held in every church every day; the usual order of services being shortened, and earnest, striking addresses given by special preachers, specially qualified for this work. These are preceded and followed by meetings for Prayer—for pleading and wrestling with God for His blessing, and the outpouring of His Spirit. Arrangements are made to bring the glad tidings to those who will not come to any place of worship, and to those who cannot attend the special Church Services. Meetings and addresses are planned for all classes—rich as well as poor. Short addresses are given in factories, workshops, and railway sheds; gatherings of different callings and classes are held; cabmen, policemen, servants, young shopmen and shopwomen, poor mothers, young ladies in boarding-schools, gentlemen in business—all are considered and arranged for.

It may not be advisable to mention names, but we could tell of many places where great and abiding blessing has rested upon the Mission Week. In one small town, the number of those who were not merely impressed at the time, but have become decided and steady Christians, is estimated at twelve hundred! In a manufacturing town, the numbers added to the church in one parish were so great, that the Incumbent had to procure an additional Curate, on purpose to take up the work arising out of the Mission Week! In another, it was the working men who seemed to obtain the greatest blessing; and such congregations of these have perhaps never been seen as in a large church in that town on the Sunday evenings after the Mission Week. In the same place, the railway men, to whom short daily addresses had been given, have requested the Vicar to continue them regularly; and the results have been such as no scoffers could ignore or explain away.

It has been remarked that the greatest blessing, in nearly every place, has been among those who have already had serious impressions, and in whom the soil was in some degree prepared, rather than among such as have had no previous care or thought about their souls. Is not this a very important note of encouragement and of warning? To those who are seeking Jesus, but have not found Him, it gives encouragement to pray very earnestly that this coming Mission Week may be the great turning-point of their lives, and the coming out of doubt and darkness and indecision into "marvellous light" and "glorious liberty." To those who care for none of these things, it gives a warning, lest this great opportunity should only add to their condemnation, if they refuse to "prepare their hearts to seek God."

Our God may work above reason, but He does not work against reason. So we may fairly ask, WHY SHOULD WE EXPECT GREAT THINGS FROM A MIS-

SION WEEK? And the answer is no mystery, to those who know the secrets and the power of PRAYER. For months beforehand, many faithful hearts have been pleading, constantly and intensely, for a blessing. As the time approaches, more and more are stirred up to join in these prayers. Their fervency and earnestness deepen day by day, till at last one great cry is ascending day and night, unheard by the sleeping souls around, but strong and loud in "the ears of the Lord God of Sabaoth." How is this? Do our own evil hearts prompt to such prayer? Does Satan set us praying? How else can it arise, but from the promptings of the HOLY SPIRIT? The God in Whose hand the blessing is hid, waiting to be gracious, pours out "the spirit of grace and of supplication" upon His people, because "He will be inquired of" for the good things which He purposes to give. And the coming shower of blessing, of which this spirit of prayer is the earnest, will be all the sweeter and more powerful for being thus, as it were, drawn down by their prayers.

"He that watereth shall be watered"; and it seems that these prayers for those around generally receive a double answer, returning in a wonderful gladness,— a very reaping-time of joy, upon the hearts of those who have been, it may be, sowing these supplications in tears. Let no Christian heart lose its share in the blessing, by neglecting or delaying to join in the prayer. Let every one resolve at once, by God's help, to make it a subject of daily prayer during the coming weeks of anticipation.

But WHY DO THE CLERGY TAKE ALL THIS TROUBLE? They are not paid for it; they will get nothing by it; they will only be wearied and worn outs after days of work, and perhaps night-hours of prayer. Why? It is because they love the people around them, and because they believe that God means what He says, when He speaks in His Word, of sin, death, judgment, eternity, and of pardon, life, salvation, and glory. Months of prayer and preparation, and a week of labour to the utmost, are a very small thing to those whose whole lives are being spent for their people, and who know that in a few years every soul under their care will be in heaven or in hell.

If so, shall it be a great thing to those for whom they toil, to give a few hours to the affairs of millions of years beyond imagination? What does it matter about any business or engagement in comparison? "What shall it profit a man, if he gain the whole world and lose his own soul?"

The Mission Week will be a golden opportunity; perhaps the very last for some who read this. Loving voices will say to you, "Jesus of Nazareth passeth by! Rise! He calleth thee!" Oh, will you not come to Him, that you may have life?

A word with those who talk about "excitement," or who throw cold water on that zeal for God, which one longs to see kindled in every heart. Do any perish through religious excitement? But are not thousands perishing of religious apathy?

There is much foolish parrot-talk about this, by persons who, having no real means or power of forming an opinion of their own, catch up clap-trap phrases of irreligious cant (and for every phrase of religious, there are ten of irreligious cant!) and talk grandly about the "danger of excitement." What *is* the danger of it? Confessedly this, that if the feelings are touched and excited, without real change of heart, they lapse into greater coldness and deadness than before. Then the danger obviously is—not of going too far, but of not going far enough! None are so illogical as those who try to argue with God. See to it, you who would hinder others by talk about the danger of "excitement," but shut your eyes to the danger of death and hell,—see to it that God does not take you at your word, and leave you, untouched by "excitement of feeling," cool and easy, outside the gate, while others are entering in. What will you feel, when the last hour has struck for you, when the door is shut, and you are outside, left to "the blackness of darkness for ever"? Will there be no "excitement" in the moment of *that* discovery, think you?

But some real Christians look a little doubtfully upon new efforts, and hold aloof, and do not see why ordinary means should not be sufficient. Have they proved all-sufficient? Do they reach all the unconverted? And if not, why not try other means, in the spirit of our Heavenly Father, who doth *"devise means that His banished be not expelled from Him"*; in the spirit of our Master, who said, "Go ye out into the highways and hedges, and compel them to come in"; in the spirit of His follower, who said, "If by *any* means I might save some." Let us not, then, hinder the Gospel of Christ by our chilling half-heartedness.

While praying for "showers of blessing" upon our country and our Church, surely it will be both right and pleasant that Christians should join their pastor in seeking and expecting a special blessing on their own parish. God's order appears to be, "The more prayer, the more blessing."

Again, the approaching Mission Week seems a new call to pray for our own home circles, that if any who are near and dear to us are not yet "on the Lord's side," they may then be brought to Christ, and thenceforth live unto Him. And, drawing the circle still closer, shall we not each, whatever be our state or need, whatever be our age or position, seek a personal blessing upon our own souls? *"Bless me, even me also, O my Father!"*

PERSIS.

Genesis 27:38 " Bless me, even me also, O my Father."

Tune Persis. 8 7, 8 7, 3.

Lord, I hear of showers of blessing
    Thou art scattering full and free;
Showers the thirsty land refreshing:
    Let some dropping fall on me,
        Even me.

Pass me not, O gracious Father!
    Sinful though my heart may be;
Thou might'st curse me, but the rather
    Let Thy mercy light on me,
        Even me.

Pass me not, O tender Saviour!
    Let me love and cling to Thee;
I am longing for Thy favour;
    When Thou comest, call for me,
        Even me.

Pass me not, O mighty Spirit!
    Thou canst make the blind to see;
Witnesser of Jesu's merit,
    Speak the word of power to me,
        Even me.

Have I long in sin been sleeping,
    Long been slighting, grieving Thee?
Has the world my heart been keeping?
    Oh, forgive and rescue me,
        Even me.

Love of God, so pure and changeless,
    Blood of God, so rich and free,
Grace of God, so strong and boundless,
    Magnify them all in me,
        Even me.

Pass me not, this lost one bringing;
Satan's slave Thy child shall be;
All my heart to Thee is springing;
Blessing others, oh, bless me,
Even me!

Elizabeth Codner, 1860.

Hymn 839 in "Songs of Grace and Glory for Mission Services." (London: Nisbet & Co.)

"WILL YE NOT COME?"

Words and Music by
F. R. Havergal.

Will ye not come to Him for *life?*
  Why will ye die, oh why?
He gave His life for you, for you!
The gift is free, the word is true!
Will ye not come? Oh, why will ye die?

Refrain,
after any
or each
verse.
}
   Will ye not come? Will ye not come,
     Will ye not come to Him, to Him?
      Oh, come, come, come to Him!
Come unto Jesus, oh, come for *life.*

Will ye not come to Him for *peace,*
  Peace through His cross alone?
He shed His precious blood for you;
The gift is free, the word is true!
He is our Peace—Oh, is He your own?
     Will ye not come, etc. . . . for *peace?*

Will ye not come to Him for *rest?*
  All that are weary, come:
The rest He gives is deep and true,
'Tis offered now, 'tis offered you:
Rest in His love, and rest in His home.
     Will ye not come, etc. . . . for *rest?*

Will ye not come to Him for *joy?*
  Will ye not come for this?
He laid His joys aside for you,
To give you joy, so sweet, so true:
Sorrowing heart, oh, drink of the bliss!
     Will ye not come, etc. . . . for *joy?*

Will ye not come to Him for *love,*
  Love that can fill the heart?
Exceeding great, exceeding free!
He loveth you, He loveth me!
Will ye not come? Why stand ye apart?
     Will ye not come, etc. . . . for *love?*

Will ye not come to Him for ALL?
  Will ye not "taste and see?"
He waits to give it all to you,
The gifts are free, the words are true:
Jesus hath said it, "Come unto Me!"
     "Will ye not come, etc. . . . to HIM?

In compliance with a request from Sankey for a Gospel Musical Call, my dear sister F. R. H. wrote these lines at Winterdyne, December 21, 1873. The same morning, I met her with the MS. in her hand, toiling up to the Wyre Hill schoolroom. She said, "Maria, will the children be out of school?" "Yes." "Then I shall lock myself in and fancy the room full for a mission service! I have been praying that the *music may be sent me*, to fit His message, 'Will ye not come?'"

Soon I heard these chords on the harmonium and her ringing voice. She called the tune "Lucius," and often sang it with pleading tenderness at mission and other meetings.

Thus in poetry, in prose, in music, in life, and in death, her silver refrain was, "*Will ye not come?*"

> "Still shall the key-word, ringing, echo the same sweet '*Come!*'
> Come with the blessed myriads safe in the Father's home;
> Come—for the work is over; Come—for the feast is spread;
> Come—for the crown of glory waits for the weary head."

MARIA V. G. HAVERGAL.

Tell it out!

Tell it out among the heathen that the Saviour reigns!
  Tell it out! Tell it out!
Tell it out among the nations, bid them burst their chains.
  Tell it out! Tell it out!
Tell it out among the weeping ones that Jesus lives;
Tell it out among the weary ones what rest He gives;
Tell it out among the sinners that He came to save;
Tell it out among the dying that He triumphed o'er the grave.

Tell it out among the heathen Jesus reigns above!
  Tell it out! Tell it out!
Tell it out among the nations that His reign is love!
  Tell it out! Tell it out!
Tell it out among the highways and the lanes at home;
Let it ring across the mountains and the ocean foam!
Like the sound of many waters let our glad shout be,
Till it echo and re-echo from the islands of the sea!

MOTTOES FOR OPEN AIR MISSION WORKERS.

THE *Open-Air Mission Magazine* introduced the verses written by F.R.H. with the following words.

MEMBERS' MOTTOES.

FOR the past six years the members of the Mission have had fellowship with each other by a printed motto, selected by the Committee. Miss Frances Ridley Havergal has woven these texts into verse. In sending them, with 6000 of her leaflets, for distribution by the Mission, she says: "I do think yours is such *brave* work for Jesus. May I pass on to you a text I never noticed till this morning? 'My glory was fresh in me, and my bow was renewed in my hand' (Job 29:20), taken with 'Christ in you, the hope of glory' (Colossians 1:27), and 'His bow abode in strength' (Genesis 49:24). May your glory thus be fresh in you, and your bow renewed in your hand." This gifted Christian sister went to her rest with God on June 3rd, 1879, aged 42.

1874. "OCCUPY TILL I COME." *Luke* 19:13.

"Occupy till I return!"
Let us, Lord, this lesson learn;
May our every moment be
Faithfully filled up for Thee.

1875. "BE NOT FAR FROM ME." *Psalm* 22:11.

"Be not far from me," we pray;
"I am with thee all the day";
This Thy answer, strong and clear,
Master, Thou art *always* near.

1876. "HE IS FAITHFUL THAT PROMISED." *Hebrews* 10:23.

Thou art faithful! Praise Thy name,
Thou art evermore the same;
Thou hast promised! Oh how blest
On Thy royal word to rest.

1877.   "He that Winneth Souls is Wise."   *Proverbs* 11:30.

> "He that winneth souls is wise"
> In the Master's gracious eyes;
> Well may we contented be
> To be counted fools for Thee.

1878.   "Redeeming the Time."   *Colossians* 4:5.

> So may we redeem the time,
> That with every evening chime
> Our rejoicing hearts may see
> Blood-bought souls brought back to Thee.

1879.   "Lay up His Words in thine Heart."   *Job* 22:22.

> Let us, by Thy Spirit stirred,
> In our hearts lay up Thy word.
> Daily, Lord, increase our store,
> Fill our treasures more and more.

FRANCES RIDLEY HAVERGAL.

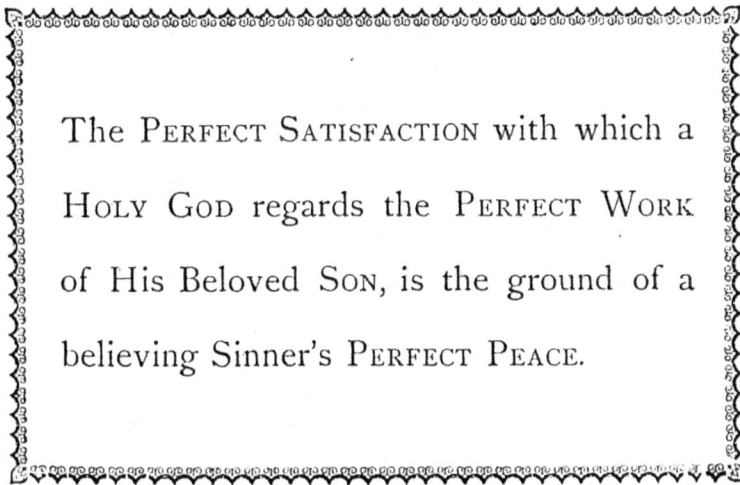

The PERFECT SATISFACTION with which a HOLY GOD regards the PERFECT WORK of His Beloved SON, is the ground of a believing Sinner's PERFECT PEACE.

Edinburgh : James Taylor, 81 Castle Street.

This small card was found among Havergal manuscripts and papers. Who wrote this is not known. Colossians 2:10 Such cards and leaflets were and are easy and inexpensive to print, a means of God to give rich truths to many people, both friends and strangers.

THE DREAM CATHEDRAL.

[*The outline of this early composition* (1857) *was a real dream.*]

I STOOD in the nave of a strangely magnificent cathedral. Such a cathedral it was as seemed to be the very embodiment of the highest ideal of beauty and grandeur. Around me were fluted columns of snowy marble, enriched with carvings of foliage, such as the artist might have seen in a vision of Eden, meeting above in pointed arches, whose upward curve seemed to beckon heavenwards and to speak of celestial aspirings; the floor was marble too, and as unsullied in its whiteness as the dewy petal of a lily, ere the dusty breath of day has passed upon it, and telling me of purity and innocence; then the vaulted roof, the union of those arching columns, with its dim twilight of undefined yet beautiful interlacings, spoke of holy mysteries. There were long shadowy aisles stretching far away, and their whispering echoes suggested sacred solitude and retirement. There were marble steps leading up to a screen of such cunning work that the very stone seemed to breathe forth beauty, and, if possible, to shadow forth the loveliness of religion. And beyond this were glimpses of such a choir, so wonderful in its transcendent beauty, as seemed scarcely fitted for mortal worshippers to kneel within. All this was seen, as it were, through the veil of a softened, shadowy radiance, poured through windows whose Gothic tracery enclosed, not stained glass, but a mosaic of the most gorgeous gems, casting the glow of their rich deep colouring on portions of the fair whiteness of pillar and arch and pavement, bathing all in a light, splendid even in the solemnity of its dimness.

Scarcely had admiration and wonder time to unfold, when the tones of cathedral music swelled through the marvellous temple. Soft and sweet as a symphony of angel harps, the sound seemed to enwreathe itself around the marble shafts, and to melt into the dark vaultings of the lofty roof, as though there were some strange affinity between them; and then, at every pause, it hovered away far down the lessening aisles, till the whole building was like one great living instrument. Then voices came floating down that glorious nave: sweet and melodious, shall I call them? words do not express what those voices were; and the anthem which they chanted was such as Handel might dream, perhaps, but never wrote.

Do you not know what it is to see something *very* beautiful, and yet feel unsatisfied? to hear the sweetest sounds, and yet feel they might be sweeter? to enjoy the greatest apparent delight, and yet feel that it is not the perfection of happiness? I cannot think that the human spirit is ever positively and absolutely *satisfied*; it is too great, too vast, (though we scarcely know it,) to be filled with anything on earth; its real ideal is never found; it is ever striving and yearning after something greater, higher, lovelier; and its Maker is its only satisfaction.

But I was satisfied. It was the perfection of beauty, the perfection of enjoyment; my longings realized, and more still. All this *seemed* to carry my heart upwards, I felt filled with joyful devotion, and adoration was the keynote of the silent anthem of my spirit. Then the thought came across me: "Can it be that such a temple is unfavourable to true devotion? can it be that a spirit could remain earthbound here, and not soar far, far upwards: in the holiest, happiest, adoration?"

Suddenly I heard a voice, clear, calm, and very grave, though I saw not the speaker. It spoke to *me*: "*Your Saviour is here*, you have long sought Him, He is about to manifest Himself to you. See! He is standing there in His own glorious Person!" In an instant all else had lost its interest. Oh! it was so strange, that sudden revulsion of feeling. Fancied devotion gave way to the reality of the intensest earnestness; the temple in all its fascinating grandeur was nothing, absolutely nothing; His Presence there was the *only* thing I longed for. I gazed intently where the voice indicated; I saw One standing alone, and knew and *felt* that it was Himself. But the many-lined shadow of one of the gem-filled windows fell upon His Form, and I could not discern its outline, much less His countenance.

"Listen!" said the voice again; "He is speaking to you. Are not His words sweet and gracious!" But a fresh burst of music pealed from the organ, the voices of the invisible choristers rose higher and louder, and the tide of melody carried away the sound of that heavenly Voice, whose words would have been more than life to me. Oh, how each note grated upon me! how I hated the music, which drowned the gentle tones of that Voice!

I determined to approach, and at least be gladdened by His look, though His words might not reach my ear. I hastened on, but the marble steps grew in height under my feet, and I could not ascend them as quickly as I thought to do, each one seemed a mountain. But He was turning to look on me, and something seemed to tell me certainly that He was going to rejoice me with one of His own sweet smiles, another instant, and His eye would have met mine, when one of the fluted pillars suddenly rose in front of me, the blessed moment was gone, and He passed away down one of the dim shadowy aisles.

In desperation I rushed on, as if every hope, every desire, of a lifetime were concentrated in that one passing instant; I gained the entrance of the aisle, when the exquisite screen, which a moment before had so charmed me, stretched it-self in defiance across it, barring the only way by which I could reach the de-parting Saviour.

He was gone! and all seemed changed to darkness and discord. In the very agonies of regret and despair I sank on the pavement, and *awoke!*

The moral, so to speak, of this dream will be apparent to every one. What is earthly beauty to a soul longing for its Saviour, and thirsting for His grace? What are externals compared to internals? But I would not be misunderstood, there is no reason why the other extreme should be advocated. I am, and always have been, a warm admirer of those time-honoured ornaments of our land, the crown jewels, as it were, of our outward and visible Church, our English cathe-drals. He who giveth us *all* things richly to enjoy must have awakened, or rather created, those thoughts of beauty which expressed themselves in these glorious temples, notwithstanding the tainted atmosphere of superstition which then darkened our land; and if their original purpose, the setting forth of Jehovah's praise and glory, is sometimes far from being attained, the fault is not in the temples, but in any who do not within them worship God in spirit and truth. It is not the grace and grandeur of their architecture which frustrate their noble object, but the earthliness of men's hearts, which rises not above pillar and roof and spire, but lies like the cold pavement itself, resting in things seen and tem-poral. If it be true that "unto the pure all things are pure," just as true is it that, to the unrenewed mind and unwatchful heart, the holiest things may and do become snares and stumbling blocks; satisfied with the beauty of earthly sanc-tuaries, and the solemnity of mere earthly forms, they yearn not for the "beau-ty of the Lord our God," who "dwelleth not in temples made with hands." But the soul of one who knows Him who is "altogether lovely," and longs for the day when he shall "see the King in His beauty," while rejoicing in, and loving, our old cathedrals in their ancient hoariness, will yet esteem them as nothing in comparison with the higher things on which his heart is set. And it will prob-ably be found that, after all, he who thus gives such things their right and sub-ordinate place has the purest enjoyment in, and the truest appreciation of, those ancient fanes [1] which have stood for centuries, the silent witnesses of the beau-ty of religion.

May each one who reads this dream find, and know, and rejoice in that Sav-iour, whose whisper of pardoning love is sweeter than earth's sweetest music, whose smile of acceptance is lovelier than earth's loveliest scene! May he him-self become a "temple of the Holy Ghost," bright with the beauty of holiness and shining in the light of the countenance of our God!

F. R. H.

---

[1] A "fane" was a temple.

CHRISTMAS DECORATIONS.

WHEN our young friends use their taste, and skill, in what seems, on the surface of things, a sacred work,—the beautifying of God's sanctuary for a holy festival, do they ever consider that, whatever the theoretical aim may be, the practical result is, necessarily and distinctly, temptation? Temptation, moreover, in exact proportion to the taste and skill displayed! The experience of every honest conscience shows that when we, who naturally love all that is beautiful, enter a church beautifully decorated, the temptation to wandering eyes and thoughts is just in proportion to the exquisiteness and elaborateness of the decorations. We have come to seek Jesus, to find the Shepherd "by the footsteps of the flock"; we want to commune with Him, and we want Him to speak to our hearts; we want to be freshly and specially "looking unto Jesus" in all the meaning of that word, looking away from all else, looking unto Him. And at once our eye is caught by an elegant festoon, and a singularly effective twining of a pillar or picking out of a moulding, and a most charming device on the reading desk, and a novel arrangement of the panels of the pulpit. It is all lovely, much prettier than last year, the general effect is so good, and so on. And suddenly we remember what we came for, and we make a great effort to turn away our eyes and fix them on "Jesus only"; but somehow the electric chain has been severed, the other things have entered in; and when we again look up, to meet the smile of the "Prince of Peace," we find there has been "something between"; our eyes have involuntarily turned away from the "King in His beauty" to the passing prettiness of garland and wreath. What have we not lost? But simple texts of Scripture I see no objection to.

The dilemma for the decorators is, do they wish their work to be looked at and admired, or do they not? If not, why put it where it must attract the eye? But if they do, let them remember that the mind cannot be equally occupied with two things at the same time; and that the moments spent in admiring gaze on their graceful work cannot be spent in adoring gaze on the Lord of Christmas, the Altogether Lovely One.

But there is something to be said for "Christmas decorations," where they will lead to no wandering thoughts in worship. If our bright young decorators could but see the gleam, on suffering or aged faces, when "a bit of Christmas" reaches the lonely lives in a hospital or workhouse ward; if they would but listen to the echo from the Mount of Olives, "Inasmuch as ye have done it unto one of the least of these My brethren, ye have done it unto Me"; surely they would gladly try to use their taste and energies for them, instead of the mere delectation, or even spiritual hindrance, of a fashionable congregation. It would be so easy; just a little bouquet of evergreens, for each poor bedside; just a little festoonery, for the bare walls; just a Christmas motto or two; they cannot tell, till they have seen for themselves, what an amount of pleasure they would give to those who have so little to cheer them! Will not some of our young friends do this little service for the Master's sake this next Christmas, each in his or her own locality? For London, they might communicate with the Hon. Secretary of the Flower Mission, 3, Clyde Street, S.W., or with the Secretary of the Mildmay Flower Mission, Deaconess House, Mildmay Park, N.; or the work might be done in the country workhouses and infirmaries, for, as a rule, far less is done to brighten them than the larger ones.

Where there is a will there is a way, and, as an old poet says, "love will find out the way." May the love of Christ constrain many, even in this, not to please themselves, but Him who came to seek and to save that which was lost.

F. R. H. (1875)

"CHRISTIAN PROGRESS" SCRIPTURE READING AND PRAYER UNION. UNITED BIBLE READING.

"WELL, Miss, as long as I *was* reading regular, I thought I might as well read what the others were reading," said a young man-servant, as his reason for joining the "Christian Progress Union."

"As well!" Yes, and much better. To begin with, we ought, every one of us, to be "reading regular." There is no doubt about that. How is any soul to "grow" on one meal a day, or on uncertain and occasional draughts of the "sincere milk of the word"? Regularly, not only as to constancy, but *as to system.* How much time is wasted in indecision, and wondering what to read next! How many are familiar only with their favourite parts of God's word, neglecting others almost entirely; thus overlooking many a royal commandment, and losing much of the royal bounty, and gaining no wide and balanced views, of the great field of His truth! How can we be "throughly furnished unto *all* good works," if we do not use God's means thereto, "*all* Scripture"?

And if we are, as every Christian ought to be, reading *both* parts of His word regularly every day, why not "read what others are reading"? Why should you read Galatians while others are reading Ephesians; Ephesians while they are in Philippians? Why not "keep rank" with all one's Christian friends, and thousands of fellow members, praying for the same light, the same teaching, day by day, for them and for ourselves? Why not lie down *together* in the green pastures, instead of scattering all about?

There are several arrangements for united reading, and membership of any will be more or less profitable. But some features of the "*Christian Progress Scripture Reading and Prayer Union*" seem to me to render it not only profitable, in a special degree, for ourselves, but peculiarly valuable, as an adjunct to our work among others.

Our members read one chapter every day in the Old Testament, going straight through; and a short evening reading in the New Testament, in consecutive portions, averaging about fifteen verses.

Personally, I believe each will find it a real help, and *not* a fetter or limit, to have these assigned portions. There is, or should be, plenty of time for any further Bible study, which may attract us. But this is a reminder to the young or unestablished Christian. It is a guard against desultoriness. It is a counteractive to one-sidedness, and a gentle guide into "the whole counsel of God." It forms a pleasant bond alike for the near and the distant. It is a connecting link for scattered families and severed friends. It is also an immense help to profitable intercourse. The mere fact of knowing that those around have certainly been reading the same chapters opens the way for questions or remarks, or mention of striking verses, which might not otherwise have been ventured on, and thus raises the tone of our household conversation. How few of us realize that we have to give account for our empty table-talk! Constantly, too, it will give easier opportunity for improvement of even a passing greeting, or enrichment of a quickly written note with a living gem of truth.

I would plead for the servants to be "partakers of the benefit." With a little kindly explanation, they are almost invariably pleased to join, and the practical benefit is perhaps even greater in the servants' hall than in the drawing-room. Children, too, if old enough to read for themselves, are important accessions. "It is so nice for our little boy and girl to join with us," said a Christian mother; "it may be the means of making them steady Bible-readers for life!" I am convinced that it would be a great blessing in schools. Many have already joined. In one young ladies' school about sixty of the pupils are members.

Most especially would I commend it to Christian workers. Those who have a settled charge will find that no amount of general exhortations, to read the Bible, will be so effectual as "Come, join with me!" This is immediate and definite, and will bring persons to a point. One lady, after joining herself, obtained some fifty members in about a week, from her two Bible-classes. Just try it! Join yourself, first; and then see if it is not a new power and blessing among those for whose souls you are labouring. Do not train them into bad ways by getting them to read only once a day. If you do that, you encourage the comfortable idea that they have done their duty very sufficiently by a chapter at night, while the whole day has been Scriptureless. Aim higher at once, and you will strike higher. There is no power in half measures. It is one of the great benefits of this Union, that it is lifting such numbers out of their easy-going, once-a-day, reading, into a more excellent way.

I believe it will be found to be a most valuable parochial agent, and that members of any congregation will be strengthening the hands of their ministers, by bringing it before them in this light. *Very* much might be said on this aspect of the Union, which it would be stepping out of my province to enlarge upon. Perhaps no item of parochial machinery would be so fraught with real spiritual blessing as this noiselessly powerful one, wherever heartily and *thoroughly* introduced.

For those who have temporary opportunities of special work with souls, this Union is simply invaluable. It is just what we want to consolidate our work. It is our best legacy when leaving those to whom we have been privileged to be

God's messengers of blessing. It is putting them on the rails; putting them in the way of further blessing; making the surest provision for their nourishment; giving them something which will be definite and perpetual help in the new path. It will be a delightful link, and a reminder to mutual prayer. It will help them to help each other, and give them something to do in trying to get others to join. Work for our young converts is often a difficulty, but this will give immediate opportunity both for confession of Christ and direct usefulness, and often lead to more.

Now, who will join us? You may do so by sending your full name and address (stating whether Rev., Mr., Esq., Mrs., or Miss, and inclosing a penny stamp) to the Rev. Ernest Boys, Bengeo, Hertford. You will receive in return a card of membership, a copy of the *Christian Progress Magazine*, and other papers containing full information respecting it. If you are not *quite* sure whether you would like it, send for the papers only, and try it for a month.

There need be no hesitation about joining, on the idea of its being a sort of irrevocable promise. You can cease to be a member any day, by *returning your card of membership*. If you forget a reading, you have not broken a vow, but missed a privilege. Those who cannot read for themselves can have the portions read to them; one of our heartiest members is "no scholar," but his little daughter reads to him.

If you shrink a little from laying aside some favourite plan, or *want* of plan, of your own, will you not remember that "none of us liveth to himself"? If you join for the sake of being in a better position to lead and lift others into the benefits of regular reading, you surely will not feel it any sacrifice! Rather you will find, as many of us thankfully acknowledge, that it is a decided personal benefit to ourselves..

"*Christian Progress*," the Organ of the Union, is well described as a "Magazine of help and encouragement in Christian life, testimony, and work." "Its aim," says the Editor, "is to encourage believers in the Lord Jesus Christ in their daily walk amidst the realities of life." Members can send questions relating to practical Christian life and work, or to the interpretation of Holy Scriptures; also special requests for prayer, which are inserted monthly. The Magazine contains tables of the readings and special notices to members.

In conclusion, let me say to every one of my friends, known and unknown, "Come *thou* with us, and we will do thee good!"

F. R. H.

WORDS ABOUT WORK.

For New Year's Day, 1879.

From *Word and Work* Magazine.

AMONG the multitude of our thoughts within us, at the solemn passing from the year for ever closed into the veiled and trackless paths of the New Year, our work, past and future, is, most likely, very prominent. Perhaps the very first thing all the true workers will be telling the patient Master, about their work, is what one of the most Christ-like workers I ever heard of said to me the other day: "It all wants forgiving." For conscience responds to the truth of His declaration, "Neither shall they cover themselves with their own works." One flash of the Spirit's light is enough to show us how true that is, and how really and truly we have been unprofitable servants. Yes, forgiveness for all our sins comes *first*, failures and successes alike all needing the sprinkled blood.

What does the next flash, or even the same flash, show? Not a promise merely, but a declaration of one of God's grand facts: "Thou hast forgiven Thy people from Egypt even until now." All along, ever since He brought us out of the house of bondage, that we might be His own happy servants, even until now, this very New Year's day, He *has* forgiven; yes, "even until now," this very minute. And so we start out upon the New Year, forgiven; our work begins again, "*forgiven.*"

What about all this forgiven work? What has become of it? Where is it? "Surely my judgment is with the Lord, and my *work with my God.*" That is where it is, yours and mine: poor, feeble, failing, forgiveness-needing, passing and past, though it be; not done with, and on the way to being forgotten; not even stored away in the archives of eternity; safer, more honoured than that, it is with our God, and "surely" so. Do not you think that what is with Him is in sufficiently safe keeping? Is it not enough that the glory of the Lord is thus our reward in our work? Well may Paul say that "God is not unrighteous to forget your work and labour of love," when it is all, just where we ourselves are, in the safe keeping of His own hand. For "the righteous, and the wise, and their works, are in the hand of God." Works past, as well as works present and future, are *there*.

Then as to the work before us. There really is nothing but encouragement in His word for His workers: not a precept without a corresponding promise; not an allusion to difficulties without ten times as many dear corresponding notes of hope and help. And, of course, what He promises He not only means, but actually does fulfil to His faithful ones.

Let us just think for a few minutes, for our comfort, what He *does* say. "Work; for I am with you, saith the Lord of hosts." That alone is the grandest, sweetest, richest "guerdon" here that any loving heart can ask. "*With* you"; not merely looking down out of the sky at you struggling in your work, but by your very side, closer than the nearest colleague, holding you by the hand, whispering words of strange power for you to use, and words of still stranger power for your own heart only, calming, and strengthening, and gladdening it; so that if you are "men wondered at" by others, you are a great deal more wondered at by yourself. You are so "marvellously helped," that you "never would have thought it!" No, of course not; but, you see, His thoughts towards you in your work were much better than yours, and you can say:

"And now I find Thy promise true,
    Of perfect peace and rest;
I cannot sigh—I can but sing
    While leaning on Thy breast,
And leaving everything to Thee
    Whose ways are always best."

Some of us know what it is to be miserably afraid of making mistakes in our work. How graciously He meets this with "I will direct their work in truth." If we could see under the surface, surely we should see that no mistakes are made when we are *really* trusting this word. Asking without trusting, *i.e.* not "in faith," or asking as a sort of experiment upon the promise, or taking it for granted in a general way that God is directing us, or going ahead in our particular line without constant uplooking, with the unacknowledged idea that, because we were directed yesterday, things will come all right to-day: all this is not the simple, implicit, and continual waiting of our eyes upon the Lord our God, which meets the constant guidance of His eye. But watching daily, and trusting simply, this promise will no more fail than any other. And this, too, is ordained in the hand of a Mediator. He who appeared to Saul and said, "It shall be told thee what thou must do," but delegated to none the showing how great things he must suffer, seems to be foreshadowed by Moses, who was not only to bring the causes of the people to God, but to "show them the work that they must do." So will our Lord Jesus Christ Himself show us the work that we must do day by day. And when we look onward, perhaps a little wearily, down the long vista of a busy year, and say, "Neither is this a work of one day or two," He answers, with quick understanding of our thoughts, "Lo, I am with you *all the days*." So, like Asaph and his brethren, we may go on "ministering *before the Ark* (*i.e.*, in the special and immediate presence of our Lord) continually, as every day's work required."

Again, in the interests of the bright side and true side of "His guerdon here," glance at the typical contrast between the labour in the house of bondage, making bricks in full tale without any straw given or provided, and the splendid supply of materials for "the work of the service of the sanctuary." "For the stuff they had was sufficient for all the work to make it, and too much!" Was not this written for our learning, dear fellow workers? We may have no "stuff" at all, to our thinking; we may be saying, "Have I now any power at all to say *anything?*" But just as these costly and fitting materials were brought to Bezaleel and Aholiab "every morning," so regularly and abundantly shall the "stuff" be supplied to "every one whose heart stirred him up to come unto the work to do it." For it is written, "My God shall supply all your need, according to His riches in glory by Jesus Christ." Surely that measure of pledged supply is "sufficient and too much." And, again, we see the hand of the Mediator, for this magnificent supply is given "by Christ Jesus," God's great Almoner.

Now for another promise, which certainly does not look like that wretched linking of "labour" with "many a sorrow," and "many a tear," of which so many seem to have a dread. But God says, "Mine elect shall long *enjoy* the work of their hands." Quite fearlessly I appeal to you to bear witness if God is not true to His word! And I would challenge the world to produce a band of men and women who "enjoy" their work as we enjoy ours! Just let the faces of the workers at any gathering bear unconscious witness whether they enjoy their work, or not. Look at them as they come away, tired, but happy and thankful! I don't think the fagged home goers from any ballroom would witness in the same way to real, downright enjoyment of *their* work, "pleasure" though they choose to call it. Or compare the faces that leave the Stock Exchange, or a political meeting, or any place where they have been simply doing their own work. Yes, there are plenty of troubles, and delays, and failures, and headaches, and much weariness, too, I know all about that; but nevertheless, when His elect are truly doing His work, sowing His seed, and reaping His precious sheaves, they enjoy that work, as He says they *shall*. And they shall *long* enjoy it, too; other enjoyments pass away in passing, but this only passes on to eternal fruition of enjoyment. No wonder if work that *abides* shall be *long* enjoyed.

When the Lord says to us, "Prepare thy work," we have the comfort of recollecting that He has prepared our works for us (Ephesians 2:10, marg.). Why not take the comfort of this as to any untried work which we may be "called unto"? That sphere did not make itself, neither did man form it into just what it is at his own will; it was God who prepared it for the worker whom He intended for it; and if there is sufficient evidence that you are called to it, then you may rest assured that He "prepared" it and "ordained" it for you. Do not let us dwell *only* on our side of the preparation; but let us recollect that He who prepares the workers prepares the works too, and prepares them for us to walk in, *i.e.*, just to go on *step by step*; for that is "walking." Then, for our own side, let us recollect, "Thou also hast wrought all our works in us"; or, as the very striking margin has it, "for us." So we see that He has wrought in us, and for us, every bit of work we have ever succeeded in doing as yet; therefore to Him be all the glory! And, no less evidently, it will be He Himself who will work in us and for us every single bit that we shall yet do; therefore in Him be all our trust! And yet (oh, wonderful condescension!), though it is all His own doing from beginning to end, "your work shall be rewarded." "Every man"; (just think; every one of us poor workers!) "shall receive his own reward," not a general premium all round. And this, too, by the hand of our Mediator. Knowing that *of the Lord* ye shall receive the reward of the inheritance, for ye serve the "Lord Christ."

May we, for, and in, and all through, the coming year, be so many individual illustrations of St. Paul's sevenfold desire for his converts as to "every good work."

May we—

1. Be "*prepared* unto every good work."
2. "Be *ready to* every good work."
3. Be "*throughly furnished* unto all good works."
4. "*Abound* in every good work."
5. "Being *fruitful* in every good work."
6. Be *stablished* "in every good word and work."
7. Be made "*perfect* in every good work."

F. R. H.

Jn.3.8.
Ps.45.1. Jo.20.18,25. CHAPTER I.

CHAPTER I.

Is.4.20. THAT which was from the *ᵃ* beginning,
Is.40.4. which we have heard, which we have
seen *ᶜ* with our eyes, which we have
looked upon, and our hands have *ᵈ* handled, of the Word of life;

2 (For the life was manifested, and we
have seen *it*, and bear witness, and shew unto you that eternal life, *ᶠ* which was with
the Father, and was manifested unto us;)

He.4.20. 3 That which we have seen and heard
Lu.2.17. declare we unto you, that ye also may
Lu.10.32. have fellowship with us: and truly our
fellowship *ˡ* is with the Father, and with
Re.1.9. his Son Jesus Christ.

4 And these things write we unto you,
that *ⁿ* your joy may be full.

Le.v.5-7 5 This then is the message which we have
heard of him, and declare unto you, that God
is light, *ʳ* and in him is no darkness at all.

6 If we say that we have fellowship
with him, and walk in darkness, we lie,
and do not the truth: *Jo.8.12. & 12.46.*

Ps.89.15. 7 But if we walk *ᵗ* in the light, as he is
1.11.9. in the light, we have fellowship one with
Re.16.30. another, and the blood *ˣ* of Jesus Christ
De.2.13. his Son cleanseth us from all sin. *He.13.12.*
1.2.6. 8 If we say that we have no sin, *ʸ* we de-
1.15.21,22. ceive ourselves, and the truth is not in us.
Jer.3.13. 9 If we confess *ᶻ* our sins, he is faithful
Ze.3.4. and just to forgive us *our* sins, and to
Je.33.8. cleanse *ᵇ* us from all unrighteousness. *Is.6.7.*

10 If we say that we have not sinned, we
make him a liar, and his word is not in us.

This is a magnification of part of the first page if I John in F.R.H.'s personal Bagster study Bible that she read, studied, annotated at the end of her life. The full page is given on page 2 of this book. Her annotations and lines were very thin and faint.

"Holiday Work" was published in *Swiss Letters and Alpine Poems*. This was Chapter V of that book (see pages 326–330 of Volume IV of the Havergal edition). This was also published by J. and R. Parlane, Paisley, with the subtitle "A Pedestrian Tour in Switzerland."

HOLIDAY WORK.

Written for *Woman's Work* Magazine in 1873.

I ONLY wish that all the tired workers at home would renew their strength and spirits by such holiday work abroad as lies within reach of many who fancy it far out of their reach. I did not know till the summer before last what a combination of keen enjoyment and benefit to health, with opportunities of usefulness and open doors innumerable, was to be found in a *pedestrian tour by unprotected females!* This, too, without difficulties or discomforts worth calling such, and at a *very* much smaller outlay than is supposed possible by those who travel in the usual expensive way, and think that going to Switzerland for six or eight weeks means spending £50 at the least. Much less than half that sum will suffice for such a tour as ours. And lest it should be thought that exceptional strength is necessary, I may premise that both my friend and myself had been thoroughly overworked, and were obliged to seek rest; that neither of us is very strong, and that a walk of a mile or two is the extent of our English powers.

Of course we chose the inexpensive route, *viâ* Newhaven and Dieppe to Paris, and thence by night train to Belfort, on the frontier, where we arrived at nine a.m., June 29th, 1871. As we had slept pretty fairly, having had a carriage to ourselves by reason of the guard's natural sympathy for unprotected females, and having been able to lie down full length by reason of going second class instead of first, we were not tired, and intended to proceed. But the train to Basle and Lucerne had just left. *"C'est une désorganisation complète!"* said a fatigued Frenchman, and rightly. No information whatever was to be had, either at Paris or at Belfort itself, as to trains beyond, unless you got hold of a German official. Moreover, every German train was arranged to depart just before the corresponding French one got in, and *vice versa,* apparently for the purpose of spite. And so it came to pass, as a result of the war, that we had nearly six hours to wait.

When there is no one to wait and be anxious for you, and no one to arrange for but your two selves, and no fixed plan beyond to-day, and that day and all its hours committed to a Father's guidance, disappointment becomes almost impossible, and the crossing of one's intentions constantly results in most evident guiding to something better. So it was with our detention at Belfort, which was no part of our own programme.

We set off through the town to the fortifications. "Why should we not begin at once?" said my friend, E. Clay. So, setting the example, she began offering French tracts and "portions" to almost every one we met. And a wonderful two or three hours we had! Such eagerness for the little books, such gratitude, such attentive listening as we tried to speak of Jesus, such tears as we touched the chord of suffering, still vibrating among these poor people, to whom war had been an awful reality! Surely God sent us! Not one to whom we spoke but told us of husbands, sons or brothers fallen in the siege or elsewhere; or else of terrible losses and poverty. Some to whom we gave tracts went away reading, and soon came back begging for another, "pour ma mère," "pour un ami." We went into a large room, where several wounded soldiers lay, while women sat at work; here again all was earnest attention and gratitude. "*Merci infiniment, infiniment!*" said one poor fellow.

At last we made our way up to the fortifications, where probably none but "unprotected females" would have been allowed! Our *petits livres* secured us the respect of the few soldiers and many workmen. We realized a little of what war means, as we wandered about the half ruined stronghold, and looked down upon a church with scarcely a square yard of roof intact, and houses in every stage of shatter and desolation, or, at best, poorly patched up for bare shelter.

Before we left, a deputation came to us from a party of workmen who had been reading our tracts during their dinner, to ask for a few more, that they might take them to some *camarades,* who were employed in another part of the town, and who "would be too happy to possess them."

As we returned through the town we found many waylaying us. At one point which they knew we must pass, at least thirty persons were waiting, and pressed round us, begging for more tracts. We had only a few leaflets left, with "Rock of ages" in French and German, and these they accepted eagerly. I have since regretted that it did not occur to me at the moment to *sing* it.

We reached Lucerne that night, and next morning steamed down the lake. It would have been contrary to our travelling principles to pay first-class fare for the privilege of sitting among the unsociable English, aft, with funnels and paddle-boxes right between us and the magnificent scenery opening out before us; so we took second-class tickets, thereby securing for half-price a clear front view, with nothing but transparent air between us and the increasing loveliness ahead, and also the advantage of being among the natives, who were all politeness to the English ladies. We thus had also the benefit of some charming Swiss

songs, sung by a girls' school out for a holiday; they lent us their little song-book
to follow the music, and were delighted at receiving little books in return, which
might by His blessing put a *new* song in their mouths.

From Altdorf, at the other end of the lake, our long anticipated *real* pedestrian tour began. Our plan was as follows. Our luggage consisted of a *small* car-
petbag apiece, every inch and ounce having been considered and economised,
though even these were discovered on further experience to contain superflu-
ities! These bags we sent on each morning by post or diligence if on *grandes
routes;* by baggage mule, country cart, or small boy, if off the track: to whatever
place we thought we could reach in the day without undue fatigue; and here we
always found them all right; average expense, a few pence.

We started at four, or five a.m., walking on till we felt inclined to stop and
rest: our first halt being given to leisurely reading and prayer in some grand and
lonely mountain oratory; a plan which we found more pleasant and profitable
than devoting the whole time to it indoors before starting. Then we strolled on
again, halting or taking refreshment, just as and when we felt inclined; resting
for several hours in the heat of the day, and making another stage or two in the
afternoon. We carried tiny knapsacks (bags are a great mistake, being more fatiguing to carry); these held tracts and "portions," a biscuit and a hard egg, and
the barest necessaries in case of missing our carpetbags, or altering our plan for
the night. As Switzerland is the land of hotels and travellers, such a tour as ours
is easier than it would be elsewhere; unless you are in *very* out-of-the-way places, you seldom go three miles without some opportunity of getting a meal, nor
six without a fair chance of beds.

We began very gradually; our first walk was only two miles, but in a fortnight we found ourselves doing from fourteen to twenty miles in the day without getting tired! Our early hours were part of the secret; one can do double the
distance before seven a.m. that one can after; the invigorating effect of the crisp
fresh mountain air from four to seven a.m. is indescribable. Those who think
eight a.m. a pretty fair start never know what this atmospheric salvolatile is. But
you cannot burn your candle at both ends, and must go to bed accordingly. If
you resolutely and *regularly* retire at eight p.m., and make no scruple about taking a good siesta in the heat of the day; (and you may lie down on the grass with
impunity in *such* open air), it will come quite natural to get up about 3.30 or
4 a.m. We felt sensitive about Dr. Watts and "wasting our hours in bed," if we
were not out of it before 5.30 on Sunday mornings.

Oh the delicious freedom and sense of leisure of those days! And the veri-
table "renewing of youth," in all senses, that it brought! How we spied grand
points of view from rocks above, and (having no one to consult, or to keep

waiting, or to fidget about us) stormed them with our alpenstocks, and scrambled and leaped, and laughed and raced, as if we were, not girls again, but downright *boys!* How we lay down on moss and exquisite ferns, and feasted our eyes on dazzling snow summits through dark, graceful pines, with intense blue sky above, and the quiet music of little torrents coming up from the dell below, and with the "visible music" all round us, in every possible colour-key, of those marvellously lovely Alpine flowers, which people never see who go "in the season," a month or two later. How entirely, we were rid of that imp, Hurry, who wears out our lives in England! "No hurry!" It took us a long while to realize that delightful fact. And how we wished that a wish could have transported the whole Association of Female Workers and Young Women's Christian Association, whom we left in London, bodily to the spot, to share the wonderful rest and enjoyment which our Father was giving us! A *"holiday"* most certainly; but how about *"work"*? So much of that, that we never wanted more opportunities, but only more earnestness and faithfulness, and courage and love, to use them. If space allowed, one would like to give each day in order and detail, with its pleasant providences and openings. But we can only indicate briefly some of the different kinds of "opportunity" so thickly strewn in our path.

Our tour was entirely through Roman Catholic cantons; its roughly sketched outline being this: from Altdorf, over the Furca, down the Rhone valley to Viesch; a detour to Æggischhorn and Bel Alp; then to Zermatt; over the pass of St. Théodule into the Val d'Aosta; Courmayeur; over the Col de Bonhomme to Chamouni; thence to Martigny, where we took rail direct home, *viâ* Neuchatel. And all the way, no Bible, no gospel, but souls walking in darkness all around! Will not some of our workers try to go, and tell them of the True Light?

At the little inns where we slept, we nearly always found young waitresses. A few kind words and smiles secured their absolute devotion to us, and we were waited on like duchesses. (N.B.—How much nicer than going to big hotels, with waiters flying about, to whom you are merely No. 79 or No. 43!). They have "no time for religion in the summer," but attend extra masses in winter to atone for it. But they find time to listen with surprise as you speak to them of salvation. They are afraid to die; *"Ah, la mort, c'est terrible!"* And it is at least something new to hear of a "sure and certain hope." We speak to them again in the morning before we go, and sometimes find that they have been lying awake thinking of what had been said. We give them a Gospel of St. John, and our own reading has not been less profitable because it has not been in our own Bibles, but in this "portion" for poor Thérése, marking as we read such bright star-texts as may catch her eye, and guide her to Jesus.

Here I may say that during our long mid-day rests, we made it our special occupation to mark the most striking passages and texts in the "portions" we were going to give away. These were *chiefly* St. Luke and St. John, while to persons of superior intelligence and education we often gave Romans, but *always marked.* Even curiosity will induce people to look attentively at marked passages.

At Zermatt, where we stayed five days in the clean, cheap, and unpretending Hotel des Alpes (which we strongly recommend), there were two maidens, and we agreed each to make special effort with one. Alexandrine had evidently never thought about religion; but Marie, a singularly gentle and loveable girl, seemed an instance of "soil prepared." She had thought much of death, and with terror; she had tried to be worthy of heaven, and had failed, and wondered why she felt so bad when she really wished to be good. She said she knew that Jesus died for sinners, but had no idea what good that was to do for her, as of course she must gain her own salvation, and *then* He might save her. She had never seen a Testament, and no one of the many English ladies whom she had served had ever spoken to her about these things.

Every evening she contrived to come to my room, and we read the German Testament and prayed together. She listened eagerly, and as if it were indeed a matter of life and death. I cannot say that when we left she was able to *rejoice* in Christ, but I think that she had, though tremblingly, touched the hem of His garment; she was trusting to none other, and saw that it must be "Jesus only," and the whole desire of her heart seemed to be toward Him.

We often turned out of the path to go to parties of haymakers. They invariably received our books with pleasure, and their acknowledgments were most courteous. If we stayed to read a few verses, they never seemed to feel it an interruption. We gave them the book out of which we read, with a leaf turned down, that they might look again at the passage. One morning I sat down by an old woman, who was knitting, and watching goats. She was an "old maid," very poor and full of troubles. She often thought of heaven, she said, and how different it would be there, and she prayed that God would show her how to get there. She was sure she should be happy if she was where the good Lord Jesus was. It seemed to me that the poor old creature had some real love for Him, and was perhaps a true child of God, though with little light; so, acting on impulse, yet with misgiving as to its being the right choice, I read to her very slowly most of the 8th of Romans, pointing with my finger to every line as she looked over me, dwelling on and repeating the most comforting words. I was little prepared for the effect of the thought, so entirely new to her, "*no separation.*" She took hold of it with unquestioning faith and with wonderful joy. "Has He said that,

that I shall never be separated from Him? Ah, how beautiful; ah, how good! I can suffer now, I can die now." And the poor wrinkled old face was positively radiant. Her tears of gratitude, when, after a long talk, I said she might keep the little book which contained such precious words, were touching indeed. At my last glimpse of her she was poring over her Romans, heeding neither her goats nor her knitting.

Children were generally proud to be taken notice of by the "*Engländerin-nen*," and so were the parents, if, on making friends with a family group, we asked the little ones to show us how nicely they could read. As they mostly read clearly and well, this seemed to answer better than our own reading, for it gave additional motives for attention, and easy opportunities for questions and simple comments.

It is a good plan to learn by heart some of the leading gospel texts; even a very few, so learnt, prove valuable weapons, and without this one feels comparatively swordless, as one cannot give a rough and ready translation with the same confidence as the exact words of the French or German version. Sometimes we quoted such a text where we could have but a minute's conversation, and if our friends seemed at all struck with it, we gave them the portion containing it, telling them that if they would look carefully they would find those words in the little book. We sometimes, on looking back, saw them sitting down at once to search for it. "*My word shall not return unto Me void*" is a grand promise; and in the faith of that it was a comfort to quote and reiterate short and easily remembered texts, when our supply of "portions" ran short.

All very well; but what are those to do who speak little or no French and German? "Where there's a will there's a way," and plenty of ways too. You can mark the "portions"; you can offer them; you can point out passages, and get the person to *read it to you;* or you can set the children to read for you; and while that promise standeth sure, who shall say that such work shall be in vain? What does it matter about *our* words, if we can, even silently, give *His* words?

We never came upon ground trodden by any other sower, except among the guides, and we did find a few of them who had at least "heard of these things." They are intelligent and superior men, and seemed more often ready and disposed to converse *seriously* and *freely* on important subjects than any *class* of men there or elsewhere.

At Bel Alp, a mountain pension about seven thousand feet high, one of the loveliest spots in the darkest canton, we engaged a guide for the ascent of the Sparrenhorn, which is nearly ten thousand feet high. (Unless going above snow level, or crossing a glacier, we never required Swiss guides. A tolerable map and the "Practical Swiss Guide" were enough for all other routes.)

We started at 3.45 a.m., and from the stillness of the hill side overlooking the great Aletsch glacier watched an Alpine dawn. In the east was a calm glory of expectant light, as if something altogether celestial must come next, instead of a common sunrise. In the south and west, "clear as crystal," stood the grandest mountains, white and saintly, as if they might be waiting for the resurrection, with the moon shining in paling radiance over them, and the deep Rhone valley, dark and grave-like, below. Suddenly the first roseflush touched the Mischabel, then Monte Leone was transfigured by that wonderful *rose-fire,* delicate yet intense. When the Weisshorn came to life (most beautiful of all, more *perfectly* lovely than any earthly thing I ever yet saw) the Matterhorn caught the same resurrection light on its dark and evil-looking rock peak. It was like a volcano, lurid and awful, and gave the impression of a fallen angel, impotently wrathful, shrinking away from the serene glory of a holy angel, which that of the Weisshorn at dawn might represent, if any material thing could. The eastern ridges were almost jet, with just a tinge of purple, in front of the great golden glow into which the "daffodil sky" rapidly heightened, till the sun rose, and the great dawn splendour was over. Would you not like to go and see such a sight?

During this excursion I had several little talks with our guide, Anton. In response to a remark, he quoted a verse from Hebrews to my surprise. He explained this by telling us that four years ago an English lady had spoken to him about his soul, and on her return to England had sent him a New Testament. This he had read daily. He had *no other help,* but found in it that he might pray for the teaching of the Holy Spirit, and from that time had constantly done so. He had learnt from it the need of a mediator, and that there is but *one* Mediator, and now prayed no longer to the Virgin or the saints, but only to and through the Saviour. He had no doubt but it was God's own word, because he felt its power and preciousness. "Life was a different thing to him now," he said, and it was evidently a life of faith on the Son of God. Possibly this may meet the eye of the faithful sower who dropped the incorruptible seed which has borne such "fruit unto life eternal."

What if but one of the words spoken or books given during a whole tour should be thus blessed! Would it not be worth all the effort, and the screwing up of courage, and the battles with shyness and nervousness and reluctance, which have to be fought again and again?

> Ye who hear the blessèd call
>   Of the Spirit and the Bride;
> Hear the Master's word to all,
>   Your commission and your guide:

"And let him that heareth say,
Come," to all yet far away.

.   .   .   .   .

Brothers, sisters, do not wait,
    Speak for Him who speaks to you!
Wherefore should you hesitate?
    This is no great thing to do.
Jesus only bids you say,
"Come!" and will you not obey?

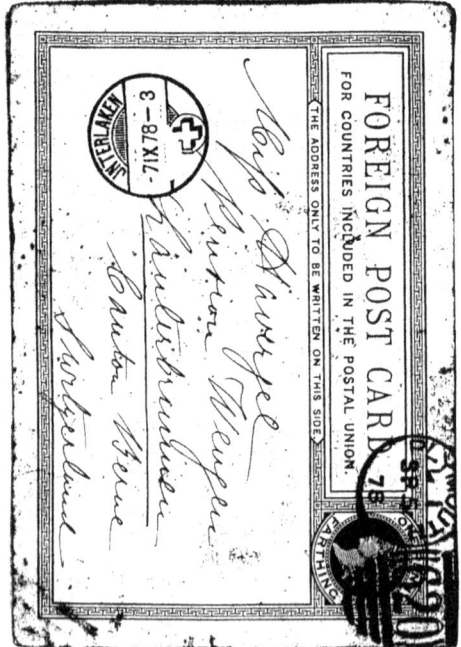

A postcard sent to Pension Wengen in Switzerland. The directions are written by F.R.H. Apparently Frances was sending this to her sister, Miss Maria V. G. Havergal.

Frances Ridley Havergal's eldest sister, Jane Miriam (Havergal) Crane (1817–1898, born 19 years before F.R.H.'s birth and living 19 years after her death) posthumously published *Swiss Letters and Alpine Poems* by Frances, a volume of letters, a few poems and two articles by F.R.H.: the first article was "Holiday Work," found on pages 61–68 of this book, and the second article was "Our Swiss Guide." The complete *Swiss Letters and Alpine Poems* is found on pages 277–366 of Volume IV of the Havergal edition. "Our Swiss Guide" was Chapter XI of that book.

OUR SWISS GUIDE.

Written in 1874.

(Reprinted from the "Sunday Magazine.")

NOT the least interesting part of mountaineering is the perpetual upspringing of lessons and illustrations and analogies. Sometimes an idea starts up which has, for one's self, all the delicious charm of a quite new thought, though very likely it may have flashed upon the minds of scores of other travellers; sometimes a very old and familiar one presents itself, and we have the pleasure of proving it, perhaps for the first time, by practical experience. In noting one little group of illustrations among many, those which cluster round the idea of a " Guide," we shall not be careful to steer clear of such old ideas, though we may hope to add some freshness to them.

The application throughout will be so very obvious to any mind accustomed to take the least interest in analogies of spiritual life, that we prefer giving the points of illustration only, leaving the reader to supply the " heavenly meaning" which shall underlie each sentence.

Curiously enough, the name of our favourite Swiss guide, the one who inspired us with most confidence, and to whom we should most like to entrust ourselves in any future tour, at once gave the keynote of thought; it was *Joseph*. While we instinctively trusted his sagacity and strength, it was additionally pleasant to find that our bright young guide was a believer in the Lord Jesus Christ, our true Joseph. He had remarked that his great physical strength and health was " the most splendid earthly gift," but on our mention of the most glorious Gift of all, our Saviour Christ himself, he rejoined fervently, " Ah, one can never estimate the value of *that* gift!"

But to proceed to our illustrations.

1. The first duty of a really firstrate guide, when arranging for a long snow or glacier excursion, is to see that we are properly provided with everything needful. He ascertains that you have snow spectacles, without which the glare of the snow is not simply inconvenient, but injurious; and veils, without which you stand a fair chance of finding your face completely flayed, if it should be a sunny day. He examines the spike of your alpenstock and the nails of your boots, and inquires after your wraps, and often gives curiously practical advice as to other points in your outfit. He not only tells you what you must have as to provision, but, if the excursion involves a night in some mountain hut, he sends on the necessary fuel and food, and sometimes even bedding. In all these matters you do not need to trouble at all; if you will only leave it altogether to him, he will think of everything, arrange everything, and provide everything; and when the time comes you will find all in order, your shoes fresh nailed, your alpenstock newly spiked, the porter sent on with provision, and the coil of strong rope and the ice axe all ready for the difficult places which you do not yet know of.

But many travellers do not even know that the guide is thus willing and competent; they do not ask, or perhaps they even decline, his aid and advice. Instead of throwing it all upon his responsibility, they take all the trouble themselves, and then generally find something gone wrong or something overlooked.

2. Before you start, the guide has disposed of all those heavier matters which you could not possibly carry for yourself. Very often they are taken completely out of your sight. Encumbered with these, you could not even set out on your journey, much less progress quickly and pleasantly.

But there are always plenty of little affairs which seem mere nothings at first, but which are soon found to be real burdens. The guide is perfectly willing to relieve you of all these. They are no weight to him; he quite smiles at the idea of its being any trouble to him to carry them, but they make a serious difference to you. He offers to take them at first; and if you decline, though he may not perhaps offer again, he will cheerfully take them when, later on, you feel their weight, and hand them one by one to him, till the very last is given up, and you walk lightly and freely. A beginner says she " would rather carry her little knapsack, it is really no weight at all! " and thinks a parcel or two in her pocket " can't make any difference," and prefers wearing her waterproof, because " it isn't at all heavy." But she has not gone far before she is very glad, if a sensible girl, to give up her knapsack, tiny though it be; and then she finds that a waterproof won't do for climbing, and she hands that over; and presently she even empties her pocket, and the guide trudges away with it all. Then she is surprised to find what a difference it does make, and understands why her friend, who knew the guide's ways better and gave up every single thing to him at first, is getting along so cool and fresh and elastically. But mark that the weight of a burden is seldom realized till we really are going uphill and in a fair way to make progress. Indeed, this very sensitiveness to weight is a quick test of increased gradient. We think nothing about it as long as we are walking on a level or slightly downhill; but as soon as we begin the real ascent the pull of the little burdens is felt at once, and the assistance, which before we did not crave, becomes very welcome. It is then that we feel we *must* " lay aside *every* weight."

3. One may almost certainly distinguish between a tyro and an old hand by watching for a few minutes the style of march. A novice will walk at an irregular pace according to the irregularities of the ground, making little " spurts" when she comes to an easy bit, and either putting on steam or lagging behind for extra steep ones; stopping to gather flowers and poke at curious boulders; taking long or short steps according to circumstances, and never thinking of such a thing as noticing, much less imitating, the steady rhythm of the guide's walk. Probably she expresses her astonishment at his unexpectedly slow pace, and would prefer getting on a little faster; very likely she dashes ahead or aside, and presently has to be recalled to the track, which is not so easy to keep as she supposed.

One with more experience is quite content to take the guide's pace, knowing certainly that it pays in the long run, and saves an enormous amount of fatigue, and therefore of time also. Very short steps, slowly, silently, and steadily placed, but as regular as martial music, never varying in beat, never broken by alternation of strides and pauses—this is the guide's example for uphill work; and yet it is what one never believes in till one has learnt by experience that one gets through twice as much by it.

4. It is wonderful what a saving of fatigue it is if from the very beginning one obeys the guide implicitly and follows him exactly. You spy such a handy " short cut," you can see so precisely where you can join the path again, it will save you such a provoking long round, you can't think why the guide does not choose it! So away you go, exulting in your cleverness, straight uphill, instead of that tiresome zigzag.

But it is rather steeper than you thought, and you get just a little out of breath; and you find an awkward little perpendicular rock right in the way and you must go round it; and then you get into rhododendron bushes which are thicker than you thought, and you get very wet; and then you see your companions reaching the point you are making for, and you scramble and hurry. And by the time you have done with your short cut you find you have not only gained no time, but that the few minutes away from the guide have heated you and taken more out of you than an hour's steady following. Later in the day you recollect your short cuts of the morning, and wish you had economised your breath.

5. The full value of exact following is not learnt in the valleys or pastures. It is on the "high places" and on the unsullied snowfields that one discovers this.

It is when we are high away above the green slopes, seeing no track but our guide's own footsteps, that we learn its safety. He set his foot on that stone: there you must set yours, for the next is loose and would betray you; he planted his alpenstock on that inch of rock: there you must plant yours, for an inch either way would give no firm hold; he climbed by that jut of rock: so must you, for the other would be too hard a step; he sprang but half way over that torrent, and you must do the same at cost of wetting your feet, for he knew that the slab of rock which you could have reached at one bound was treacherously slippery and dangerous.

It is here also that we get into the way of instant and unquestioning compliance with every word our guide utters. I was struck with the remark of a Swiss Alpine Clubbist in a description of his ascent of the Tödi. His guide suddenly shouted to him, "Turn sharp to the right!" He saw no reason whatever for this, but obeyed instantly. The next moment an immense block of stone fell upon the spot where he would have been had he hesitated an instant or even looked round to satisfy himself. The quick and practised eye of the guide saw the trembling of the loosened mass which the traveller could not see. A query would have been fatal. He added, "In these high places one learns to obey one's guide without stopping to ask 'Why?'"

But when the snow slopes, so cool and pure and beautiful, are reached, another phase of following is learnt. There is not the excitement and effort of the rock climbing, and at first it seems very quiet and easy work, with a special exhilaration of its own, making one feel as if one had started quite fresh, all the rest of the journey counting for nothing. Once we set out on such a slope, tracking after our guide in a general sort of way, rather interested in making our own footprints, and hardly distinguishing his from those of our companions. If we turned to look back, it was surprising what a number of unconscious little curves our feet had made. But the snow was rather soft, and we soon found it much harder work than we expected. One of us was walking, as she always did, close behind the guide, because she was not quite so strong as the rest, and was therefore under his especial care. Suddenly she called out, "Oh, do set your feet *exactly* in the guide's footsteps, you can't think how much easier it is!" So we tried it, and certainly should not have believed what a difference it would make. All the difficulty and effort seemed gone; the fatiguing sinking and laborious lifting of our feet were needless; we set them now exactly where the guide's great foot had trodden, keeping his order of right and left, and all was easy, a hundred steps less toil than twenty before. But, to have the full benefit of this, one needed to keep also very near to the guide, for the last comers trod rather in their companions' footmarks, and were often misled by some false or uncertain treading of these, which marred the perfectness of the original steps.

6. Thorough knowledge of the guide's language adds both to the enjoyment and safety of our following. He has much to tell us by the way, and is always ready to answer questions and give information. One who does not easily understand loses a great deal. A companion may be very willing to translate, but may do so incorrectly, and in any case the freshness and point of many a remark is lost; while it often happens that the usual interpreter of a party is not near enough for appeal or too tired to keep up the interchange. In sudden emergencies too it may be really important that each should personally understand, and thus be able instantly to obey, the guide's directions.

Moreover, it is very desirable not only thus to "know his voice," but to be able to speak to him for one's self. Once one of us slipped in a rather awkward place. She called out, "Stop a moment!" but the guide in advance knew no English, and therefore did not heed her, and but for the quick call in German of another who saw the slip, she might have been frightened and hurt.

7. When we come to really difficult places, or glaciers with hidden crevasses, we find the use of the coil of rope. This is fastened first round the guide himself, and then round the rest of the party, allowing a length of eight or ten feet between each. Once I questioned the strength of the rope, upon which the guide untwisted it a little, and showed me a scarlet thread hidden among the strands. He told me that this was the mark that it was a real Alpine Club rope, manufactured expressly for the purpose, and to be depended upon in a matter of life and death. It is remarkable that this typical "line of scarlet thread" should have been selected as the guarantee of safety.

Once roped thus, you have a sense of security in passing what would otherwise be very dangerous places, especially concealed crevasses. And not only a sense but a reality of security. You feel the snow yield beneath your feet, you sink in, and you have neither hand nor foothold; you get perhaps a glimpse of a fathomless blue depth below you. If you struggle you only break away the snow and enlarge the cavity. But you are in no real danger, and if you have confidence in your guide and the rope, you wait quietly, perhaps even smilingly, till you are hauled out of the hole, and landed on firm snow again. Why? Because you are firmly knotted to your guide, and also to all the rest of your party. You had not even time to call out ere he felt the sudden strain upon the rope, and instantly turned to help you, drawing you easily up to his side without hurt. Your friends felt the shock too but they could not do much to help, only they watched and admired the guide, and found their own fears (if they had any) lessened, and their confidence in him and his rope greatly increased.

But it is the guide himself who bears the brunt of these difficulties. He goes first, carefully sounding the snow, avoiding many a crevasse which we should never have suspected, and sometimes getting a fall which would have been ours but for his trying the way for us. If we really follow his steps exactly and patiently, the probability is that we never go in at all, for the snow that has borne his weight never gives way under ours. But if we swerve even a few inches from his footmarks, we may soon find ourselves in the predicament described above.

8. Sometimes we come to a slope of frozen snow so steep that it looks absolutely impossible to climb it. And so it would be, but for our guide. Our impossibilities only develop his resources. Now he unshoulders his ice axe, and with wonderful rapidity cuts steps by which we ascend even more easily than hitherto. And we notice that these extra-difficult slopes are a positive advantage to us, because while he has all the hard work we have time to take breath. When the steep bit is passed, we have gained greatly in height, and yet we feel quite freshened for further ascent, instead of fatigued.

9. The guide decides your rest as well as your progress, if you are wise enough to let him. He very soon measures your powers, and not only knows precisely when a crevasse is just too wide for you to leap without help, or a rock just too awkward for you to climb, but he also seems to know precisely when you had better make longer or shorter halts. Sometimes you are unwilling to rest when he proposes it, and perhaps he lets you have your own way and go on, and then you are quite certain to be sorry for it. But more often he insists, and then you always find he was right, and that he had timed the halt better than you would have done. Then, without waiting to be asked, he unfastens your wraps, contrives a seat upon the snow, and folds a shawl round you. It is no use saying you do not feel cold, he is responsible for you, and knows what is safe, and will not let you risk getting chilled by the subtle glacier wind. Then he gives you the provision he has carried for you, meat, and bread, and wine, and leaves no little stone unturned towards making your halt as refreshing and pleasant as possible. There is no need for you to be calculating time, and fidgeting about going on; he knows how much is yet before you, and he will tell you when it is time to be moving again.

10. I mentioned that the weakest of our party was specially cared for. Sometimes while the others had merely general orders, she had his strong arm, and thus escaped the slips which the more independent ones now and then made. Weakness or ailments proved his patience and care. On one occasion the

"mountain sickness" which sometimes befalls travellers on great heights suddenly attacked one not accustomed to fail in strength, and then nothing could
exceed Joseph's kindness and attention. He made a wonderfully comfortable
couch on the snow, told us what was the matter, administered advice and wine,
and waited patiently and sympathetically till his patient, completely prostrate
for an hour, felt able to stand. Then in a firm decided tone he said, "*Ich* überne-
hme die Kranke!" (*I* undertake the sick one!) and leaving the other guides to
attend to all else, his powerful arm helped "die Kranke" down to a level where
the less rarefied air soon set all to rights.

11. It is understood that a true Swiss guide is literally "faithful unto death,"
that he does not hesitate to risk his own life for the sake of his charge, and that
instances are known in which it has not only been risked but actually sacrificed.
We have never been in a position to prove this, but the undoubted fact com-
pletes the illustration. Yet this completion only shows the imperfection. For
that poor faithful guide may perish *with* the traveller, and not *instead* of him;
the sacrifice may be all in vain where the power and the will are not commen-
surate. In such illustrations we may learn as much by the contrasts as by the si-
miliarities; and how often, as in this instance, does the very failure of an earthly
type bring out the glory and perfection of the Antitype. Our glorious Guide,
who has called us to the journey, and whose provision for it is "without money
and without price," cannot fail in His undertaking. All who are in His covenant
hands are "kept by the power of God through faith unto salvation," and "shall
never perish." What He hath begun He will perform, for He "is able to keep
you from falling, and to present you faultless before the presence of His glory
with exceeding joy." He is not merely willing to lay down His life, but He hath
laid it down for us, and now death cannot touch our Leader any more; He hath
"the power of an endless life," and we are united to that life by the strong cords
of His eternal purpose and His everlasting love, which no friction can weaken
and no stroke can sever. However tremendous the gulf beneath us, if thus united to Him, He will lead us on till our feet, no longer weary, stand far above the
clouds upon the mountain of our God, never to repass the toils and dangers of
the ascent, never to return to the valley, never to part from the strong and loving Guide who has led us to such a Hitherto of rest and wonder, and to such a
Henceforth of joy and praise.

These are rough draft notes in F.R.H.'s handwriting for My King. The notation "F's rough outline of My King 1876" looks like the handwriting of her sister Maria Vernon Graham Havergal. Two other pages of these 1876 rough draft notes on My King are given on page 98.

This was a small booklet published by James Nisbet & Co., one of three in the "Bright Thought Series." The other two were "All Things" and "Most Blessed For Ever."

HINDERERS AND HINDRANCES.

Part I

HINDERERS! Whoever set to work in real earnest without finding them? Yet they act like centrifugal and centripetal force, producing a tolerable equipoise—the ice and the steam resulting in lukewarm water, in which you can wash your hands very comfortably. Some temperaments need a little cold water, yet the world is the warmer for them. Some are of the wet blanket nature, and they are useful when the chimneys are on fire.

All who bend their minds to the attainment of some object soon find out the existence of hinderers. There are few who do not at some time or in some way hinder some one. The men hinder the women, the women the men, and children hinder both. Yet, in society as a whole, the various and mutual hindrances so fit into each other that they act like the opposing forces of gravitation and attraction.

Perhaps workers for God, and those who are longing to work for Him, longing to win souls and advance the glory of their Lord and Master,—these know vividly, and often bitterly, what hinderers mean. There are hinderers from *without*: world-loving friends, secret or open opponents, false reasoners, and many others, which one's own life-experience supplies.

There are hindrances from *within*: restless and ambitious thoughts, weary doubts, and down-heartedness; coldness of spirit, darkness of vision, impatience and over-anxiety. Do we not know these and thousands more?

And are there not hinderers from *below*? Yes, grim legions,—dark-winged opposers, hovering around both work and workers. But they cannot pierce the invisible shield, they cannot efface the invincible prayer and promise, "I have prayed for thee, that thy faith fail not," and, "Thou shalt have good success."

There are *no* hinderers from above! only blessed helpers, holy watchers, a cloud of witnesses, and One who ever whispers, "In me is thy help." The garrison may be shut in on all sides, but the free, bright sky will always be open above.

But all *these* hinderers are as a matter of course, a thing to be taken for granted; as soon may the soldier be astonished at encountering an old and well-known enemy as expect to be exempt from these.

There are other hinderers than those without, within, and below: the un-intentional ones, well-meaning ones, hard-working ones, affectionate, ay, over-affectionate ones; and it is these classes of hinderers we shall now consider, and by a few conversations illustrate and enforce our meaning.

"Mother, dearest, I have a favour to ask you. Are you too busy to listen?"

"What is it, Alice?"

"I think you will grant it, mother; but I am half afraid, too."

"If it is anything right and reasonable, you know I shall be glad."

"I have been thinking about it all the week, mother, ever since last Sunday's sermon about, 'She hath done what she could;' and I am wondering if you would mind letting me go to the Sunday school with Lizzie, and taking a little class,—I should like it so much." And Alice drew closer to her mother, and laid her arm along the back of her chair.

"My dear Alice, I think you are quite too young—not sixteen yet. It will be quite time enough to teach when you are seventeen or eighteen. Besides, you have a great deal to learn yourself; and your Bible questions take up all your Sunday afternoons, and I like you to read before morning service."

"But, mother dear, if you would only let me go once a day, say in the morning, I could easily do part of my questions on Saturday, and so get time for reading."

"There are plenty of older people to teach besides you, Alice. You will be able to do it much better when you leave school."

"But, mother, this is the only thing I could think of; and I don't know what else I could begin with."

"You have a great deal to do, Alice, a great deal that is very important,—your own education, your own heart and mind to improve. You can set a good example to your sisters out of school-hours, and be kind and helpful to them, and other ways in which you can earn the commendation, 'She hath done what she could.'"

"But can I not try to do all this, mother, and yet undertake just this little class? May I not, mother dear? It seems so long to wait till I am eighteen; and I might not live till then," said Alice thoughtfully.

Her mother looked up from the table, which was strewn with tracts, carefully sorted, and in process of being supplied with neat brown paper covers. For Alice's mother was an energetic and useful district visitor, and hoped in due time to lead her children to follow in similar paths of usefulness.

Alice was an impulsive girl, and required to be rather held in check than otherwise. Yet she had given many evidences of such care for her own soul that might have encouraged her mother to let her undertake what she might have done faithfully and perseveringly. But Alice was little for her age, and childish and merry in her ways, so that few gave her credit for ever being thoughtful, and possessing some tact and brightness when talking to her younger school-fellows.

Her mother did not know how Alice had thought and prayed over this seemingly sudden request, nor how her child longed to "do something for the Lord Jesus"; so she could not measure the depth of disappointment, the crushing out of the loving desire, as she replied:

"Alice, dear, if God has work for you to do, He will spare your life to do it—that is in His hands, not yours. Wait two or three years, and then I promise you we will see about it. But just run and fetch me the ball of string out of the dining-room."

All these objections were perfectly true, and the mother thought she was acting rightly in restraining her child, though sorry to disappoint what she thought only a momentary fancy. But did she pray that God's will might be known and done in this matter? Was she not her child's *hinderer?*

An elder and a younger sister's conversation will be our next illustration.

"Ada, it's no use your thinking of going to the night-school; it will be pouring with rain before we get back,—it's beginning to spot now." And the speaker turned from the window, where she had been scanning the clouds.

"I don't much think so, Mary. I can put on goloshes and waterproof, and then it is no matter if it does."

"There is no occasion for you to run the risk of catching another cold. Jessie White can look over the writing; and as for the Scripture, your class can join mine."

"But, Mary, dear, it never answers to put so many girls together. I would rather go. Please, don't say any more. If we don't attend regularly, how can we expect the girls to come?"

"There's a difference between going regularly and going imprudently, Ada; and you look tired to death now, and nothing comes of over-exertion. You really must not be so foolish as to go. I shall just have to nurse you with a cold."

Ada felt annoyed; but Mary's manner was determined, and to save further fuss she gave up her wish.

However, things did not go smoothly at the night-school. Mary found a note of excuse from Jessie, and the hope that the day-schoolmistress would take her class. But the mistress was gone out to tea, and Mary found herself with three or four classes on her hands. She was clever and energetic, but had some difficulty in getting so many girls to attend to the Bible lesson, and certainly the thought half intruded, "I wish I had not hindered Ada from coming!"

Shall we glance in a curate's home, that centre of struggle and devotion, where burning zeal and loving labour are often sorely unpaid and unrequited?

"Charlie! it's all very well for you to undertake one thing after another, but I know what the end of it will be—breakdown, doctor's bills, and next to nothing to live upon."

The said Charlie was a hard-working curate, with a wife whose affection was most devoted to him, and to his parish, to a certain extent, for his sake. The immediate subject of attack was a cottage-lecture, voluntarily undertaken, but involving a long walk. He had already walked five or six miles that morning, visiting from house to house, besides a good set-to at his sermon and taking a funeral in the afternoon.

"I am perfectly well and strong, Agnes dearest, and so long as God gives me such powers, why should I not use them?"

"Perfectly well and strong! Oh, Charlie! Who had such a headache last week that he couldn't bear to have the fire poked, and who had such influenza and had to pay two guineas for a Sunday's rest?"

"But I have neither headache nor influenza, and when I had I omitted the lecture. Walking really does me good, and the lecture is quite a refreshment to me. You must not grudge your husband his parochial pleasures," and he put his hand caressingly on her shoulder.

"Oh, yes, I know it's very nice, and the people listen, so it's encouraging, but that's no reason you should wear yourself out."

"Would you have me give up the lecture, and disappoint those who are just beginning to value what they hear?"

"I wish you would distinguish things that differ, Charles. I never wanted you to give it up (you'll be late if you go on talking), only I do think it very wrong to go on work, work, work. You don't consider what it will be to me if you are ill for weeks, like Mr. J——'s curate, and then I shall break down too."

This was not a pleasant view of the subject for a man who loved his wife as men *should* love their wives, and as Charles did. An expression of endurance came over his face. "Dear Agnes, don't talk so!" was all he said.

"Talk how, Charlie? You know it's true, and you can't deny it. Why, there's another hole in your glove! If you mean to be in time, you must start, and please don't step into those ruts in that dark lane. I shall have you brought home with a broken leg, I expect, for you dash on so!"

Charles departed; but the discussion had an irritating effect upon him, and he felt dispirited, and almost disheartened, and almost disinclined for his usually loved work.

His subject was, "Bear ye one another's burdens, and so fulfil the law of Christ." But the practical commentary upon the precepts which he had just experienced was unfortunate. He felt that his burdens had been momentarily at least added to by one who would have given her life to lighten them. And, like a sudden gust of wind, his wife's remarks had utterly blown away many of the thoughts which he was intending to give his waiting people, and so ruffled and disordered the rest that he thought it best to give up that subject and take some other.

Was it any marvel that his lecture was less full of the powerful simplicity of gospel truth which drew and kept that little congregation together? Yet who would have thought that the help-meet had been the *hinderer?*

Again, and let our illustration warn the unconscious hinderers.

It is night, and the candle is almost burnt down in a double-bedded room shared by two brothers. The elder is still intently reading—he had read in that book an hour ago, and since then has knelt long by his bedside, and now he has returned to its pages again. There was a reason for that return. He had been walking many days in darkness, without light or comfort, almost without sensible love to the Saviour whose service both brothers had chosen. That evening Edgar had striven hard, with wandering thoughts in prayer which often wellnigh overcame him, and, after long wrestling, something of the old fervour of spirit had returned, and he thirsted to read again the words of pardon and comfort, which had been as a sealed roll to him. How could he wait for morning hours? He rose from his knees and sought out the passages which had been as living waters to him in days past, and oh! that they might be so again.

"Edgar, my good fellow, are you going to sit up all night, and be frozen to death?"

"I shan't be long," he quietly replied, without raising his eyes.

Two or three minutes elapsed.

"I say, when are you going to come? What would father say if he sees the light?"

"Oh, don't chatter, John, please; I'm coming directly."

"But just see the time—twenty minutes to twelve; why can't you read after tea?"

Edgar did not answer. He knew his father wished them to be in bed early, but as they had come to years of discretion he had issued no special rule, and only too gladly would he have seen his boy over the open Bible; but seeing that

John had set his head upon enforcing "regular hours" that night, he shut up his Bible and put out the light.

When spiritual realities are trembling in the balance, it needs but little to turn the scale to the wrong side.

Edgar's train of thought and prayer was broken by this little cloud. Was it not unkind of his brother to interrupt him, and how could he think out that chapter? The wheels went heavily enough already, now they were still more clogged. John would not knowingly hinder his brother from the heavenward way, and yet his few impatient, though well-meant words, had done so, and the step so nearly gained was for that night lost.

Shall *all* hindrances prove to be furtherances? Some there are which seem as if they could not so be resolved. Our whole life may have hinged upon some well-meant yet not the less fatal hindrance; a shortsighted pointsman may have turned our train on to the wrong line, we may have travelled far from what seemed our true terminus, and there is no possibility of return ere "the night cometh." It was no doing of ours—why should we and the Master's work suffer loss by it? There are life-enigmas of this kind which admit of *no* solution, hindrances which remain such in grim reality unsoftened by past or future as far as our eye can reach, and beyond. What are we to think of these? Turn the others, the minor ones, the solvable ones, into so many arguments for the *probability*, to take the lowest ground, that these also have their solutions, quite as clear when once revealed, only a little farther to seek.

Last May we stood on a hill and looked down into the valley just flushing out into its early summer smile of leaf and blossom. The opposite slope was wooded, but the foliage was late, and did not hide the ground below. That ground was covered with a soft blue mist, pale and lovely, melting and thinning away towards the summit, and showing the wild undergrowth of spring greenery. We gazed long—it was surely mist. After awhile we went down into the valley and crossed the stream from which the blue haze must have arisen. As we gained the other side our feet stepped upon beds of wild hyacinths, delicately blue, paling with the advancing season into tenderer tints and stretching away up the bank, and along the brook till, in the distance, the blossoms blended again into the semblance of blue mist.

But we knew then that as far as we could see, and farther, it was only flowers. We cannot expect all blue mists to resolve themselves into flowers *here*. But there is a hill to be descended, a valley beneath, and a stream to be crossed, and *Then!*

So much for analogy. But there is more certainty to go upon. We come back to the grand old pillar Promise, which shall stand without a quiver "though the earth be removed, and though the mountains be carried into the midst of the sea." "*All* things work together for good to them who love God." Or, to change the figure, that "work together" makes one think of a mighty current, far too strong for mortal engineer to turn or dam, steadily and grandly rolling on to the ocean of perfect ultimate good—hinderers and hindrances dash noisily down from the hill-sides to meet it, their course at right-angles to the current, but do they impede it? does the splashing torrent counteract one inch of its flow? do its little sticks and stones delay it for one moment? Not one inch, not one moment! They only join the great stream, and the larger they are the more they swell it and add to its force and volume. Yes, they too, *hinderers* and *hindrances,* are among the "all things," and therefore, whether within sight or beyond sight, they never work *against,* but only and always "work *together for* good."

> "The ills we see,—
> The mysteries of sorrow deep and long,
> The dark enigmas of permitted wrong,—
> Have all one key:
> This strange sad world is but our Father's school;
> All chance and change His love shall grandly overrule.
>
> "He traineth so
> That we may shine for Him in this dark world,
> And bear His standard dauntlessly unfurled,
> That we may show
> His praise, by lives that mirror back His love—
> His witnesses on earth, as He is ours above."

Part II.

Are our illustrations exaggerated? We appeal confidently to any one placed in close contact with fellow-workers. But what if your own conscience replies, "I have been a hinderer?"—that is, consciously to yourself, for who may tell the "secret faults" in this particular? Who may tell the unknown times that word or example of yours has hindered the soul's work? Seek to amend the habit, if habit it be, of impeding those around you in efforts for good, and hold out a helping, not a hindering, hand.

It is not to be denied that there are people who will go out district-visiting for hours at the expense of being laid up for weeks; others who will act in diametrical opposition to medical and parental advice—who will go out in east winds, who will sit up for hours in their bedrooms after the household are asleep instead of early rising, who, in fact, seem bent upon annoying their friends and shortening their usefulness: of such extremes we do not speak. But how many needless anxieties arise about infections and colds, and long walks! How many worrying and useless objections are started regarding undertakings which the objectors have no intention of seriously opposing! How many lions in the way of others are seen by those who tread on fierce ones themselves! How many a nervous semi-invalid is kindly prevented from working off his or her nervousness! How many a dispirited one is still further discouraged by gloomy remarks and prognostications! How many an ardent one damped and dulled by the same! Let us consider one another to provoke unto love and to good works, that the crown of no beloved one may be the less radiant for our hindrances!

The previous illustrations affect only passing circumstances, but we must not forget those more serious hindrances, which may embitter a very lifetime, or thwart the purpose of some heaven-sent aspiration. Parental ambition may check some high resolve of dedication to God's service. It may be some of England's daughters who are startled from their silken dreams and homes of peace and joy, where truth and light are shining fair as the stars of night, and they long to rise and go,

> "Laying their joys aside,
> As the Master laid them down,
> Seeking His love and lost in the veiled abodes of woe,
> Winning His Indian gems, to shine in His glorious crown!"

And so some hasty home decision quenches the bright flame. Or may be some son, with no definite opening, no call of home duty, hears the Master's call, and his true-hearted response is, "Here am I; send me," and he is ready to go and—

> "Tell it out among the heathen that the Lord is King,
> Tell it out, tell it out!
> Tell it out among the nations, bid them shout and sing!
> Tell it out, tell it out!"

A letter from Ernest at last! And the sister eagerly gives her father the morning budget at the breakfast table. Her mother watches, for gloom gathers on the father's face as he reads it. Silently the letter is given to the mother, and he passes through the open window to the pleasant terrace-walk beneath. The sister guesses in vain, "What can Ernest have written?" The father paced up and down, thinking of the position he himself had won, and which he had hoped would be a stepping-stone for his son to one far higher, in which his many gifts of mind and heart would shine with no common effulgence. He had hoped his son would carry out and develop many schemes of benevolence he had set on foot. But that morning's letter was as a mighty crucible, wherein the man's devotedness to Him who had given him that darling son was to be tested and analyzed. What was that letter?

—College, Cambridge.

Dear Father,—Will you listen to your son's request for your consent, your blessing, your prayers? Father, there is a burning impulse within me, a new life-pulse seems beating in my soul, a still deep voice ever sounding in my ears, "Go ye into all the world, and preach the gospel to every creature." Years ago that same voice called me, when I first heard stories about the heathen and their idols, and when standing by my mother I looked at the Church Missionary Society's green picture-book (*Juvenile Instructor*), of white men preaching to the heathen. Silently, but surely, has that call followed me. I have cried earnestly, "Lord, what wilt thou have me to do?" and again the heavenly whisper comes, "Go ye." Therefore, though never before breathed to any but God, this is no sudden thought, no unconsidered plan. Father, let me go, let me take the cup of living water to him that is ready to perish. I should like to tread the very footsteps of Him who came to seek and to save that which was lost, to search in His name for the "other sheep, which are not of this fold."

I know the hopes and intentions which you have cherished for my future; but is not a missionary's joy a nobler gain, the missionary's crown a nobler ambition than any other? And what if the time came when, among the multitude out of all nations and kindreds and tongues, I might be permitted to recognise some who first heard a Saviour's name from my unworthy lips. My own dear mother! her heart will be with me in this; I know she lent me to the Lord.

Dearest father, I believe Christ has called me, will you not let me obey His voice?—Your loving son,

Ernest.

Reader, what would *your* answer have been? Would you have hindered? The father could not brook that the talents of his son, the pride of his ancestral hall, should go forth into the gloom and obscurity of distant shores. But who can tell how bitterly that question, "Father, will you hinder me?" returned to his mind when the bell tolled for the early death of that loved and devoted son!

"Man's hindrances may be God's furtherances." Not that this is any excuse for the "hinderers" we have described. No thanks or praise to them that medicine is distilled from their poison, heavenly sparks struck from their cold steel and flint. We have no consolation for "hinderers," in their thoughtless jarrings upon the strings tuned for God's music. But for the *hindered* there is honey out of the rock, honey upon the ground; sweet and abundant and ever-flowing. Put forth the end of the rod that is in your hand, ye hindered ones, weary and discouraged with the rocks, the boulders, the stones in your way, perhaps merely the grit of a fairly smooth path, which others do not see, but which you feel and wince at, because your feet are sensitive and bare. Dip your rod in the honeycomb of God's own ruling gentleness and love, and, like Jonathan, your eyes shall be enlightened, and you shall no more be faint.

It is a wide subject, that of hindrances. Even a catalogue of the varieties known to any one person's experience would occupy too much time and patience to write or even read. They fall into two classes, God's hindrances and man's hindrances. On the former we need not dwell. It is more easy to see that they are furtherances; it is easier to say, "Thy will be done" with regard to that which is unmistakeably and directly God's will, and which has not to be painfully traced back to it through some distorting human medium, and therefore more easy to open the heart to receive comfort at first, and profit afterwards; more easy to weave them into the web of our work, and to believe that the design will be all the richer for the troublesome insertion of a dark thread. In these hindrances from God the element of bitterness is wanting, even when the trial is otherwise deep and heavy. For bitterness can only grow out of evil, evil that has sin for its essence or foundation, and this cannot be from God; this cup, though divinely *permitted,* must be humanly *presented.* The heart knows the difference, the essential difference between a trial which comes only and purely from God's hand, in which we say, not only "Himself had done it," but Himself *only,* and the trial which comes through a human medium, which treachery, faithlessness, ingratitude, heartlessness have brought about. There is a sting, a gall, a smart in the one which appertains not to the other. Let us fall into the hand of God, and not into the hands of man, said David, and he knew the depths of both.

In God's trials, moreover, the chief earthly alleviation of sympathy is enjoyed to the full, and its ministration is almost invariably co-extensive with the circle of our friends—often far wider.

Not so with the trials of man's hindrances; often we have but partial sympathy or none at all, and we bear them in smiling but heartbreaking silence.

Take the case of illness *simple,* by which you are laid aside for a few weeks or months. (We speak not of excruciating agony or consequent poverty.) You are hindered from all work, rendered utterly useless and helpless, debarred from ordinary pleasures; you lie in uncertainty of the issue, and you seem a very hinderer and drag to the willing and kindest friends.

And so you are driven to trust, and lean and rest on the bosom of the Father. You are drawn closer to Him; even if you cannot think continuously, nor read, nor listen to reading, you have far more communion on the whole with the Invisible but felt Presence than was possible in your busy days and sleepful nights. You know it *is* the Lord's chastening, and so you look for a "nevertheless afterward" of blessing. You cannot struggle against the trial; by no planning, no wakeful contrivings, can you slip away from His hand, and so you lie still under it; and there are no rankling regrets, no struggles to forgive and forget anything or any one who has caused pain.

The Master's voice does not bid you "Enter the thick of the conflict," but "Come ye yourselves apart into a desert place and rest awhile." It *is* a desert place, and you leave all the pleasant fruits and fair flowers of life behind, but you leave its turmoil too; and is there not *enough* to make you glad when you are alone with Jesus, so utterly weary that He lays your head upon His bosom; is that not rest?

Contrast this with any trial from the hand of man—some one great wound or succession of blows from one whom you trusted and loved. You are withdrawn by it from none of your ordinary work or calls, these are superadded; you cannot speak about it; you cannot speak about your trial, it would not be half understood, or it might injure and even exasperate the listener if you sought the solace of sympathy. You puzzle yourself vainly and wearily; you torture yourself with suppositions as to what might have been, if this or that had not been said or done. If you have any cause for self-reproach, you are miserable; if you have none, you almost wish you had, that the matter might be less wrong, less unreasonable. There is *evil* in it that you are sure is not God's will; how are you to say, "Thy will be done?" You grieve over your friend's sin, and you grieve over the evil it stirs up in your own heart, and you lie wakefully with worse than pain. And perhaps you get letters alluding to some of your blessings,—your happy home, your pretty study, and "nothing to do but write poetry!" and other felicitations on your supposed unclouded lot. You sigh over the kind, ignorant letter, and say, "How little they know!" Or you must keep an engagement to sing, and it is for your King, and strangers shall not misjudge your loyal love. You sing sweet words of "Comfort ye!" but they little ween[1] the tight tension on your own heart as you sing, "Whom having not seen ye love ... though now for

[1] ween: think

a season if need be, ye are in heaviness through manifold temptations";—and yet, oh yet, you do trust in Him, whose love seems more precious still in the fires.

F. R. H.

[These thoughts on Hinderers and Hindrances were written some time ago by my dear sister, F. R. H. By experience she keenly felt for many a young disciple, whose first desires to follow Christ are often checked instead of being cherished and encouraged. Unconsciously F. R. H. lifts the veil from some of her own life-enigmas most patiently borne, till shone for her—

> "Light after darkness,
>   Gain after loss,
> Strength after suffering,
>   Crown after cross.
> Sweet after bitter,
>   Song after sigh,
> Home after wandering,
>   Praise after cry."

M. V. G. H.]

F.R.H. wrote and published a pamphlet entitled "I also . . . for thee" which is very similar—most of it is identical—to Chapter 13 of *Kept for the Master's Use*. This pamphlet, likely published in the middle 1870's, has first all of the verses of the Consecration Hymn "Take my life;" then next a different introduction (different from the first part of the last chapter of *Kept for the Master's Use* near the end of her life); and then finally the twelve points which are identical to the twelve points in Chapter 13 of *Kept* (see pages 495–500 of Volume II of the Havergal edition).

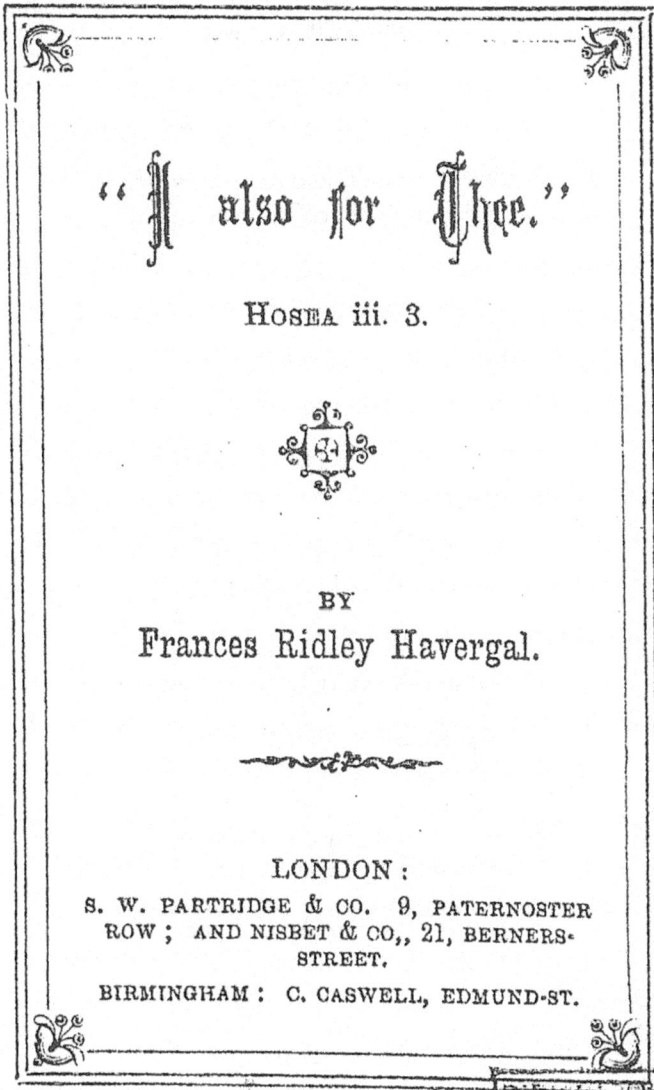

"I also for Thee."

HOSEA iii. 3.

BY

Frances Ridley Havergal.

LONDON :
S. W. PARTRIDGE & CO. 9, PATERNOSTER ROW ; AND NISBET & CO,, 21, BERNERS-STREET.
BIRMINGHAM : C. CASWELL, EDMUND-ST.

The title page of the pamphlet "I also . . . for thee."

"I also . . . for thee."

HOSEA 3:3.

———

TAKE my life, and let it be
Consecrated, Lord, to Thee.

Take my moments and my days;
Let them flow in ceaseless praise.

Take my hands, and let them move
At the impulse of Thy love.

Take my feet, and let them be
Swift and 'beautiful' for Thee.

Take my voice, and let me sing
Always, only, for my King.

Take my lips, and let them be
Filled with messages from Thee.

Take my silver and my gold;
Not a mite would I withhold.

Take my intellect, and use
Every power as Thou shalt choose.

Take my will, and make it Thine;
It shall be no longer mine.

Take my heart, it *is* Thine own;
It shall be Thy royal throne.

Take my love; my Lord, I pour
At Thy feet its treasure-store.

Take myself, and I will be
Ever, *only*, ALL for Thee.

HAVE we said, humbly and heartily, "Yes, let Him take all"? Do we really mean *all*, down to the deepest depths of our hearts, and up to the farthest possibilities of our lives? Without any reserve? Is it really "*all* for Jesus,"—yes, ALL for Jesus?

Is there any misgiving lest the surrender which we honestly meant to make of "ourselves, our souls and bodies," has not been actually and fully made? Are we "not quite sure" about it? Then pause now, yes, even *now*, and give up the very citadel of our being to the King. "Ye sought, in times past, for David to be king over you, NOW, THEN, DO IT!" (2 Samuel 3:17,18.)

> In full and glad surrender I give myself to Thee,
> Thine utterly and only, and evermore to be!
> O Son of God who lovest me, I will be Thine alone,
> And all I have, and all I am, shall henceforth be Thine own.

Now, has your heart said it? And you do not want ever to take it back? "Doubt ye not then, but earnestly believe that He hath favourably received" you, and "embraced you with the arms of His mercy," and that your offering is "accepted in the Beloved."

And what then? First,—He will not let you take it back. He is able to keep that which you have committed unto Him. Knowing, better than you know it, "how weak is thine heart," He says, "Thou *shalt* abide for me." Let us honour His faithful love by joyfully trusting His promise, the brightness of which is quite enough to dispel any rising cloud of fear, or haze of uncertainty.

But He says more,—"I also for thee!" It is a marvel of love how He meets every detail of our consecration with this wonderful word.[1]

1. His Life "for thee!" "The Good Shepherd giveth His life for the sheep." Oh, wonderful gift! not promised, but *given*; not to friends, but to enemies. Given without condition, without reserve, without return. Himself unknown and unloved, His gift unsought and unasked, He gave His life for thee; a more than royal bounty—the greatest gift that Deity could devise. Oh, grandeur of love! "I lay down My life for the sheep!" And we for whom He gave it have held back, and hesitated to give our lives, not even *for* Him (He has not asked us to do

---

[1] At this point, after the first five paragraphs, the pamphlet "I also . . . for thee" continues with the identically same twelve points found in Chapter 13 of *Kept for the Master's Use* (on pages 495–500 of Volume II of the Havergal edition), a verbatim quotation, with only minor, completely unimportant differences in typesetting (for example, small capital letters instead of italicized words at the start of each point).

that), but *to* Him! But that is past, and He has tenderly pardoned the unloving, ungrateful reserve, and has graciously accepted the poor little fleeting breath and speck of dust which was all we had to offer. And now His precious death and His glorious life are all " for thee."

2. His ETERNITY "for thee!" . . . All we can ask Him to take are days and moments—the little span given us as it is given, and of this only the present in deed and the future in will. As for the past, in so far as we did not give it to Him, it is too late; we can never give it now! But His past was given to us, though ours was not given to Him. Oh, what a tremendous debt does this show us!

Away back in the dim depths of past eternity, "or ever the earth and the world were made," His divine existence in the bosom of His Father was all " for thee," purposing and planning " for thee," receiving and holding the promise of eternal life " for thee."

Then the thirty-three years among sinners on this sinful earth: do we think enough of the slowly-wearing days and nights, the heavyfooted hours, the never-hastening minutes, that went to make up those thirty-three years of trial and humiliation? We all know how slowly time passes when suffering and sorrow are near, and there is no reason to suppose that our Master was exempted from this part of our infirmities.

Then His present is "for thee." Even now He "liveth to make intercession"; even now He "thinketh upon me"; even now He "knoweth," He "careth," He "loveth."

Then, only to think that His whole eternity will be "for thee!" Millions of ages of unfoldings of all His love, and of ever new declarings of His Father's name to His brethren. Think of it! and can we ever hesitate to give *all* our poor little hours to His service?

3. His HANDS "for thee." Literal hands; literally pierced, when the whole weight of His quivering frame hung from their torn muscles and bared nerves; literally uplifted in parting blessing. Consecrated, priestly hands; "filled" hands (Exodus 28:41, 29:9, etc., margin)—filled once with His great offering, and now with gifts and blessings "for thee." Tender hands, touching and healing, lifting and leading with gentlest care. Strong hands, upholding and defending. Open hands, filling with good and satisfying desire (Psalm 104:28, and 145:16). Faithful hands, restraining and sustaining. "His left hand is under my head, and His right hand doth embrace me."

4. His FEET "for thee." They were weary very often, they were wounded and bleeding once. They made clear footprints as He went about doing good,

and as He went up to Jerusalem to suffer; and these "blessed steps of His most holy life," both as substitution and example, were "for thee." Our place of waiting and learning, of resting and loving, is at His feet. And still those "blessed feet" are and shall be "for thee," until He comes again to receive us unto Himself, until and when the word is fulfilled, "They shall walk with me in white."

5. HIS VOICE "for thee." The "Voice of my beloved that knocketh, saying, Open to me, my sister, my love"; the Voice that His sheep "hear" and "know," and that calls out the fervent response, "Master, say on!" This is not all. It was the literal voice of the Lord Jesus which uttered that one echoless cry of desolation on the Cross "for thee," and it will be His own literal voice which will say, "Come, ye blessed!" to thee. And that same tender and "glorious Voice" has literally sung and will sing "for thee." I think He consecrated song for us, and made it a sweet and sacred thing for ever, when He Himself "sang an hymn," the very last thing before He went forth to consecrate suffering for us. That was not His last song. "The Lord thy God … will joy over thee with singing." And the time is coming when He will not only sing "for thee" or "over thee," but with thee. He says He will! "In the midst of the church will I sing praise unto Thee." Now what a magnificent glimpse of joy this is! "Jesus Himself leading the praises of His brethren," [1] and we ourselves singing not merely in such a chorus, but with such a leader! If "singing for Jesus" is such delight here, what will this "singing *with* Jesus" be? Surely song may well be a holy thing to us henceforth.

6. HIS LIPS "for thee." Perhaps there is no part of our consecration which it is so difficult practically to realize, and in which it is, therefore, so needful to recollect—"I also for thee." It is often helpful to read straight through one or more of the Gospels with a special thought on our mind, and see how much bears upon it. When we read one through with this thought,—"His *lips* for me!"—wondering, verse by verse, at the grace which was poured into them, and the gracious words which fell from them, wondering more and more at the cumulative force and infinite wealth of tenderness and power and wisdom and love flowing from them, we cannot but desire that our lips and all the fruit of them should be wholly for Him. "For thee" they were opened in blessing; "for thee" they were closed when He was led as a lamb to the slaughter. And whether teaching, warning, counsel, comfort, or encouragement, commandments in whose keeping there is a great reward, or promises which exceed all we ask or think—all the precious fruit of His lips is "for thee" really and truly *meant* "for thee."

[1] See A. Newton on the Epistle to the Hebrews, ch. 2. ver. 12.

7. His WEALTH "for thee." "Though He was rich, yet for our sakes He became poor, that ye through His poverty might be made rich." Yes, "through His poverty" the unsearchable riches of Christ are "for thee." Sevenfold riches are mentioned; and these are no untainted treasure or sealed reserve, but all ready coined for our use, and stamped with His own image and superscription, and poured freely into the hand of faith. The mere list is wonderful. "Riches of goodness," "riches of forbearance and long-suffering," "riches both of wisdom and knowledge," "riches of mercy," "exceeding riches of grace," and "riches of glory." And His own Word says, "All are yours!" Glance on in faith, and think of eternity flowing on and on beyond the mightiest sweep of imagination, and realize that all "His riches in glory" and "the riches of His glory" are and shall be "for thee!" In view of this, shall we care to reserve anything that rust doth corrupt for ourselves?

8. His "TREASURES OF WISDOM AND KNOWLEDGE" "for thee." First, used for our behalf and benefit. Why did He expend such immeasurable might of mind upon a world which is to be burnt up, but that He would fit it perfectly to be, not the home, but the school of His children? The infinity of His skill is such that the most powerful intellects find a lifetime too short to penetrate a little way into a few secrets of some one small department of His working. If we turn to Providence, it is quite enough to take only one's own life, and look at it microscopically and telescopically, and marvel at the treasures of wisdom lavished upon its details, ordering and shaping and fitting the tiny confused bits into the true mosaic which He means it to be. Many a little thing in our lives reveals the same Mind which, according to a well-known and very beautiful illustration, adjusted a perfect proportion in the delicate hinges of the snowdrop and the droop of its bell, with the mass of the globe and the force of gravitation. How kind we think it if a very talented friend spends a little of his thought and power of mind in teaching us or planning for us! Have we been grateful for the infinite thought and wisdom which our Lord has expended upon us and our creation, preservation, and redemption?

Secondly, to be shared with us. He says, "All that I have is thine." He holds nothing back, reserves nothing from His dear children, and what we cannot receive now He is keeping for us. He gives us "hidden riches of secret places" now, but by and by He will give us more, and the glorified intellect will be filled continually out of His treasures of wisdom and knowledge. But the sanctified intellect will be, must be, used for Him, and only for Him, now!

9. His WILL "for thee." Think first of the *infinite might* of that will; the

first great law and the first great force of the universe, from which alone every other law and every other force has sprung, and to which all are subordinate. "He worketh all things after the counsel of His own will." "He doeth according to His will in the army of heaven, and among the inhabitants of the earth." Then think of the *infinite mysteries* of that will. For ages and generations the hosts of heaven have wonderingly watched its vouchsafed unveilings and its sublime developments, and still they are waiting, watching, and wondering.

Creation and Providence are but the whisper of its power, but Redemption is its music, and praise is the echo which shall yet fill His temple. The whisper and the music, yes, and "the thunder of His power," are all "for thee." For what is "the good pleasure of His will"? (Ephesians 1:5). Oh, what a grand list of blessings purposed, provided, purchased, and possessed, all flowing to us out of it! And nothing but blessings, nothing but privileges, which we never should have imagined, and which, even when revealed, we are "slow of heart to believe"; nothing but what should even now fill us "with joy unspeakable and full of glory!"

Think of this will as always and altogether on our side—always working for us, and in us, and with us, if we will only let it; think of it as always and only synonymous with infinitely wise and almighty love; think of it as undertaking all for us, from the great work of our eternal salvation down to the momentary details of guidance and supply, and do we not feel utter shame and self-abhorrence at *ever* having hesitated for an instant to give up our tiny, feeble, blind will, to be—not crushed, not even bent, but *blent* with His glorious and perfect Will?

10. His Heart "for thee." "Behold… He is mighty… in heart," said Job (Job 36:5, margin). And this mighty and tender heart is "for thee!" If He had only stretched forth His hand to save us from bare destruction, and said, "My hand for thee!" how could we have praised Him enough? But what shall we say of the unspeakably marvellous condescension which says, "Thou hast ravished (margin, *taken away*) my heart, my sister, my spouse!" The very fountain of His divine life, and light, and love, the very centre of His being, is given to His beloved ones, who are not only "set as a seal upon His heart," but taken into His heart, so that our life is hid there, and we dwell there in the very centre of all safety, and power, and love, and glory. What will be the revelation of "that day," when the Lord Jesus promises, "Ye shall know that I am in my Father, *and ye in Me*"? For He implies that we do not yet know it, and that our present knowledge of this dwelling in Him is not knowledge at all compared with what He is going to show us about it.

Now shall we, can we, reserve any corner of our hearts from Him?

11. HIS LOVE "for thee." Not a passive, possible love, but outflowing, yes, *outpouring* of the real, glowing, personal love of His mighty and tender heart. Love not as an attribute, a quality, a latent force, but an acting, moving, reaching, touching, and grasping power. Love, not a cold, beautiful, far-off star, but a sunshine that comes and enfolds us, making us warm and glad, and strong and bright and fruitful.

His love! What manner of love is it? What should be quoted to prove or describe it? First the whole Bible with its mysteries and marvels of redemption, then the whole book of Providence and the whole volume of creation. Then add to these the unknown records of eternity past and the unknown glories of eternity to come, and then let the immeasurable quotation be sung by "angels and archangels, and all the company of heaven," with all the harps of God, and still that love will be untold, still it will be "the love of Christ that passeth knowledge."

But it is "for thee!"

12. HIMSELF "for thee." "Christ also hath loved us, and given Himself for us." "The Son of God... loved me, and gave Himself for me." Yes, Himself! What is the Bride's true and central treasure? What calls forth the deepest, brightest, sweetest thrill of love and praise? Not the Bridegroom's priceless gifts, not the robe of His resplendent righteousness, not the dowry of unsearchable riches, not the magnificence of the palace home to which He is bringing her, not the glory which she shall share with Him, but HIMSELF! Jesus Christ, "who His own self bare our sins in His own body on the tree"; "this same Jesus" "whom having not seen, ye love"; the Son of God, and the Man of Sorrows; my Saviour, my Friend, my Master, my King, my Priest, my Lord and my God—He says, "*I* also for thee!" What an "*I*"! What power and sweetness we feel in it, so different from any human "*I*," for all His Godhead and all His manhood are concentrated in it, and all "for thee!"

And not only "all," but "*ever*" for thee. His unchangeableness is the seal upon every attribute; He will be "this same Jesus" for ever. How can mortal mind estimate this enormous promise? How can mortal heart conceive what is enfolded in these words, "I also for thee"?

One glimpse of its fulness and glory, and we feel that henceforth it must be, shall be, and by His grace *will* be our true-hearted, whole-hearted cry—

> Take *myself*, and I will be
> *Ever*, ONLY, ALL for Thee!

[That is the end of the essay pamphlet "I also for thee."

This pamphlet, "I also . . . for thee," likely written a few years earlier, was apparently the seed of one of Frances' last completed books, and, except for the introduction, became the end of that book, *Kept for the Master's Use*.

C. Caswell & Co., Birmingham, England, published four prose essays by F.R.H., likely in the mid-1870's: "One Hour with Jesus" (the first item, pages 1-9, in Volume II of the Havergal edition), "The Five Benefits," "I also . . . for thee," and "The Perpetual Presence."

In a handwritten list of items published by Caswell that she had written, Frances wrote that "The Five Benefits" was "for the New Year." In a letter that she wrote to Maria in 1874 (in "Division V" of *Letters by the Late Frances Ridley Havergal* edited by Maria), Frances wrote that "Caswell will publish one [a penny book] for the New Year, *The Five Benefits*." She wrote to Julia Kirchhoffer on March 19, 1876, "Caswell had to reprint my *Five Benefits* four times in as many weeks, the demand was so great!"

The Thirtieth Day of *Royal Bounty* is entitled "The Perpetual Presence," and the Caswell small book may be the same as, or similar to, the Thirtieth Day of *Royal Bounty*, or an enlargement upon it. We do not know.]

This brief hymn, a single verse, was written in July, 1876:

> Now, Lord, I give myself to Thee;
>   I would be wholly Thine,
> As Thou hast given Thyself to me,
>   And Thou are wholly mine.
> Oh, take me,—seal me as Thine own,
>   Thine altogether—Thine ALONE!
>   Frances Ridley Havergal

"I also . . . for thee" very much follows the 12 couplets of the Consecration Hymn "Take my life" (found on the first page of this pamphlet, on page 90 of this book). We should give each part to Him, after He has given each part—infinitely more of Himself—to each one of His people, His bride.

These are rough draft notes in F.R.H.'s handwriting, for My King. These two pages of notes were found with the two other pages given on page 76.

These "Excerpts on Music" were published by Maria in the Appendix to her biography *Memorials of Frances Ridley Havergal* (in Volume IV of this edition). Maria likely found these comments in various letters and papers. F.R.H. was a true musician to the core, remarkably gifted. Much more is shown in Volume V of this edition, *Songs of Truth and Love: Music by Frances Ridley Havergal and William Henry Havergal.*

EXCERPTS: ON MUSIC, ETC.

To me the overture to the Lobgesang[1] *is a vision of Christian life* with its own peculiar struggles and sorrows as well as joys. It is the sixth, seventh, and eighth chapters of the Epistle to the Romans in essence. The mingling of twilight yearnings, ever pressing *onward*, with calm and trustful praise, ever pressing *upward*, is an almost unbearably true echo of the heart, especially in the 6/8 Allegretto agitato; then the Andante religioso is the still, mellow glow of "light at eventide," to which one looks forward; then I go just one step farther, and find a fore-echo of the eternal song in the burst of *vocal* praise, after the long tension of the voiceless overture.

On no form of "The Beautiful" is "passing away" *so engraven* as on music; I have felt this with painful vividness. In "passing away" lies its very *essence*, not merely its *accidents*. The most exquisite passage, if lingered on, loses its very existence as well as beauty; the time, the motion, is the life, the actual notes only a dead letter without it; while to *hold* it is simply an inherent impossibility.

Is not the tendency of the human voice to fall from the true pitch, one of the results of "*the* Fall"? Adam and Eve must have sung in tune, like the birds. How wonderful it is, that the birds not only sing their own songs in tune, but all

---

[1] This is the first movement of Felix Mendelssohn's *Symphony* Number 2 in B-flat major, Opus 52, for soloists, chorus, amd orchestra, entitled *Lobgesang* (German, *Song of Praise*). F.R.H. had a special love for Handel's and Mendelssohn's music, and extensively studied their scores. Mendelssohn wrote on the front of his manuscript of this *Symphony* a quotation of Martin Luther: "*Sandern ich walt all Kunste, sanderlich die Musica, gern sehen im Dienst des der sie geben un geschaffen hat.*" "But I would that all the arts, and especially music, glorify Him Who created them and gave them life."

the songs always seem in tune with each other, except the cuckoo, when passing from his major third in May to his minor third (or even second) in June!

May not one apply this to the dissonances within, that stun and bewilder and weary us, and believe that if we are indeed God's chosen praise-harps, all that is not as yet *tune* is but the *tuning*, which is *not* in itself beautiful.

Next after prayer, nothing is so healing and calming as pouring out oneself in music. Not in singing; there, one is limited by words, but playing, it restores the balance marvellously. Conventionality would forbid this "antidote of medicated music" in *some* sorrows, but in *such* one can have the outlet of words and the balm of human sympathy; music seems an especial medicine, for all things in which this is not to be had, or could not be sought.

Gregorians are to me only curious and interesting, like dried plants or fossils, not living and lovely.

Of the chorus "And the glory of the Lord" (Handel's "Messiah") I shall never forget the impression of its first bars at the Birmingham Festival, 1867; it gave such a sense of clear *sunny* grandeur, massive open-browed stateliness, and fearless, glorious, overwhelmingness; a musical expression of one's ideal personification of TRUTH, majestically going forth conquering and to conquer.

Beethoven's 95th Psalm is a grandly jubilant thing, with contrasts of sternness and melancholy.

I believe that everything earthly contains analogies of the heavenly, but that we have not yet the key to *all* the golden ciphers; and it may be that our yet "unpurged vision" is not capable of reading them, beyond a certain point. This too, all *designedly*, is the material fitted and planned to reflect the spiritual.

Rubens' sacred paintings impress one with his wonderful *art*, Vandyke's with the reverent love he betrays for the subject itself.

Poetry is a *second translation* of the soul's feeling; it must be rendered into thought, and thought must change its nebulous robe of semi-wording into definite language, before it reaches another heart. *Music* is a *first* translation of feeling, needing no second, but entering the heart direct.

Music seems the only universal language understood by men of every tongue and age, and by the angels too. It is an alphabet of the language of heaven, not any more equal to it than an A B C book is to Milton. Why should such a mysteriously subtle and unaccountable gratification have been provided for us? Verily He is Love!

The magnificent massive choruses in the "Israel in Egypt" need a gigantic orchestra to give scope for their great swing of grandeur. The mighty flinging of sound from side to side, in some of the double choruses, is what might be carried out if Handel had Salisbury Plain for his concert room, cannon for his basses, an army for his tenors, and angelic legions for his sopranos.

As to the "infinite suggestiveness" of music, the "Israel in Egypt" choruses exemplify this to a marvellous degree; so does "Let their celestial concerts" with its *blaze* of light; so does Beethoven's Pastoral Symphony.

A hush comes over one at the very thought of one so loved being on the very threshold of eternal rest and joy, so near Christ's own immediate presence. It is as if the veil were growing half transparent, which hangs between life and its dreams, eternal life and its realities.

The shadow of orphanhood has now fallen upon you; and therefore His blessed name of Father acquires depth and reality; "doubtless Thou art our Father." Some day, when we are where they reckon not by days and years, He will tell you *why* He has tried you, and let you look back on your life story and see the golden thread of His fatherly love and care shining over and around it all,—not as it is now, winding in and out, and only seen by glimpses.

"Faithful and True." What a keystone to the grand bridge which His promises have made for us, over the abyss of despair and misery! Faithful as regards us; True, essentially and inherently.

Experience of life is a great commentary on the Bible, and a sort of realization of it. At first, the Bible is a detailed map, which we study and admire; but on the road we find the very same things noticed, but not realized, in one's map. Many of the hills and valleys I read of (and *only* read of), in the Psalms, seem to have come across my own journey of late. It has been so to-day with Isaiah 26:3, which is rather like sitting under the shadow of a great rock, which was marked in one's map, but was not in sight a few days ago.

"I have given them Thy word": John 17. To me this has been a golden key to many other texts, or a sort of seal upon them; the Father's and the Saviour's gift. Apply this first to *the* "word of reconciliation," the Father's message of salvation through Christ. Then to the whole Bible; it makes it ten times dearer, and it seems our claim to appropriate every sweet promise.

Mrs. Stephen Menzies wrote *Hints on Bible Marking*, which F. R. H. appreciated and recommended, herself using the same method for Bible marking that Mrs. Menzies presented. Mrs. Menzies edited a book of 165 brief stories, statements, and pieces, *The Traveller's Guide from Death to Life*. Published jointly by S. W. Partridge & Co., London (who published pieces by Frances during her life), and the British Gospel Book Association, Liverpool, without date (likely 1880 to 1900), at least 200,000 copies were printed, likely more. That now extremely obscure but truly, richly beneficial book contains a one-page piece, copied below, "I do not fear death."

"I DO NOT FEAR DEATH."

Extract from F. R. H.'s MS., in answer to a remark: "Death, which we ALL dread."

No, not "All!" One who has seen and *accepted* God's way of salvation, does *not* dread death. Perhaps I shall best express myself by doing it very personally —just giving my own experience.

I do not fear death. Often I wake in the night and think of it, look forward to it, with a thrill of joyful expectation and anticipation, which would become impatience, were it not that Jesus is my Master, as well as my Saviour, and I feel I have work to do for Him that I would not shirk, and also that *His* time to call me home will be the *best* and *right* time; therefore I am content to wait.

One night I was conscious of certain symptoms preluding an all but fatal attack (of erysipelas[1]) I had had once before on the brain.

I knew, if means failed, it was probably my last night on earth. I let my mother attend to me, but alarmed no one, and I was left alone in bed. Then, alone in the dark, I felt it might be my last conscious hour on earth, and that either sleep or fatal unconsciousness would set in. I never spent a calmer, sweeter hour than that. I had not one shadow of fear! only happy rest and confidence in Him "Whom I have believed."

Was this delusion? Could it be so in the very face of death, that great *unmasker* of all uncertainties? I knew it was not delusion, for "I know Whom I have believed."

It was not always thus. I know as well as any one, what it is to "*dread death*," and to put away the thought of its absolute certainty, because I dare not look it in the face.

---

[1] erysipelas: an acute disease of the skin, streptococcal infection causing red inflammation of the skin and mucous membranes

There was a time when I saw clearly I could *not* save myself—that I deserved hell in many ways, but in one most of all, this—that I owed the whole love of my heart to God, and had not given it to Him; that Jesus had *so* loved me as to *die for me,* and yet I had treated Him with daily, hourly ingratitude. I had broken the first commandment, and as I owed all my life—future and past—to God, I had literally *"nothing to pay"*; for living to Him, and keeping His commands for the future, would not atone for the past. I saw the sinfulness of my heart and life. I could not make my heart better. *"The soul that sinneth it shall die."* So, unless sin *is* taken away, my soul *must die and go to hell.*

Where then was my hope? In the same Word of God (1 John 5:10), it is written, "He that believeth on the Son hath the witness in himself," and (John 3:36), "He that believeth on the Son *hath everlasting life:* and he that believeth *not* the Son shall not see life; but the *wrath* of God abideth on Him."

Believe what?—that He *must* keep His word and punish sin, and that He *has* punished it in the person of Jesus, *our Substitute,* "Who His own self bare our sins in His own body on the tree" (1 Peter 2:24).

If Jesus has paid *my* debt, and borne the punishment of *my* sins, I simply accept this, and believe Him, and it is all a true and real transaction. I did this—I believed it, and cast myself, utterly hopeless and helpless in myself, at the feet of Jesus, took Him at His word, and accepted what He had done for me.

Result?—Joy, peace in believing, and a happy, FULL trust in Him, which death cannot touch.

Now it is a reality of realities to me—it is so intertwined with my life, that I know nothing could separate me from His love.

I could not do without Jesus. I cannot and I do not live without Him. It is a *new* and different life; and the life and light which takes away *all fear of death,* is what I want others to have and enjoy.

"Death is swallowed up in *victory.* O death, where is thy sting? O grave, where is thy victory? The sting of death is sin; and the strength of sin is the law. But thanks be to God, which giveth us the victory through our Lord Jesus Christ" (1 Cor. 15:54-57).

Note: In the same volume, *The Traveller's Guide from Death to Life* edited by Mrs. Menzies, is a piece entitled "The Transferred Burden." This piece in Mrs. Menzies' book is an abbreviated quotation of "The Transferred Burden" which is the Sixth Day of *Royal Commandments* by F. R. H. (page 108 of Volume II of the Havergal edition).

Mrs. Menzies and F.R.H. almost surely knew well about each other (Frances highly valued Mrs. Menzies' *Hints on Bible Marking*) and very possibly or likely met or wrote to each other. We do not know. The same piece is given in *Letters by the Late Frances Ridley Havergal* edited by her sister, Maria V. G. Havergal (London: James Nisbet & Co., 1885), original pages 267–270, page 222 of Volume IV of the Havergal edition. There are differences between the two texts, and Maria's text is given here also.

(Extract from F. R. H.'s answer to a remark, 'That death which we all dread.')

"NOT ONE SHADOW OF FEAR."

1876.

No, not "all!" One who has seen and accepted God's way of salvation, does *not* dread death. Perhaps I shall best express myself by doing it very personally—just giving my own experience.

I do *not* fear death. Often I wake in the night and think of it, look forward to it with a thrill of joyful expectation and anticipation, which would become impatience, were it not that Jesus is my Master, as well as my Saviour, and I feel I have work to do for Him that I would not shirk, and also that His time to call me home will be the best and right time, and therefore I am content to wait.

One night I was conscious of certain symptoms preluding an all but fatal attack of erysipelas[1], I had once before, on the brain.

I knew, if means failed, it was probably my last night on earth. I let my mother attend to me, but alarmed no one, and I was left alone in bed. Then, alone in the dark, I felt it might be my last conscious hour on earth, and that either sleep or fatal unconsciousness would set in. I never spent a calmer, sweeter hour than that. I had not one shadow of fear! only happy rest and confidence in Him "in whom I have believed."

Was this delusion? Could it be so in the very face of death, that great *unmasker* of all uncertainties? I knew it was not delusion, for again, "I know in whom I have believed."

Now, *how* has this come to be so with me, for it was not always thus; and I know as well as any one what it is to "dread death," and to put away the thought of its absolute certainty, because I dare not look it in the face.

There was a time when I saw clearly I could *not* save myself—that I deserved hell. In many ways, but in one most of all, this—that I owed the whole love of my heart to God, and had not given it to Him; that Jesus had so loved me as to die for me, and yet I, unmindful of it, had treated him with daily, hourly, practical ingratitude. I had broken the first commandment, and as I owed all my life,

---

[1] erysipelas: an acute disease of the skin, streptococcal infection causing red inflammation of the skin and mucous membranes

future and past, to God, I had literally "nothing to pay"; for living to Him, and keeping His commands for the future, would not atone for the past. I saw the sinfulness of my heart and life. I could not make my heart better. "The soul that sinneth it shall die." So, unless sin *is* taken away, my soul must die and go to hell; anyhow I must "stand before the judgment-seat of Christ."

Where then was my Hope?—in the same Word of God, 1 John 5:10, it is written, "He that believeth on the Son, hath the witness in himself," and John 3:36, "He that believeth on the Son hath everlasting life: and he that believeth not the Son shall not see life; but the wrath of God abideth on him."

Believe what? "Whom God hath set forth to be a propitiation through faith in His blood," Romans 3:25. He must keep His word and punish sin, and He has punished it in the person of Jesus, our Substitute, "who His own Self bare our sins in His own body on the tree," 1 Peter 2:24.

Thus being "just," and having set forth Jesus as the propitiation for sin—if Jesus has paid my debt and borne the punishment of my sins, I only simply accept this, and believe Him, and it is all a true and real transaction. It is no theorizing but acting. I did it—I believed it, and cast myself utterly hopeless and helpless and lost in myself, at the feet of Jesus, and took Him at His word, and accepted what He had done for me.

Result?—joy, peace in believing, and a happy full trust in Him, which death cannot touch. Now it is a reality of realities to me—it is so intertwined with my life, that I know nothing could separate me from His love.

I could not do without Jesus. I cannot and I do not live without Him. It is a new and different life, and the life and light which takes away all fear of death is what I want others to have and enjoy.

I can say that such a light has shone upon all the dark bits of my life, that even if I was in heaven itself, I could not more clearly see why I was so led— that all the training was needed. And nothing tries me now; things that would so have disappointed me do not now. Even when I am suffering severe pain, I would not have it otherwise. And then in daily life, daily temptations, I find a victory in Jesus against sin, without any struggle.

And what was trial to me,—keen scathings, blightings,—is all taken from me, lifted out of me. It is really miraculous, I cannot say HOW; certainly it was not my own strength, but things that were such agony and bitterness—it is all gone. All was needed—and all that might have been a cloud between me and this full sunshine is taken away. Now it is utter calm and quietness, a realization constantly that—

> Life is a gift to use for Thee,
> Death is a hushed and glorious tryst
> With Thee, my King, my Saviour, Christ!

This was published as a leaflet by C. Caswell & Co., Birmingham, and later included in or after a letter (Oakhampton, 1871) in *Letters by the Late Frances Ridley Havergal.*

THANKFULNESS FOR CRUMBS.

"Thy words were found, and I did eat them; and Thy word was unto me the joy and rejoicing of my heart."—Jeremiah 15:16.

An old woman of ninety lives in a lonely country cottage. It is pretty enough, half-covered with roses and honeysuckle, but it is years since poor Mrs. Lane has seen them; she is blind. A few years ago ministering steps came often to her door, but now they are silent for ever on earth, and the little garden-path is never trodden by any lady visitor. While spending a few weeks in the neighbourhood, I went to see her now and then, and at each visit taught her a short text, and other young visitors did the same.

The last time I saw her, she repeated all the texts she had thus learnt with the greatest delight. She seemed to think the possession of these little texts— only about half a dozen—a perfect treasure, and counted them over like pieces of gold.

"Oh dear, Miss, this summer's gone too quick for me; it made the time pass so pleasant, having all them beautiful texts. I couldn't tell you how it's passed away the time. There's '*I am poor and needy, but the Lord thinketh upon me;*' there's a many as don't think about a poor old blind body like me, but the Lord does; and that *must* be for me, Miss, because I'm very poor, Miss, just like it says in the verse. And then there's '*When thou passest through the waters, I will be with thee;*' that's my companion, I call it, Miss; you wouldn't believe what company that is to me, and it seems to take me through all my little troubles of every day; I don't think that's been out of my mind an hour since you learnt it me. Ah! I know what came *next*—'*Having loved His own which were in the world, He loved them unto the end;*' that was right, wasn't it, Miss? I couldn't say it rightly at first, but I've got it faster than any now, since you taught it me over again; that's always my comfort when I feel so sinking like, and I think perhaps it's the end coming near, and then He'll love me unto the end. But that last one I learnt— '*Thine eyes shall see the King in His beauty*'—that *is* beautiful; oh, it *is* a beauty! My poor eyes, Miss, that can't see you, it says they shall see Him; to think of that now! well, to be sure now!" and the dear old woman's voice lowered, murmuring on in broken exclamations of happy anticipation, till she seemed almost to forget her visitor's presence.

What a lesson of thankfulness for crumbs! Far too infirm to reach any service, no one to read to her, her only companion being a somewhat graceless great-grandson, away at work all day; no treasures of earlier teaching to fall back upon, nothing but six little texts, and these filling the poor blind woman's heart with comfort, making the lonely summer pass "too quick," and being "company" to her, night and day! What an illustration of the satisfying power of the Spirit's teaching, and what a reproof to those who, with access to all the full and precious promises of the Word, give scanty time and thought to their appropriation!

And may it not suggest the value of trying to fasten God's own words in the memories of those whom we visit? A whole chapter read and explained may leave a happy impression, but a few words actually learnt are often far more useful. Never mind if the weak or aged memory cannot at first retain them,—go over the same tiny text next time, and then add another, and by dint of constant repetition, it is wonderful how many will at last be retained, while the increasing stock is increasingly valued, and becomes not only a source of fresh, bright interest, but of true, deep influence upon heart and life.

My sister has a weekly reading with the old women of a cluster of almshouses, and has for some time pursued the plan of teaching them a short text every time. They repeat them after her, over and over, just like little children, always saying over in chorus all the previously-learnt texts; and the pleasure which this appears to give them is almost amusing. Many of the texts thus learnt have been indeed "songs in the night," cheering long hours of pain and loneliness, and giving new proof of His faithfulness, who says, "My word shall NOT return to Me void."

TO THE MEMBERS OF THE

Young Women's Christian Association.

"We believe, and therefore speak."
2 Corinthians iv. 13.

DEAR sister-workers, may we, prayerfully depending on the Holy Spirit's teaching, find in these words a stimulus to greater faithfulness to our membership, greater effort for our Master.

WHAT *do we believe?* "The glorious Gospel of Christ." A true belief in this is no light thing. Could we sever it from our hearts, what would be left but a very death in life? However feeble, it is *precious* faith.

HOW *do we believe?* What is the practical result for others? We meet with those who have not "like precious faith," and we are content to speak only of what is nothing worth. If we believed that she with whom we have fled, each has the same soul-needs. If we believed that she with whom we are lightly exchanging pleasant or necessary remarks, must perish for ever unless Jesus saves her, should we not "therefore speak?" Let us try to realise. The young friend or stranger at my side, if she does not know Jesus, has no Friend, no Comforter, no share in all my happiness, nothing to fill an aching void within. But more:—This very one, if she does not know Jesus, must be shut out from Him for ever, and endure the unknown terrors of God's wrath for ever, and ever, and ever. There is but a step between her and death, and this may be her last opportunity to hear of the Saviour's love. Can I believe these truths, and part from her with smiling nothings, without one word to arouse, to win, to save?

WHAT *shall we speak?* Say that to God. He will give us words. With our highest skill, we can but draw the bow at a venture, for the mark is hidden. Let us trust in Him who can and will both give and guide the arrow. An imperceptible pause in conversation is time enough for an unworded prayer, a heart-glance up to Him for the right words, and for those words to be flashed into our minds, in swift and gracious answer. Let our hearts be filled with Christ and His salvation, and out of their abundance our mouths will speak.

WHEN *shall we speak?* Conscience will tell us. It will tell us, too, that we do not want more opportunities so much as grace to see and to use those which are continually given. Which of us can count lost opportunities?

Yet our Master noted each one as it passed. Let not the number be increased this year. It may be that a sense of coldness and sin is heavy upon us, and we hardly dare to speak of truths which have so little power over ourselves. Yet it does not say—"We *feel*, and therefore speak," but "We *believe*." Could we say that we do *not* believe? or quietly endure to hear our Saviour's name and work denied? Even in our suffering we may tell a fellow-sufferer of a cure; and while laying her case before the Great Physician, we shall find that He is nearer than we thought, and that His healing and reviving hand is laid upon ourselves. "The Lord turned the captivity of Job when he prayed for his friends." "He that watereth shall be watered."

HOW *shall we speak?* One who has had long experience among degraded Eastern women lately said:—"If we would do them good, *we must love them.*" This is the secret of reaching English girls, as well as Syrian maidens; the feather that wings our arrow must be *love*, and if love be real it will be seen and felt. It flows spontaneously to some, but how shall we command it for all whom we would reach? Only believe the word—"He died for all." Realise that Jesus so loved them that He died for them, and you will catch your Master's spirit, and speak with that winningness which love alone can give.

Let us make a second application of our motto, which yet must come first in practice. If we believe, let us therefore speak much *to* our God for every one to whom we would speak *of* Him. Does He anywhere set any limit to expectant prayer except His will? And "He willeth not the death of a sinner." What unknown blessings we may have lost by restraining prayer! What unknown blessings may be granted us, even this year, only for the asking! Will every one connected with the Association pray especially that God would pour "the spirit of grace and of supplication" upon every Branch and every Member through the coming year? Then how many prayers will be transmuted into praise! Let us look forward, not merely with hope, but expectation; believing that not we alone, and not the angels only, but our beloved Master Himself, will rejoice and be very glad over those for whom we pray. Sooner or later, we who "believe, and therefore speak," shall see, and therefore sing.

LORD, INCREASE OUR FAITH. LORD, OPEN THOU OUR LIPS.

F. R. H.

[*Copies on application to* MISS E. ROBARTS, *Barnet.*]

Original leaflet copy of the Open Letter.

This "Open Letter" was a printed leaflet, found among Havergal manuscripts and papers.

TO THE MEMBERS OF THE

Young Women's Christian Association.

"We believe, and therefore speak." 2 Corinthians 4:13.

Dear sister-workers, may we, prayerfully depending on the Holy Spirit's teaching, find in these words a stimulus to greater faithfulness to our membership, greater effort for our Master.

What *do we believe?* "The glorious Gospel of Christ." A true belief in this is no light thing. Could we sever it from our hearts, what would be left but a very death in life? However feeble, it is *precious* faith.

How *do we believe?* What is the practical result for others? We meet with those who have not "like precious faith," and we are content to speak only of what is nothing worth. Yet each is in the danger from which we have fled, each has the same soul-needs. If we believed that she with whom we are lightly exchanging pleasant or necessary remarks, must perish for ever unless Jesus saves her, should we not "therefore speak?" Let us try to realize. The young friend or stranger at my side, if she does not know Jesus, has no Friend, no Comforter, no share in all my happiness, nothing to fill an aching void within. But more:—This very one, if she does not know Jesus, must be shut out from Him for ever, and endure the unknown terrors of God's wrath for ever, and ever, and ever. There is but a step between her and death, and this may be her last opportunity to hear of the Saviour's love. Can I believe these truths, and part from her with smiling nothings, without one word to arouse, to win, to save?

What *shall we speak?* Say that to God. He will give us words. With our highest skill, we can but draw the bow at a venture, for the mark is hidden. Let us trust in Him Who can and will both give and guide the arrow. An imperceptible pause in conversation is time enough for an unworded prayer, a heart-glance up to Him for the right words, and for those words to be flashed into our minds, in swift and gracious answer. Let our hearts be filled with Christ and His salvation, and out of their abundance our mouths will speak.

When *shall we speak?* Conscience will tell us. It will tell us, too, that we do not want more opportunities so much as grace to see and to use those which are continually given. Which of us can count lost opportunities? Yet our Master noted each one as it passed. Let not the number be increased this year. It may be that a sense of coldness and sin is heavy upon us, and we hardly dare to speak of truths which have so little power over ourselves. Yet it does not say— "We *feel*, and therefore speak," but "We *believe*." Could we say that we do *not* believe? or quietly endure to hear our Saviour's name and work denied? Even in our suffering we may tell a fellow-sufferer of a cure; and while laying her case before the Great Physician, we shall find that He is nearer than we thought, and that His healing and reviving hand is laid upon ourselves. "The Lord turned the captivity of Job when he prayed for his friends." "He that watereth shall be watered."

How *shall we speak?* One who has had long experience among Middle Eastern women lately said:—"If we would do them good, *we must love them*." This is the secret of reaching English girls, as well as Syrian maidens; the feather that wings our arrow must be *love*, and if love be real, it will be seen and felt. It flows spontaneously to some, but how shall we command it for all whom we would reach? Only believe the word—"He died for all." Realize that Jesus so loved them that He died for them, and you will catch your Master's spirit, and speak with that winningness which love alone can give.

Let us make a second application of our motto, which yet must come first in practice. If we believe, let us therefore speak much *to* our God for every one to whom we would speak *of* Him. Does He anywhere set any limit to expectant prayer except His will? And "He willeth not the death of a sinner." What unknown blessings we may have lost by restraining prayer! What unknown blessings may be granted us, even this year, only for the asking! Will every one connected with the Association pray especially that God would pour "the spirit of grace and of supplication" upon every Branch and every Member through the coming year? Then how many prayers will be transmuted into praise! Let us look forward, not merely with hope, but expectation; believing that not we alone, and not the angels only, but our beloved Master Himself, will rejoice and be very glad over those for whom we pray. Sooner or later, we who "believe, and therefore speak," shall see, and therefore sing.

LORD, INCREASE OUR FAITH. LORD, OPEN THOU OUR LIPS.

F. R. H.

[*Copies on application to* MISS E. ROBARTS, Barnet.]

PREFACES AND ITEMS BY F.R.H. ON MUSIC.

Frances Ridley Havergal was a musician to the core of her. She was rarely gifted in music, and rarely diligent with her gifts, and her musical gifts were very important in her life and works. Since the time of those who knew or heard her, few people have realized the specialness and importance of her music, both scores she composed and performances she played or sang before others. Volume V of this edition (*Songs of Truth and Love: Music by Frances Ridley Havergal and William Henry Havergal*) has nearly all of her published scores. The Preface to Volume V (by far the longest preface of the five in this edition) is an attempt to show the value and richness of her music, the rareness and rich benefit of her gifts in music. There were no recordings of her (there are clear, strong accounts of her playing and singing by ones who heard her), and we have now only her scores, important, beneficial scores. Her compositions and performances were given by the Lord and used by Him, truly to His glory and to others' benefit and enrichment, true worship, true edification.

Her father, Rev. William Henry Havergal (1793–1870), was the foremost church musician and composer of sacred music in his day in England. After his death, Frances edited his *Old Church Psalmody* (1847) and his *A Hundred Psalm and Hymn Tunes* (1859), adding a few scores by her, published in the goldmine volume *Havergal's Psalmody and Century of Chants*. She also worked with Rev. Charles Busbridge Snepp, a pastor and hymnologist, to publish *Songs of Grace and Glory*, almost surely the largest and most comprehensive hymnbook in the Church of England till that time. Rev. Snepp edited the texts and led the work, and Frances edited the music. This is an enormous and enormously impressive body of work. Her "Supplementary Remarks" (which she wrote after two Prefaces by her father) in *Havergal's Psalmody and Century of Chants* is given first. After that, her 1875 Preface to the "Musical Edition" of *Songs of Grace and Glory* (the hymnbook was published also with words only, without music) is given. Then an article by F.R.H. on *Songs of Grace and Glory* published in the *Perry Barr Magazine* is given next. Then a second article (authorship uncertain, possibly written by F.R.H.) on the hymnal is given, followed by an advertisement and published reviews of *Songs of Grace and Glory*.

Late in her life, Charles Henry Purday wrote Frances for approval to set poems by her to music. Purday (himself a composer and a fine singer, who had sung at Queen Victoria's Coronation in 1837, who corresponded with William

Henry Havergal and was highly esteemed by him) proceeded to set poems by her to music, corresponding with her and later sending her his scores, which she examined and corrected shortly before her unexpected early death. This collection was published the same year in a volume entitled *Songs of Peace and Joy* (words by F.R.H., music by Purday). Excerpts from three letters by her to Purday and her "Prefatory Note" to *Songs of Peace and Joy* are given, followed by Purday's "Composer's Preface."

David Chalkley

HAVERGAL'S PSALMODY
AND
CENTVRY OF CHANTS
FROM
"Old Church Psalmody".
"Hundred Tunes" & Unpublished Manuscripts
OF THE LATE
Rev. W. H. Havergal, M.A.
Honorary Canon of Worcester.
with Prefaces, Indices and Portrait.
Edited by his daughter, Frances Ridley Havergal.

LONDON,
Robert Cocks & Co. New Burlington Street.
By Special Appointment.
Music Publishers to her Majesty the Queen, H.R.H. the Prince of Wales, and the Emperor Napoleon III.
MDCCCLXXI.

Supplementary Remarks.

1871.

MANY will be surprised at the large number of well-known and favourite tunes in *Havergal's Psalmody*. The fact is, that *Havergal's Old Church Psalmody* has been the fountain from which editors of subsequent collections have drawn—either at first or second hand—and the original guide to many valuable tune-sources, both English and foreign. It was the Columbus of tune-books; the pioneer, not to a New, but to an Old World of musical treasure. *Now*, the route is open and easy.

The retiring and unselfish spirit of its editor, as well as his devotion to yet higher work, prevented that assertion of its true position before the multitude, which has always been accorded to it by the highest musical authorities. "Little more than a sovereign was expended in advertising it"; and only once did he pen a remark upon any unfair treatment of his work. "To the multitudinous applications for permission to reprint tunes from the *Old Church Psalmody* no refusal was ever given, nor was any remuneration named. But the permission, when granted, has not always been duly acknowledged. Some tunes have been properly acknowledged; but others, taken *wholly* or chiefly from the same source, have been printed as though they belonged to the editor of the collection in which they appear. These oversights, which ought not to be made, have too frequently occurred." Also,—"It was due to *Old Church Psalmody* that they who were allowed to borrow its tunes, should likewise have adopted its names."

The selections from "*A Hundred Psalm and Hymn Tunes, by the Rev. W. H. Havergal,*" will be found, as experience has proved them to be, easily learnt, greatly liked, and practically adapted for congregational singing. Of one of these, Dr. Lowell Mason, the great American promoter of choral singing, wrote as follows:—

> I have lately introduced into my choir, and sung with admirable effect, your tune, "ST. NICHOLAS" [now called "EDEN," No. 38 in this volume]. The effect of it was truly magnificent. My choir consists of about sixty singers; the different parts are well sustained, and about equally balanced. I have never heard anything come nearer to my *beau ideal* of Church Music than did the singing of this tune, on a fine Sabbath morning, in a church filled with people. It made a deep impression; and the next day, one and another was

asking, "What tune did you sing yesterday morning?" "Where did you get that tune?" etc. The performance of "St. Nicholas" [Eden] makes one feel as did Jacob at Luz, and involuntarily exclaim, "This is none other but the house of God, and this is the gate of heaven." Wonderful would be the effect of the Psalmody were all the people to unite in such lofty and majestic strains.— April 30, 1847.

In order to meet the increasing proportion of "peculiar measures," a number of tunes have been adapted from the Rev. W. H. Havergal's own melodies, (chiefly from unpublished MSS.), while, for extra measures which could not be thus supplied, a few tunes have been added by another hand. The present volume, therefore, contains tunes for all measures in the best modern hymnals. It is, however, specially adapted to the new hymnal, *Songs of Grace and Glory*, with its 1,000 carefully selected hymns, edited by the Rev. C. B. Snepp, to whom the editor of *Havergal's Paslmody* is greatly indebted for much kind counsel in the work.

Any clergyman or organist will be willingly supplied with a Tuneal Key for whatever hymnal he may wish to use in connection with *Havergal's Psalmody*.

The arrangement of the tunes is strictly metrical. After the regular L.M.'s, C.M.'s, and S.M.'s, the P.M.'s follow *in order of length of measure*, beginning with 5555, and ending with 12 10.[1] When several tunes belong to one measure, they are carefully arranged *in order of character*, beginning with the jubilant, and shading gradually to the plaintive, so that if an alternative tune for any hymn be desired, it will never be far to seek.

The nomenclature of *Havergal's Psalmody* is systematic. The *name* of each tune at once supplies information as to its origin. Old English, Scotch or German tunes, bear respectively English, Scotch or German names; those by the Rev. W. H. Havergal are named (with a few exceptions), from the natural geography of the Bible; the added tunes are named from "the friends of St. Paul." No departure from these rules has been made without some necessitating reason.

Amens have been appended for optional use, wherever such a close is not unsuitable to the "suitable words."

May this memorial, to one "whose works do follow" him, be to the glory of his God, who has now "made him most blessed for ever."

F. R. HAVERGAL.

---

[1] (N.B.—15 15, 15 15, will be found under 87, 87 D.)

Original Preface to the Musical Edition

OF

"Songs of Grace and Glory."

(BY FRANCES RIDLEY HAVERGAL.)

MANY will be surprised at the large number of well-known and favourite tunes in "Havergals' Psalmody." The fact is that "Havergal's Old Church Psalmody" has been the fountain from which editors of subsequent collections have drawn, either at first or second hand, and the original guide to many valuable tune sources, both English and foreign. It was the Columbus of tune-books; the pioneer, not to a New, but to an Old World of musical treasure. *Now*, the route is open and easy.

The retiring and unselfish spirit of its editor, as well as his devotion to yet higher work, prevented that assertion of its true position before the multitude which has always been accorded to it by the highest musical authorities.

The selections from "Havergal's Psalmody" will be found, as experience has proved them to be, easily learnt, greatly liked, and practically adapted for congregational singing. Of one of these, Dr. Lowell Mason, the great American promoter of choral singing, wrote as follows:

> I have lately introduced into my choir, and sung with admirable effect, your tune "Eden." The effect of it was truly magnificent. My choir consists of about sixty singers; the different parts are well sustained, and about equally balanced. I have never heard anything come nearer to my *beau ideal* of Church Music than did the singing of this tune, on a fine Sabbath morning, in a church filled with people. It made a deep impression; and the next day one and another was asking, "What tune did you sing yesterday morning?" "Where did you get that tune?" etc. The performance of "Eden" makes one feel as did Jacob at Luz, and involuntarily exclaim, "This is none other but the house of God, and this is the gate of heaven." Wonderful would be the effect of Psalmody were all the people to unite in such lofty and majestic strains.— April 30, 1847.

In order to meet the increasing proportion of "peculiar measures," a number of tunes have been adapted from the Rev. W. H. Havergal's own melodies (chiefly from unpublished MSS.), while, for extra measures which could not be thus supplied, tunes have been added by other hands [F. R. H. and others].

The *name* of each tune at once supplies information as to its origin. Old English, Scotch, or German tunes bear respectively English, Scotch, or German names; those by the Rev. W. H. Havergal are named, with a few exceptions, from the natural geography of the Bible; the tunes added by F. R. H. [Frances Ridley Havergal] are named from " the friends of St. Paul."

" Havergal's Psalmody," a memorial to one whose works do follow him, was originally given to the church by his devoted widow, and " dedicated to his beloved, honoured, and cherished memory." The Large Type or Organ editions of " Havergal's Psalmody" contain Kyries, Glorias, and other additions not included in the present hymnal edition; while editions A and B contain Prefaces and Historical Notes, which are quoted as " a treasury of information and an armoury of defence of the principles of Church Music." A and D include " A Century of Chants." [1]

As the tunes have not been affixed to the hymns without much thought and prayer, and very careful consideration as to which tune will best develop the spirit of each hymn, and emphasize its most important points, it is strongly advised that, generally speaking, the tunes indicated should be adhered to.

On the other hand, as the great aim of making our singing congregational is not attained if too many new tunes are attempted at once, it is well to introduce them *gradually*, repeating each newly learnt tune at short intervals, until quite familiar. It is advisable to begin with a few tunes in such metres as occur abundantly.

The following selection of peculiar metres may be found useful at first, as giving a wide range of hymns. Hermas, for 6 5, 6 5. D.; Zoan I., for spirited and joyous hymns in 7 6, 7 6. D.; and Mahanaim (or Goldbach), for quieter hymns in the same metre; Lubeck and Patmos, respectively, for the two classes of hymns in 7 7, 7 7; Nassau and Sihor, for 7 7, 7 7, 7 7; Culbach and Frankfort (or Godesberg), for 8 7, 8 7; Zaanaim and Idumea, for 8 7, 8 7, 4 7 (or 8 7, 8 7, 8 7); Magdalene College and Kedron, for 8 8 6. D.; and Paran, for 11 11, 11 11.

1875.   FRANCES RIDLEY HAVERGAL.

---

[1] All of which can be obtained from Nisbet and Co., 21, Berners Street, London.

The following article by F.R.H. (found among Havergal manuscripts and papers, date not known, almost surely 1872) was published in the *Perry Barr Magazine*. (F.R.H. was "Our Own Correspondent.") She describes the hymnbook *Songs of Grace and Glory*, edited by Rev. Charles Busbridge Snepp, Vicar of St.John's Church, Perry Barr, near Birmingham, England. Rev.Snepp was the architect and leader of the work. Frances was very modestly silent about her part in the volume. She was the editor of all the music for the hymnbook, preparing, checking, finalizing every measure of music, an enormous and enormously impressive body of work. She also composed a number of hymntunes and wrote the words of a number of the hymns for *Songs of Grace and Glory*, and collaborated with Rev. Snepp extensively, invaluably. This hymnbook was first published in 1872 with the words only, and the hymnbook had a "Companion Volume," *Havergal's Psalmody and Century of Chants*. This "Companion Volume" was published in 1871, edited by F.R.H., and most of the music in it had been composed by her father, Rev. William Henry Havergal, with a few tunes composed and added by F.R.H. *H.P.C.C.* contained the music for all the hymns in *Songs of Grace and Glory*, and with each text of words in *S.G.G.* was written the number of the hymntune for that hymn in the Companion Volume. In 1876 the "Musical Edition" was published, with both the words and music together in *Songs of Grace and Glory*. This very valuable, richly beneficial hymnal became very obscure, though a copy dated 1883 says "Three Hundred and Thirteenth Thousand."

Though a number of the articles written by her were unsigned, anonymous, here her name Frances Ridley Havergal is printed at the end of this article. Like most of the articles published in periodicals and found among Havergal manuscripts and papers, the date is not known.

PARISH EVENTS.

From "Our Own Correspondent."

(Extract from "Home Words" Perry Barr Magazine.)

———

A COMING "PARISH EVENT."

A LONG anticipated *"Parish Event"* will, it is hoped, take place before the next Magazine reaches all its readers, viz., the introduction of the new hymnal, *"Songs of Grace and Glory,*" into the churches and homes of Perry Barr. People ask what it will be like, and how it will differ from other hymn books; so a few words of explanation of the nature and results of their Pastor's long and laborious work for the Church of God in general, and for his parish in particular, may not be out of place.

"*Songs of Grace and Glory*" contains more than a thousand hymns. Some of them have been treasures of the Church for centuries, others are quite new. All our old favorites will be found in it, as well as many which are even more beautiful and admirable.

The hymns are arranged according to a very perfect and comprehensive scheme of subjects, embracing every Scripture doctrine, every season of our Church's year, every phase of Christian experience, and every duty, sorrow, or joy of our homes. It is not too much to say that there cannot be a throb or a thrill in any heart among us which will not find a true and touching echo in some strain of "*Songs of Grace and Glory.*"

But we must *sing* them! And so, to save all trouble of wondering—"What tune can we have?"—the name of a suitable tune is printed at the top of every hymn. In many cases two tunes are given; so that, if we do not know the first, we have the chance of finding that the second is more familiar. These tunes will all be found in the "*Companion Volume*," advertised at the end of this Magazine.

Who wrote all these hymns?—It is interesting to know; for often the very name of the writer makes us love a hymn the more. We shall know all about it now, for at the foot of each hymn stands not only the name of the author, but the date. So, when a hymn is given out, and we see "Eighth Century," it will surely add to our interest to know that it was sung "to the praise and glory of God" by voices which went up to sing the "New Song" eleven hundred years ago. But it has been no easy thing to find out all these names and dates; and many an hour of patient search or repeated correspondence has been devoted to this by him who has spared no toil to make his work in all respects complete, and worthy of its great object, its dedication to the Triune Jehovah.

Beautiful hymns have often been altered and re-altered till the saintly or sainted writers would hardly know them again; and we feel that, if possible, we should like to have them as they were really written at first. This, again, has cost more labour than any one who had had no share in it would imagine. Mr. Snepp has discovered and restored the original reading of numbers of mutilated hymns. Sometimes, however, our old writers used expressions which are now considered ungrammatical or otherwise faulty; sometimes a line, which might be made to sound all right in reading, was found to be very imperfect for singing, owing to inattention to the correct placing of accented syllables; and sometimes an alteration was such an obvious improvement that, having been adopted by general consent, it would be a pity to return to the original; in these cases alterations have been either made or retained, and this is indicated by (*a*) placed after the writers' names. Wherever correction has appeared absolutely necessary, the greatest care has been taken to adhere as nearly as possible to the originals.

Our beautiful hymns should lead us to love and value all the more the music of God's own Word. So, over every hymn we shall find a text, the key note of the "song" which follows. Often we find that what an earthly writer has taken many lines to express, the One Inspirer has already summed up in a few words; and while the hymn explains the text, the text sums and seals the truth and beauty of the hymn.

Perhaps we think it will take a long time to learn to find our way about such a large collection,—we fancy we shall not be able to find what we want, even if we are sure it is there. This is met by a set of such full and carefully planned indices as no other hymnal can show; so that if we wish to lay our finger upon any particular hymn, text, tune, author and date, subject, or Sunday service, we shall be able to do so in a minute. Special attention, however, should be given to Index No. 1., as, if we study that, the whole scheme of the book will be within our grasp at once.

The *outside* of "*Songs of Grace and Glory*" will need no introduction, as it is quite attractive enough to stand on its own merits at first sight. There will be seven editions, marked A, B, C, D, E, F, and G, so we shall have plenty of choice. "G" will be wonderfully cheap, as Mr. Snepp will supply it at one shilling, by a sacrifice upon it. That is, we shall get hymns at the rate of very little more than 1*d*. per 100, with strong and handsome binding into the bargain. "A" is a special and very beautiful edition on large paper, intended as a drawing room table or gift book. It is well that this will be in plenty of time for Christmas presents; for what could be a better gift than "*Songs of Grace and Glory*" at that holy and happy season? Far better than useless ornaments, or books which rather hinder than help the "onward and upward" progress. "B", "C", and "D" are in large and clear type, "D" in plain binding, "C" cloth gilt, and "B" very handsome leather gilt; "E" and "F" are smaller, but also very clear type.

Those who have already seen the work, now so nearly completed, cannot but feel that Mr. Snepp is giving, not to his people only, but to his Church and country, a treasure which will outlive the present generation of its singers and readers. The outlay, not merely of money (which is very great), but of far more precious time and health, is not grudged but laid at his Master's feet, in the earnest hope and belief that He will not only accept it, but by the power of His blessing make His servant's work a wide and mighty means of cheering and quickening His people, of spreading the truths of His gospel, and of setting forth His praise from generation to generation.

FRANCES RIDLEY HAVERGAL.

[The following, unsigned article on *Songs of Grace and Glory* was also published in the *Perry Barr Magazine*. F.R.H. wrote articles and pieces for this periodical without giving her name, and though we do not know, this may have been written by her. This researcher thinks this was likely her writing. David Chalkley]

Songs of Grace and Glory, for Mission Services, etc. Price 2d.; cloth 4d.; gilt 6d., and *Children's Songs of Grace and Glory*. Price 1-1/2d.; cloth 4d.; gilt, 6d. Edited by the Rev. Charles B. Snepp, LL.M., Vicar of Perry Barr. London: James Nisbet & Co.

THE so-called "Mission Week" movement in the Church of England is one of the brightest features of the day, indicating as it does life and love, zeal and energy; and resulting, in most instances, in the quickening of spiritual life and the adding of many to the Church. But new work requires new adjuncts. A want of precisely suitable hymns there has been greatly felt; and the attempt to supply it by little sheets or handbills, useful only for once and soon torn or lost, has been very unsatisfactory. A collection was needed, small and cheap, yet in good type, containing hymns which should combine that refinement and sobriety which harmonize with our beloved Church, with the clear ring of Gospel invitation, and the tone of favor and spirituality which should be the characteristics of a Mission Service. It should contain the standard Gospel Hymns with which all are familiar; and also others which, having arisen from the needs and the spirit of our own day, are perhaps even more adapted to present and special use.

These requirements have been admirably met in a selection of 130 Hymns from the Rev. C. B. Snepp's most valuable Hymnal, "Songs of Grace and Glory." While specially suited for Mission Week use, this little book is all that can be desired for the many occasions on which hymns of the character described above are a desideratum, whether schoolroom services, prayer meetings, drawing room or cottage Bible readings, mothers' meetings, Bible classes, or family worship. It will also serve as an Appendix in churches where the need of such hymns is felt, while yet a change of Hymnal may not be considered feasible.

"Children's Songs of Grace and Glory," contains a selection of 110 Hymns from the Full Editions, being "partly Children's Hymns, in the strict sense of the term, and partly such hymns as, from their winning sweetness, important teaching, or standard character, should be early familiar to the little ones."

Congregations already using the Full Edition of "Songs of Grace and Glory" will find both these little handmaids very useful for various forms of parochial work, and for the schools. "For convenience of reference and simultaneous use, the number to each hymn remains the same in all the editions." We may add that while the paper copies meet the cry for a very cheap supply, the cloth and gilt copies of both these little books are particularly attractive in appearance.

———🎗———

vows in the strength of God's confirming grace, but to those who have long ago done so. For it is well to have vividly brought before us the recollection of the day when we, too, said that solemn word "I do," and heard, with bowed head and hushed heart, that thrilling prayer, "That they may continue *Thine for ever.*"

"*Come and let us join ourselves to the Lord in a perpetual covenant that shall* NOT BE FOR-GOTTEN."—Jer. l. 5.

BAPTISMS, IN THE MONTHS OF DECEMBER AND JANUARY, IN ST. JOHN'S CHURCH, PERRY BARR.

Dec. 8, Walter Herbert Grimmett; Jan. 5, Hannah Beatrice White; Jan. 12, Edward James Unite Turner; Jan. 12, John Judd; Jan. 19, Eleanor Davenhill.

MARRIAGE.

Dec. 26. Mr. John Stephen Turner, of Perry Barr, to Jemima, daughter of the Rev. Charles Brooke.

Miss Brooke's long and valued work in connection with the schools of this parish, gives this "parish event" a special interest, and many are the readers of *Home Words* who will wish her all happiness and blessing in her new sphere, in which good wishes both parents and children will cordially unite.

BURIALS.

Dec. 5, Joseph Wright, aged 2 years; Dec. 11, Eliza Morse, aged 2 years; Dec. 12, John Richard Wright, aged 6 months; Dec. 21, Emily Morse, aged 6 months; Dec. 24, Lucy Emily Lena Snepp, aged 12 years; Jan. 19, Alfred William Wallis, aged 5 weeks.

The Burial Register for the past two months is indeed a singular and touching one, and full of solemn lessons for the little ones. Not one grown up person, but six little boys and girls, laid to rest in Perry Churchyard! It was on Christmas Eve that one was laid there, "in sure and certain hope of a joyful resurrection." Only a month before that she was strong and well. But though the call was so early, she was ready, and this will always be the greatest comfort to her sorrowing parents and sisters. All through her short and suffering illness her heart seemed set on heavenly things. It was very remarkable that a copy of her dear uncle's hymnal, "Songs of Grace and Glory," given to her as a reward for learning thirty hymns, was her constant comfort, and was always beside her till the last. One night, when very ill, she fell asleep singing softly, "I lay my sins on Jesus," and she woke again far in the night with the words, "Oh, for the robes of whiteness!" And now, while, as these words are being written, the snow is falling fast upon her grave, she is arrayed in those "robes of whiteness," and joining in the new song of praise to Him who is the Friend of little children.

"*Suffer the little children to come unto Me.*"—Mark x. 14.

A page in the Perry Barr Magazine. *The text above the advertisement of* Songs of Grace and Glory *is found on pages 145–146 of this book.*

The preceding advertisement and the following set of reviews of *Songs of Grace and Glory* were published in the *Perry Barr Magazine*.

SONGS OF GRACE AND GLORY.

OPINIONS EXPRESSED.

" The external appearance is beautiful, and I can see at a glance that very great care has been bestowed upon the compilation."—The Right Rev. the Lord Bishop of Lichfield.

" A very comprehensive and valuable book, and the beauty of its outward form and type leave nothing to be desired."—The Right Rev. The Lord Bishop of Worcester.

" In your precious book I find an endless fund of Divine instruction. It is the best 'Preacher's Assistant' I ever met with, next to the Word itself."—John T. Maley, Vicar of Tunbridge.

" The more I peruse it, the more I like it."—Marcus Rainsford, Belgrave chapel, Eator Square.

" 'Songs of Grace and Glory.'—Just the book I wanted—TRUE POETRY, DEEP SPIRITUALITY, GREAT TASTE, AND GREAT VARIETY."—H. O. Sterland, Vicar of St. Edmund's Gateshead.

" I have carefully read 'Songs of Grace and Glory,' and have no hesitation in saying that the volume is, in my opinion, one of the most admirable and comprehensive collections of Hymns I have ever seen. The labour in research and arrangement undergone by the Editor must have been very great indeed. I shall rejoice to hear of its wide circulation. It is a marvel of cheapness." [1]—R.W. Forrest, Vicar of St. Jude's South Kensington.

" I like your Collection of Hymns very much."—Rev. J. C. Ryle

" The selection of old Hymns is admirable, and the new ones, with which you have enriched your pages, deserve the gratitude of the Church of Christ. Those by Frances Ridley Havergal are particularly pleasing. Their perusal has proved a source of great comfort and instruction to us."—John Stevenson, D.D. (Author of "The Lord our Shepherd," etc.)

" My brother clergymen are greatly taken with it. It is without exception, the best ever published. I look at it and at those indices with astonishment. We

---

[1] Rev. Forrest unquestionably meant by "cheapness" non-expensive affordableness, economically priced. David Chalkley.

have been perfectly reveling in the book."—D. A. Doudney, D.D., Incumbent of St. Luke's Bedminster.

"At Walton, I found the change to your full and faithful Hymn book most acceptable."—Canon John Babington, Rector of Walton-le-Wolds.

"The demand for 'Songs of Grace and Glory' (just adopted in the writer's church), is so unprecedented. They win golden opinions on every side."—C. T. Rolfe, Rector of Shadoxhurst Kent.

———— ❧ ————

[This next item was a small review published in a periodical, found among Havergal manuscripts and papers. Only the cut-out clipping was found, with no indication of the periodical name or date.]

We cordially welcome a musical edition of *The Songs of Grace and Glory* (Nisbet and Co.), edited by the Rev. C. B. Snepp and Miss F. R. Havergal. This excellent hymnal has, by the addition of the tunes, been rendered suitable for all purposes, and should prove of service in supplanting other compilations of a less satisfactory character. Miss Havergal has done well in drawing largely from her father's collection of tunes, and from this and other sources she has provided a really useful tune-book which is sufficiently extensive to meet the requirements of any ordinary congregation. At the same time we cannot but regard it as a mistake to include in a volume intended for permanent use any of the tunes so recently popularized by Messrs. Moody and Sankey. These tunes are very taking at first, but they soon wear out, and it is hardly likely that any of them will be heard amongst us except as musical curiosities half-a-dozen years hence.

———— ❧ ————

[The next items are excerpts from three letters by F.R.H. to C. H. Purday and Prefaces to *Songs of Peace and Joy*.]

THE MUMBLES, October 14, 1878.
Your note has touched and interested me most deeply. "Heart answereth to heart." I do trust that ere now you are still further on the way to recovery. Yet there is, I *know*, so much real blessing in the touch of our Lord's hand, even when we have to say, "Thy hand presseth me sore," that somehow, ever since a very long and suffering illness of my own, I have hardly been able to say sin-

cerely to any really Christian friend, "I am *sorry* you have been ill." And the "afterward" is surely promised. Every time of calling apart leads us to know and understand a little better "Him with whom we have to do." How much these words imply! . . .

I am so glad you like my *Royal Commandments,* though I should not have expected you to like it so well as *Royal Bounty.* Mr. Snepp is charmed with your tune to "Yes, He knows the way is dreary," and would be very glad to include it in his new edition.

Possibly the enclosed tiny books may give you some pleasant thought—I shall be so thankful if they do. (*Precious Things,* and *I also for Thee.*)

THE MUMBLES, October 30, 1878.

. . . I am so glad to hear you are raised up again. It is curious that in the night I was thinking so much of the promise, "Thou shalt glorify Me," specially in its connection as following deliverance from trouble (Psalm 50:15). And then your letter came in the morning, speaking of your desire to do something for His glory! Whatever He has promised, surely we may and should claim and expect, however much better and greater it may be than we should have thought of asking. Oh yes, if one may but do anything for Him "who loved us and washed us from our sins in His own blood," it is worth coming back from the very golden gates to do it. If He has made us for His glory He will surely "be glorified in us." That He will even *now,* and there is 2 Thessalonians 1:10 to come! It is so wonderful.

December 30, 1878.

I have been on the shelf, or should have replied sooner. And now the few days' illness has thrown me all behind with letters and work, so pardon haste. The only tune I do not like, and cannot possibly sanction, in your *Songs of Peace and Joy,* is the setting of my Consecration hymn, "Take my life," to that wearisomely hackneyed kyrie of Mozart. It does not suit the words either, and I was much vexed with Mr. Mountain for printing it with it in his *Hymns of Consecration,* and it would just spoil your book to let it pass. I *particularly wish* that hymn kept to my dear father's sweet little tune, "Patmos," which suits it perfectly. So please substitute that, and your book will be the gainer. You have rather taken the wind out of my own sails by your book, as Hutchings & Romer have for a good while wanted me to set *Loyal Responses* to music (now published by them); but I have so many irons in the fire, that I can barely find time to heat a musical one. However, I could not find it in my heart to hinder you in your wish, with which my whole heart sympathizes, to do this thing for God's glory. I do so very much like many of your tunes.

"Therefore, being justified by faith, we *have* peace with God." Dear friend, why say, "May that peace be mine," when it is yours already, purchased for you, made for you, sealed for you, pledged to you—by the word of the Father and the "precious blood of Jesus"! Forgive me for touching up your words, but I have recalled them so many times since you wrote.

May 1, 1879.

Glad it is all straight now for Nisbet! Shall leave form and style and everything to you and Mr. N.

Thanks, I rarely have anything the matter with me except what arises from over-pressure. God has given me an exceptionally healthy set of organs, so all doctors tell me, only they add, "Your physique is not equal to the brain and nerves." "If you could live as an oyster, you might be a little Hercules," said one to me! But *I cannot* live as an oyster! I have always more to write and do and talk and attend to than I *can* get through in the day without just so much fatigue and pressure as keeps me nearly always more or less suffering or exhausted. It is the little things that do it—"only just" this note and that letter, and the other ten minutes' interview, and so on—all day long! And I cannot live near a poor village (Newton Mumbles) and not get doing anything for the people—and one thing always involves and leads on to another, and the very success that God gives to really everything I put my hand to, wears me out. A special branch of work for the Irish Society, which I started only two years ago, thinking merely to have about a dozen juvenile collectors in tow, forthwith grew, so that there are now more than 100, all in my own hands, and this will ere long be multiplied and be kept organized with lots of other things growing out of it. I only name this as one out of many similar *growths,* and your kind interest deserved an explanation of the state of things once for all! Then every time I pay a visit, I always get a whole following of fresh friends, and readers and correspondents! I can't imagine where into it will grow! And sometimes I look longingly to the land that is very far away just for *rest.*

———— ✤ ————

PREFATORY NOTE.

————

This little book contains upwards of Thirty musical settings of selected verses from

"The Ministry of Song" and "Under the Surface."

It may be interesting to mention that, with the exception of three or four, they are the production of an octagenarian friend, whose desire is that his work may be to the glory of that faithful God who has led him for more than twice forty years through the wilderness; and that his chosen titile for these little melodies

"Songs of Peace and Joy"

may be true of the experience of all who shall sing them.

Frances Ridley Havergal.

May 13, 1879.

———— ❧ ————

COMPOSER'S PREFACE.

————

In publishing this little volume, I desire to say that I had never read any of Miss Havergal's beautiful Poems until the summer of 1878, when I was so charmed with the natural flow, lyrical aptitude, and truly Christian sentiments of her poetry, that I felt an intense desire to set some of her Hymns to music. I accordingly wrote to ask her permission to do so, which she readily and most kindly granted, by a short not to me dated August 10, 1878. I then set three of them, which I sent for her approval—viz., "Ministry of Song," v. 1 and 11, "Be not Weary," and "Wait patiently for Him,"—when she replied, August 24, 1878: "Some of the Hymns have been set already; it would save possible disappointment if you would say beforehand which you would like to set. . . . Your name is so well known to me, and was so honoured by my dear father, that I am specially gratified at your music and my little words being linked together. May our God grant his special blessing on your plan." Thus encouraged, I went on adapting and occasionally sending her my tunes until they had reached about thirty, corresponding with her at intervals, until it became necessary that we should determine how they should be published. This suggested an interview, and an invitation was sent me to go to Wales for the purpose of going through the M.S. together. "Man proposes, but God disposes," and it was ordered otherwise. Consequently a request was made that I should send the M.S. down, as Miss H. said she could look it over then, and return it before she went on her projected tour to her Irish mission. This was done and the M.S. returned with copious notes and valuable suggestions, to which I had much pleasure in giving effect,—when it pleased the Disposer of all events to call her hence,—how gloriously prepared has been fully stated.[1] And I have reason to bless God for my acquaintance with her and her works.

C. H. P.

Oct. 1, 1879.

[1] "The Last Week."

Stay and Think.

1. Know-ing that the God on high, With a ten - der Fa - ther's grace,

Waits to hear your faint - est cry, Waits to show a Fa - ther's face :—

Stay and think! Stay and think!

Stay and think! Stay and think! How He loves! oh, should not you Love this gracious Fa -ther too?

2.

Knowing Christ was crucified,
　Knowing that He loves you now
Just as much as when He died,
　With the thorns upon His brow ;
　　Stay and think—
How He loves ! oh, should not you
Love this blessèd Saviour too ?

3.

Knowing that a Spirit strives
　With your weary wandering heart,
Who can change the restless lives,
　Pure and perfect peace impart :
　　Stay and think—
How He loves ! oh, should not you
Love this loving Spirit too ?

Words and music by F.R.H. This was published posthumously in Loyal Responses The Last Melodies of Frances Ridley Havergal with Other Poems and Tunes. *See Volume V of the Havergal edition,* Songs of Truth and Love: Music by Frances Ridley Havergal and William Henry Havergal. *"Stay and Think" was also entitled "Love for Love" with the quotation, "We have known and believed the love that God hath to us" in I John 4:16.*

In 1878 F.R.H. published the fifth, final book of the set of five "Royal" books she regarded as a set, *Loyal Responses*, 31 poems. In the list found in her desk after she died (entitled "Work for 1879 'If the Lord will.'"), one of the items was "Set 'Loyal Responses' to music." Her music publishers, Hutchings and Romer, posthumously published the volume *Loyal Responses. The Last Melodies of Frances Ridley Havergal. With Other Poems and Tunes* in 1881, with this preface by Maria and her quotation of F.R.H. at the end:

PREFATORY NOTE.

SOME of these melodies were the very last composed and sung by Frances Ridley Havergal. So rapidly did they occur to her that they were only pencilled down, but her hand was stayed from the chords of earth before the musical completion of "Loyal Responses." Other melodies by F.R.H. have therefore been chosen and fitted to her hymns, in order to complete the thirty-one days.

The following extract will express F.R.H.'s feeling on the subject of

SACRED SONG.

"I am delighted to have an opportunity of adding to the very meagre supply of Sacred Songs, and I hope they will be sufficiently tuneful and sufficiently easy for drawing-room singing. Some of those extant are such pathetic and dismal affairs! Why put off joyous singing till we reach the happier shore? Let us sing words which we feel and love, with clearness of enunciation, and looking up to meet His smile all the while we are singing. So shall we loyally sing for our King, yes for Him, whose voice is our truest music."

MARIA V. G. HAVERGAL.

Caswell Bay Road,
    Aug., 1881.

Established 1818.

IRISH SOCIETY

FOR PROMOTING

The Scriptural Education and the Religious Instruction of

IRISH ROMAN CATHOLICS,

Chiefly through the Medium of their own Language.

COLLECTING BOOK.

OFFICE:
17, Upper Sackville-st., Dublin.

AGENCY AT PRESENT EMPLOYED, &c.

One **General Clerical Superintendent.**
53 Clerical Superintendents (including nine Missionaries).
One **Re-Inspecting Agent.**
23 Inspectors of Irish Schools, who also act as Scripture-readers.
47 Scripture-Readers.
8 Schoolmasters, } in charge of Mission Schools.
2 Schoolmistresses, }
10 Mission Schools (including three Ragged Schools), in which upwards of 350 Children are under instruction.
229 Irish Schools, in which about 7,589 Pupils are under instruction.

AUXILIARY TO ITS MISSIONARY WORK, THE SOCIETY SUPPORTS—

Two Bedell Irish Scholarships, and a Premium, in the University, for the encouragement of the study of the Irish Language.

THE following facts connected with the work of the IRISH SOCIETY, since its establishment in the year 1818, are commended to the prayerful attention of every true friend of Ireland.

I.—3,000 Irish-speaking people—the vast majority Roman Catholics—have, each year, been instructed by its Agents in the art of reading their native language.

II.—165,000 Irish-speaking people *are thus known* to have been brought into contact with the Word of Life: while it is believed that as many more, relatives and friends of those instructed, have likewise been made acquainted with the same Word, 'whose entrance giveth light.'

III.—More than 500 Scripture-Readers and 50 ordained Missionaries—mostly converts of the Society—have been successively employed in the Irish-speaking districts.

IV.—20 Churches—19 in Ireland, and 1 in America—with several School-houses, have been built for the reception of Convert congregations, and the instruction of their children.

V.—The Society's work has exercised a wholesome influence even over those who may not have left the Church of Rome. From the several agitations which of late have disfigured the historic annals of our country, the Bible-taught Roman Catholics have stood aloof, being remarkable no less for their peaceful demeanour, than for their loyal attachment to the Throne and Constitution.

VI.—The Irish language is still extensively spoken; 1,105,536 persons were returned as Irish speakers in 1861.

VII.—To reach this Irish-speaking population, widely scattered throughout the land, the present agency of the Society must be sustained. Every friend of Ireland is therefore earnestly requested to aid the Society's cause—by prayer, by subscribing to its funds, by prevailing upon others to subscribe, or by collecting and getting others to collect.

PETER ROE, Printer, 42 Mabbot-street, Dublin.

This was F.R.H.'s personal Irish Society Collecting Book.

This was published in *Lilies and Shamrocks*, a posthumous, small book of letters and other items by F.R.H., many concerning her work for her Irish Society. F.R.H. led a growing number of children who raised funds to support Missions work in Ireland, a cause very dear to her.

HINTS FOR IRISH SOCIETY COLLECTORS.

By Frances Ridley Havergal.

————

1. Never consider your work done; set your new card going the very week the old one is sent in.

2. At the beginning of your collecting year make a list of every one, near or distant, likely or unlikely, whom you could possibly ask during the twelve months, keeping the list where it may often catch your eye, adding names whenever they occur to you, and marking off each as soon as you have applied.

3. Never be without a card; keep two in hand—one to be enclosed in letters, hoping for its return with stamps; the other should lie on the drawing-room table, and thus do some possible passive work when not in active use.

4. *Watch* for opportunities, and you will see them.

5. Ask unlikely people, and you will get delightful surprises.

6. Keep an eye to shillings, and even sixpences, as well as sovereigns.

7. Aim definitely at progress. Determine that, God helping, you will *never* retrograde, but always send an increase upon the last year.

8. Unless very sure of your ground, ask for a "contribution" rather than "subscription" or "donation." The former is alarming, because it implies continuance; the latter is objectionable, because it precludes asking next year. "Contribution" neither frightens the contributor nor hinders the collector, and nearly always results in a "subscription" in course of time.

9. Carefully read and *mark* your Reports or other papers, before lending, turning down leaves at the more important or attractive pages, and using the pencil freely. Persons who never touch an ordinary Report will and do seek out and read all your marked passages.

10. Lose no opportunity of gaining any information for yourself on the subject. Do not hesitate to talk about it and tell striking facts or statistics, even when you are not actually collecting. You may thus awaken interest in unexpected quarters, and seed, thus casually dropped, sometimes yields a golden harvest.

11. Remember that one collector is more real gain than several contributors; and, therefore, aim rather at getting others to undertake a card than to contribute to yours. This widens interest as well as increases funds, for persons always take more interest in what they work for than what they merely give to.

12. Be ready to sacrifice your own apparent results to the real gain of the society. We may often gain a new collector by handing over some of our own subscribers. They will shrink less from gathering in subscriptions already assured, and will generally double the amount thus transferred.

13. Pray, not occasionally, vaguely, and doubtfully, but (1) *Systematically.*— Fix one morning in the week all the year round for the praying part of your work. (2) *Definitely.*—Ask for exactly *what* you want and *all* you want in connection with your collecting; ask for faith, zeal, courage, and love; ask that names may be suggested to you, and openings made for you; ask *where,* and *when,* and *how* to appeal; ask that in each case you may be guided whether to write or speak, that hearts may be prepared before you come, and that the very words may be given you; ask beforehand, and ask at the moment, for wisdom, willingness, and, if it be His will, success. (3) *Expectantly.*—Do not look at *probabilities,* but at *promises;* work only for God's glory, and only in the Master's name, and then joyfully trust Him to "fulfil *all* thy petitions."

NAME	SUBSCRIPTION		
	£	s.	d.
Miss Fisher		2	-
Mrs Nicholls	2	-	-
Mrs Usborne		10	-
Mrs Bullock		5	
Mrs Moir		5	
Mrs Gough		1	
Miss Cobb		1	
Mrs Riddell		5	
F. R. H.		1	
Edges		10	
Carried forward .. .. £			

NAME	SUBSCRIPTION		
Brought forward	£	s.	d.
Carried forward .. .. £			

The work of the Irish Society was very dear to F.R.H.

ITEMS PUBLISHED IN PERIODICALS.

These next items published in periodicals were found among Havergal manuscripts and papers. Several of these texts were small clippings cut out from the magazines or newspapers, often with no dates nor name of the periodicals.

This first article was published in the *Episcopal Register*, and a clipping of the newspaper article was found among Havergal manuscripts and papers. This article was also published in *Ben Brightboots and Other True Stories, Hymns, and Music*, a posthumous volume of items by F.R.H. for children, compiled and published by her sister, Maria V. G. Havergal.

(For the Episcopal Register.)

"HOW MUCH FOR JESUS?"

BY FRANCES RIDLEY HAVERGAL.
Author of "Ministry of Song," and other Poems.

A little group of boys and girls were gathered around me on a pleasant evening in the Easter holidays. We were talking about the Lord Jesus, and all the wonderful and solemn things which our Church services had so lately brought before us,— His agony and bloody sweat, His Cross and Passion,—His precious Death and Burial, and His glorious Resurrection. There was such a quieted and tender tone among them, such wistful looks and gentle voices, and the hearts of more than one were so evidently burning within them, that one could not doubt that "Jesus Himself drew near," and that while we spoke one to another, He not only hearkened and heard, but was really present in our midst. Then we spoke of what we owed to Him who had done so much for us. How much do we owe Him? And how much shall we give Him? Can there be any hesitation as to the answer? Shall it not be, joyfully and gratefully, "All! yes, *all* for Jesus!" But "all" means a great deal; it really does mean *all;* all our hearts, all our lives, all that we have, all that we are. And if truly "all," it must be for *always*, too; no reserve, and no taking back. I heard a little sigh by my side, as we spoke of this. Did it seem too hard? Could we ever hope to keep to it? Was it more than we dared say? Then we looked at the bright side of it,—the grand shining of gladness which Satan tries to hinder us from seeing. If we are "all for Jesus," He will be all for us, and *always* all for us, too. When we give Him all, He gives us all,—all His tender love, all His wonderful peace and joy, all His grace and strength. On His side there will be no reserve and no taking back. And with "all" this, we shall find, nay, we *do* find that life is quite a different thing, ever so much happier than we imagined it could be, and that He does for us exceeding abundantly above all that we ask or think.

As this was dwelt upon, I saw a very bright smile on a face that was generally the merriest of the party. After a little while, "good-night" was said, and we separated. But I went up-stairs to two quiet rooms. In the first I found the author of that little sigh. She was, I had every reason to hope, a dear Christian child, who had for some time past "known and believed the love which God hath for us," and had tried to follow her Saviour in the little steps of home and school life. I put my arms round her and said, "Well, Alice, how much for Jesus?" The great dark eyes that just before had looked up so lovingly into my face fell, with such a mournful look that I shall never forget it. There was no answer. "How much, darling? Is it not *all* for Jesus?" Again came the little sigh, and a sad whisper, "I don't know!"

In the other room another warm kiss awaited me, and there was a something in the merry face which made me ask very hopefully, "Well, Meta, how much for Jesus?"

Oh, if I could describe to you the utter gladness in the bright eyes, and the very joy that seemed to overflow the lips, as she answered, not hastily, but very firmly and resolutely, "All, auntie, *all!*" That, too, was a look never to be forgotten—the words and the tone were sweet and strong, but the look told more than either. One could not but take knowledge of her that she had been with Jesus. She had given her heart to Him, and He had given His joy to her.

Let me put the question to you—"How much for Jesus?" Is your answer a sigh or a smile?

(For the *Episcopal Register*.)

"HOW MUCH FOR JESUS?"

By Frances Ridley Havergal.

Author of "Ministry of Song" and other poems.

A LITTLE group of boys and girls were gathered around me on a pleasant evening in the Easter holidays. We were talking about the Lord Jesus, and all the wonderful and solemn things which our Church services had so lately brought before us; His agony and bloody sweat, His cross and passions, His precious death and burial, and His glorious resurrection. There was such a quieted and tender tone among them, such wistful looks and gentle voices; and the hearts of more than one were so evidently burning within them, that one could not doubt that "Jesus Himself drew near," and that while we spoke one to another He not only hearkened and heard, but was really present in our midst.

Then we spoke of what we owed to Him who had done so much for us. How much do we owe Him? and how much shall we give Him?

Can there be any hesitation as to the answer? Shall it not be, joyfully and gratefully, "All! yes, *all* for Jesus!"

But "all" means a great deal; it really does mean *all*; all our hearts, all our lives, all that we have, all that we are. And if truly "all," it must be for *always* too; no reserve, and no taking back.

I heard a little sigh by my side as we spoke of this. Did it seem too hard? Could we ever hope to keep to it? Was it more than we dared say? Then we looked at the bright side of it, the grand shining of gladness which Satan tries to hinder us from seeing. If we are "all for Jesus," He will be all for us, and *always* all for us, too. When we give Him all, He gives us all; all His tender love, all His wonderful peace and joy, all His grace and strength. On His side there will be no reserve and no taking back. And with "all" this we shall find, nay we do find, that life is quite a different thing; ever so much happier than we imagined it could be, and that He does for us exceeding abundantly above all that we ask or think.

As this was dwelt upon, I saw a very bright smile on a face that was generally the merriest of the party. After a little while, "good-night" was said, and we separated. But I went upstairs to two quiet rooms. In the first I found the author of that little sigh. She was, I had every reason to hope, a dear Christian child, who had for some time past "known and believed the love which God hath for us," and had tried to follow her Saviour in the little steps of home and school life.

I put my arms round her, and said, "Well, A——, how much for Jesus?" The great dark eyes that just before had looked up so lovingly into my face fell, with such a mournful look that I shall never forget it. That was no answer. "How much, darling? Is it not *all* for Jesus? Again came the little sigh, and a sad whisper, "I don't know."

In the other room another warm kiss awaited me, and there was something in the merry face which made me ask quite hopefully, "Well, M—— how much for Jesus?"

Oh if I could describe to you the utter gladness in the bright eyes, and the very joy that seemed to overflow the lips, as she answered, not hastily but very firmly and resolutely, "All, auntie, all!" That too was a look never to be forgotten; the words and the tone were sweet and strong, but the look told more than either. One could not but take knowledge of her that she had been with Jesus. She had given her heart to Him, and He had given His joy to her.

Let me put the question to you—"How much for Jesus?" Is your answer a sigh or a smile?

ONLY one heart to give,
    Only one voice to use;
Only one little life to live,
    And only one to lose.

Poor is my best, and small:
    How could I dare divide?
Surely my Lord shall have it all,
    He shall not be denied.

All! for far more I owe
    Than all I have to bring;
All! for my Saviour loves me so;
    All! for I love my King.

All! for it is His own,
    He gave the tiny store;
All! for it must be His alone;
    All! for I have no more.

All! for the last and least
He stoopeth to uplift:
The altar of my great High Priest
Shall sanctify my gift.

(*Hymn Chant* THYATIRA)

———— ✣ ————

These are notes in F.R.H.'s handwriting.

FIVE INTERESTING TRUTHS ILLUSTRATED.

From "Our Own Correspondent."

(1)

"THERE IS FORGIVENESS WITH THEE."—A famous pirate infested the seas in the days of Augustus Cæsar. So dangerous had he become, that the emperor offered a fabulous reward for his head. The pirate, hearing of it, went at once to the royal presence, and laid his head at his sovereign's feet. Augustus was so struck with the robber's confidence in his clemency, that he forgave him all his past offences, and bestowed on him the reward also. And so we, though just sentence has been passed against us, will surely find mercy if we come and cast ourselves humbly at our Sovereign's feet, trusting in His forgiveness for the sake of Jesus Christ. For He invites us, who have robbed Him these many years, to come and accept His mercy. He knows all our sins, but if we come in His appointed way, He will "bid us be of good cheer," and say, "Thy sins are forgiven thee." "*Him that cometh to me, I will in no wise cast out.*"

(2)

(3)

CHRIST A REAL SAVIOUR.—When Luther was in deep anguish about his soul, he cried out one day in the presence of one who already knew the gospel, "*Oh, my sin, my sin, my sin!*" "Well; would you be only the *semblance* of a *sinner*," said his friend, "and have only the *semblance* of a SAVIOUR?" And then he added, with authority, "Know that Jesus Christ is the Saviour of real and great sinners who are deserving of utter condemnation." "*This is a faithful saying, and worthy of all acceptation, that Christ Jesus came into the world to save sinners, of whom I am chief.*"

(4)

(5)

GRATITUDE FOR REDEMPTION.—A penitent and believing sailor said, "To save such a sinner as I am! *He shall never hear the last of it!*" This expression, so frequently made use of by unforgiving persons, never was, that I know, applied in a Christian sense before this case. It was remarkably scriptural, for the hallelujahs of heaven will be *eternal.* "*I will praise Thy name for ever and ever.*"—*Rev. Dr. Marsh.*

"CONGREGATIONAL TEA PARTY."—See page 3 of Cover.

These "Five Interesting Truths" were almost surely published in the *Perry Barr Magazine*, a parish magazine for St. John's Church, Perry Barr, where F.R.H. labored with the vicar, Rev. Charles Busbridge Snepp, editing with him the hymnbook *Songs of Grace and Glory* and working in his church. Frances was extensively involved in this magazine, and she is "Our Own Correspondent." This text was found among Havergal manuscripts and papers, with only the first, third, and fifth of the "Five Interesting Truths" found, with the second and fourth ones apparently cut out for use and never returned to be the complete text.

After the "Five Interesting Truths," several other items published in the *Perry Barr Magazine* are given next, various ones being definitely written by F.R.H. and others being likely written by her.

FIVE INTERESTING TRUTHS ILLUSTRATED.

From "Our Own Correspondent."

(1)

"There is forgiveness with thee."—A famous pirate infested the seas in the days of Augustus Caesar. So dangerous had he become, that the emperor offered a fabulous reward for his head. The pirate, hearing of it, went at once to the royal presence, and laid his head at his sovereign's feet. Augustus was so struck with the robber's confidence in his clemency, that he forgave him all his past offences, and bestowed on him the reward also. And so we, though just sentence has been passed against us, will surely find mercy if we come and cast ourselves humbly at our Sovereign's feet, trusting in His forgiveness for the sake of Jesus Christ. For He invites us, who have robbed Him these many years, to come and accept His mercy. He knows all our sins, but if we come in His appointed way, He will "bid us be of good cheer," and say, "Thy sins are forgiven thee." "*Him that cometh to me, I will in no wise cast out.*"

(2)

(3)

Christ a real Saviour.—When Luther was in deep anguish about his soul, he cried out one day in the presence of one who already knew the gospel, "*Oh, my sin, my sin, my sin!*" "Well; would you be only the *semblance* of a *sinner*," said his friend, "and have only the *semblance* of a SAVIOUR?" And then he added, with authority, "Know that Jesus Christ is the Saviour of real and great sinners who are deserving of utter condemnation." "*This is a faithful saying, and worthy of all acceptation, that Christ Jesus came into the world to save sinners, of whom I am chief.*"

(4)

(5)

Gratitude for Redemption.—A penitent and believing sailor said, "To save such a sinner as I am! *He shall never hear the last of it!*" This expression, so frequently made use of by unforgiving persons, never was, that I know, applied in a Christian sense before this case. It was remarkably scriptural, for the hallelujahs of heaven will be *eternal*. "*I will praise Thy name for ever and ever.*"—Rev. Dr. Marsh.

———— ✖ ————

No. 18.

Feb., 1873.

HOME WORDS

FOR

HEART AND HEARTH.

ST. JOHN'S CHURCH, PERRY BARR.

PERRY BARR MAGAZINE.

May be obtained at PERRY SCHOOL, OSCOTT SCHOOL, BIRCHFIELD'S INFANT SCHOOL, and of Mr. BURNS, News-agent, Birchfields.

Butler & Tanner.]   [Frome, and London.

PARISH EVENTS.

From " Our-Own Correspondent." F. R. H.

THE Parish Events of Perry Barr for the past month (which for magazine purposes reckons from 20th to the 20th) consist chiefly of "Entertainments." Never yet has "Our Own Correspondent" been present at one of these without wishing that a great number of clergy from all parts of the kingdom could be onlookers, that they might take notes, and go and do likewise in hundreds of out-of-the-way parishes, where nothing so nice as these Perry entertainments is ever attempted. The sunny side of religion, which is the *true* side, is always shown at them, and the lively, happy tone of each is felt to be in harmony with the music of the One Name, which is always the key-note of the whole. That is a grand old rendering of William Kethe's, written in 1562, "Him serve with *mirth*," (Hymn 624 in "Songs of Grace and Glory"), and the spirit of it was admirably illustrated on Dec. 30, 1872, at Entertainment No. I., and not less so on Jan. 2nd and 3rd, 1873, at Entertainments Nos. II. and III. These were given by the Vicar and congregation to the parents of the school-children, and the aged people, in the respective Schoolrooms of Perry, Birchfields, and Oscott. Evergreens, lights, and music; roast-beef, cake, and tea; pleasant information, cheery encouragement, and holy counsel;—surely this three times three at each of the three gatherings deserved, as it received, hearty expressions of appreciation and gratitude to Mr. and Mrs. Snepp, and all who had kindly and energetically worked to provide and arrange. "*Send portions unto them for whom nothing is prepared. . . . And there was very great gladness.*"—Neh. viii. 10, 17.

On January 14, 1873, Entertainment No. IV., a Musical one, took place at Christ Church Schoolroom. Whatever may be the vocal difficulties of singing in a crowded room, they are far more than counterbalanced by the sense of sympathy, warmth, and appreciation, and the throng of pleasant faces must have been most encouraging to the Choir. It is so difficult to specify where everything gave pleasure, but we may mention that an extremely pretty part-song by the choir, "Shepherds, tell me," and a bright duet by Miss Sharp and Mr. Hill, were deservedly encored. Mr. Turner sang Gounod's beautiful Christmas song, "Nazareth," and Mrs. Blewitt kindly played two brilliant pianoforte solos. Mendelssohn's exquisite tenor solo, "If with all your hearts," sung by Mr. Brown, and followed by a happy little Christmas carol, made a characteristic close to the evening's enjoyment. "*With my song will I praise Him.*"—Ps. xxviii. 7.

Parish events do not cease to become such because annually repeated, and who that heard the midnight peal of Perry bells as the old year passed away, could help feeling that it was itself a summary of parish events! Just enough of sadness in their sweetness, too, to make them true to life. It was pleasant to think, as they changed the midnight silence into music, that, even so, the many solemn prayers then going up from earnest hearts might in the coming year be changed into songs of praise. "HITHERTO *hath the Lord helped us.*"—1 Sam. vii. 12. "HENCEFORTH *live . . . unto Him.*"—2 Cor. v. 15.

On Jan. 5, the first Sunday in the New Year, the Rev. C. B. Snepp preached three different sermons at Perry, Oscott, and Christ Church, from four words, "*Jesus Himself drew near*" (Luke xxiv. 15). He offered them to his people as a motto for the year, full of encouragement and anticipation, praying that they might often have the joy of realizing these words as a blessed fact and a bright prospect. Could Perry Barr have a sweeter motto than—

"JESUS HIMSELF DREW NEAR"?

Another parish event is approaching—the Confirmation, perhaps the most important event in the whole life of some who are now prayerfully looking forward to it. May it be a time of great blessing to all, not only to those who are about to renew their baptismal

Continued on Page 3 of Cover.

I was furiously encored in "When thou passest" being sung a solo, & "O loved Peace" with one "Tell it out" opened; & "Whom having not seen" was sung very nicely by a Y.W.C.A. girl

See pages 999–1001.

These next three items were published in the *Perry Barr Magazine*. While various articles and pieces by F.R.H. were not signed, published anonymously, on the copy of the next item found among Havergal manuscripts and papers, at the top of the text "F.R.H." was written by hand. At the bottom of the same page Frances wrote a note in her handwriting (the text of her note given here with a footnote below the printed, published text).

PARISH EVENTS.

From "Our Own Correspondent."

———

THE Parish Events of Perry Barr for the past month (which for magazine purposes reckons from the 20th to the 20th) consist chiefly of "Entertainments." Never yet has "Our Own Correspondent" been present at one of those without wishing that a great number of clergy form all parts of the kingdom could be onlookers, that they might take notes, and go and do likewise in hundreds of out of the way parishes, where nothing so nice as these Perry entertainments is ever attempted. The sunny side of religion, which is the true side, is always shown at them, and the lively, happy tone of each is felt to be in harmony with the music of the One Name, which is always the key note of the whole. That is a grand old rendering of William Kethe's, written in 1562, "Him serve with mirth," (Hymn 624 in "Songs of Grace and Glory"), and the spirit of it was admirably illustrated on December 30, 1872, at Entertainment No. I., and not less so on January 2nd and 3rd, 1873, at Entertainments Nos. II and III. These were given by the Vicar and congregation to the parents of the school children, and the aged people in the respective schoolrooms of Perry, Birchfields, and Oscott. Evergreens, lights, and music; roast beef, cake, and tea; pleasant information, cheery encouragement, and holy counsel;—surely this three times three at each of the three gatherings deserved, as it received, hearty expressions of appreciation and gratitude to Mr. and Mrs. Snepp, and all who had kindly and energetically worked to provide and arrange.

"*Send portions unto them, for whom nothing is prepared. . . . And there was very great gladness.*"—Nehemiah 8:10,17.

———

On January 14, 1873, Entertainment No. IV., a Musical one, took place at Christ Church Schoolroom.[1] Whatever may be the vocal difficulties of singing in a crowded room, they are far more than counter-balanced by the sense of sympathy, warmth, and appreciation, and the throng of pleasant faces must have been most encouraging to the Choir. It is so difficult to specify where everything gave pleasure, but we may mention that an extremely pretty part-song by the choir, "Shepherds, tell me," and a bright duet by Miss Sharp and Mr. Hill, were deservedly encored. Mr. Turner sang Gounod's beautiful Christmas song, "Nazareth," and Mrs. Bleweitt kindly played two brilliant pianoforte solos. Mendelssohn's exquisite tenor solo, "If with all your hearts," sung by Mr. Brown, and followed by a happy little Christmas carol, made a characteristic close to the evening's enjoyment.

"With my song will I praise Him."—Psalm 28:7.

———

Parish events do not cease to become such because annually repeated, and who that heard the midnight peal of Perry bells as the old year passed away, could help feeling that it was itself a summary of parish events! Just enough of sadness in their sweetness, too, to make them true to life. It was pleasant to think, as they changed the midnight silence into music, that, even so, the many solemn prayers then going up from earnest hearts might in the coming year be changed into songs of praise.

"Hitherto *hath the Lord helped us.*"—1 Samuel 7:12
"Henceforth *live . . . unto Him.*"—2 Corinthian 5:15

———

On Jan. 5, the first Sunday in the New Year, the Rev. C. B. Snepp preached three different sermons at Perry, Oscott, and Christ Church, from four words, *"Jesus Himself drew near"* (Luke 24:15). He offered them to his people as a motto for the year, full of encouragement and anticipation, praying that they might often have the joy of realizing these words as a blessed fact and a bright prospect. Could Perry Barr have a sweeter motto than—

"JESUS HIMSELF DREW NEAR"?

[1] Frances placed an asterisk by this section, and at the bottom of the page she wrote this: "I was <u>furiously</u> encored in 'When thou passest.' Amy [unsure of word] sang a solo, and 'O lovely [unsure of word] peace' with me. 'Tell it out' opened, and 'Whom having not seen' was sung <u>very</u> nicely by a Y.W.C.A. girl." [See page 142.]

Another parish event is approaching—the Confirmation, perhaps the most important event in the whole life of some who are now prayerfully looking forward to it. May it be a time of great blessing to all, not only to those who are about to renew their baptismal vows in the strength of God's confirming grace, but to those who have long ago done so. For it is well to have vividly brought before us the recollection of the day when we, too, said that solemn word "I do," and heard, with bowed head and hushed heart, that thrilling prayer, "That they may continue *Thine for ever*."

"*Come and let us join ourselves in the Lord in a perpetual covenant that shall not be forgotten*."—Jeremiah 1:5

BAPTISMS, IN THE MONTHS OF DECEMBER AND JANUARY, IN ST. JOHN'S CHURCH, PERRY BARR.

Dec. 8, Walter Herbert Grimmett; Jan. 5, Hannah Beatrice White; Jan. 12, Edward James Unite Turner; Jan. 12, John Judd; Jan. 19, Eleanor Davenhill.

MARRIAGE.

Dec. 26, Mr. John Steven Turner, of Perry Barr, to Jemima, daughter of the Rev. Charles Brooke.

Miss Brooke's long and valued work in connection with the schools of this parish, gives this "parish event" a special interest, and many are the readers of *Home Words* who will wish her all happiness and blessing in her new sphere, in which good wishes both parents and children will cordially unite.

BURIALS.

Dec. 5, Joseph Wright, aged 2 years; Dec. 11, Eliza Morse, aged 2 years; Dec. 12, John Richard Wright, aged 6 months; Dec. 21, Emily Morse, aged 6 months; Dec. 24, Lucy Emily Lena Snepp, aged 12 years; Jan. 19, Alfred William Wallis, aged 5 weeks.

The Burial Register for the past two months is indeed a singular and touching one, and full of solemn lessons for the little ones. Not one grown up person, but six little boys and girls laid to rest in Perry Churchyard! It was on Christmas Eve that one was laid there, "in sure and certain hope of a joyful resurrection." Only a month before that she was strong and well. But though the call was so early, she was ready, and this will always be the greatest comfort to her sorrowing parents and sisters. All through her short and suffering illness her heart seemed set on heavenly things. It was very remarkable that a copy of her dear uncle's hymnal, " Songs of Grace and Glory," given to her as a reward for learning thirty hymns, was her constant comfort, and was always beside her till the last. One night when very ill, she fell asleep singing softly, " I lay my sins on Jesus," and she woke again far in the night with the words, " Oh, for the robes of whiteness! " And now, while, as these words are being written, the snow is falling fast upon her grave, she is arrayed in those " robes of whiteness," and joining in the new song of praise to Him who is the Friend of little children.

"Suffer the little children to come unto Me."—Mark 10:14

Parish Events.

From " Our Own Correspondent."

THE FLOWER SHOW.

THE report of a September Flower Show may seem rather late in a November magazine! But " I cry you mercy," as our forefathers used to say. For the local pages of October were occupied with a far more important subject,—the announcement of an infinitely more momentous " parish event," than all the Flower Shows and Festivals that ever were held.

A most delightful Floral Society is this of Perry, for it seems that everybody gets prizes who makes any respectable attempt. So it is all encouragement and no discouragement, which can hardly be said of any other scheme of prizes in the kingdom. This Thirty-First Exhibition stood above all previous ones in one important respect,—a larger number of competitors and competing articles being entered than ever before. Mr. Wright, whose opinion is beyond appeal in such matters, appeared greatly pleased with the show, especially considering the unusual disadvantages of weather under which such good results had been obtained. It is easy enough to pull down the stream, but the test of strength is to pull against wind and tide, as the Perry cottage gardeners have done this year.

The Gardeners' Prizes were obtained by Messrs. Heeks, Hughes, Young, Grimmett, Tomlinson, Ellson, and Cotterill. To the last-named, a silver cup, presented by Mr. Hawkins, was given, as a testimonial to steady and uniform excellence and neatness for many years. The Cottage Garden Prizes were awarded to Baldock, Talbot, C. Rose, Cooksey, George Rose, and Boneham. The Birchfield Prizes were gained by H. Prowse, Lees, J. Harris, W. Meeking, H. Brown, Damment, Stanton, H. Adkins, Ingram, and Walker. As for the prizes for different kinds of fruit, flowers, and vegetables, they seemed so numerous that "our own correspondent" cannot possibly find room for them.

The prizes for NEATNESS IN COTTAGE HOMES were gained by Mrs. Bush, Cooksey, Dale, Damment, Ingram, Smith, Stanton, Tomlinson, and Walker, consisting of 10s. each, and the handsome card, which is the proudest ornament of any Perry cottage wall. Secondary prizes of beautifully bound books were given to Mrs. Baldock, Bradley, Eyre, Garbett, Grimmett, Judd, Reynolds, Rogers, Rose, Talbot, Unite.

The prizes for Patchwork had so many competitors, that half a dozen prizes were given instead of two, as advertised; viz., Mrs. Pickering, Crisp, Heeks, S. Cooper, Widow Williams, and Jane Dale. The Prize Loaves made one hungry to look at; these were made by Mrs. Talbot, Crisp, Boneham, and Rose. But how as it that no one competed for a prize shirt? And no one for prize stockings? The long winter evenings might be worse employed than by getting beforehand against next year, and having some first-rate stitching and knitting ready for the 1873 exhibition. I would advise the darning to be also looked to, for next year's list will probably contain prizes for the best *darned* socks or stockings.

Mr. Browne's prizes for Scripture Texts on the "Trees, Fruits, and Flowers of the Bible," were gained by Mrs. Heeks, with 578 texts, and Sylvia Young, with 119. Extra prizes were given by Mrs. Snepp and Mrs. Philip Browne, in memory of beloved Parents.

It seems a long time till next year; but if those who are spared till 1873 will take the hint, it may be remarked that much difficulty and delay was occasioned by holders of prizes not being present in time to receive them when their names were called; and it is particularly desired by the President that this should not again occur. At future exhibitions, those who are not present in time must wait until the following day. Many pleasant matters were unavoidably omitted, owing to the delay caused by this unpunctuality.

May all who compete for these earthly prizes be earnest competitors for a far nobler and more enduring one, even the "true riches" here, and the "incorruptible crown" hereafter. "*I press towards the mark for the prize of the high calling of God in Christ Jesus.*" (Philippians 3:14)

[At the bottom of the following piece, at the end of the printed, published text, the initials "F.R.H." were written by hand.]

THE HARVEST THANKSGIVING FESTIVAL.

SEPTEMBER 24.

————

THERE never was a more practical proof that—

> "Religion never was designed
> To make our pleasures less,"

than this Harvest Festival of 1872. "What is going to be done?" was asked. "We are going to have a *holy* and happy evening," replied your pastor; "looking up for God's blessing, and rejoicing in His goodness, and singing sweet and hearty hymns to His praise." "Dear me, how very slow it must have been!" some ignorant folks would say who were not "there to see!" *Was* it "slow"? *Was* it dismal? "Our own correspondent" challenges every one and *any* one present to say if they ever spent a happier and pleasanter evening in their lives! So many persons have said exactly the same words about it, that it has become quite an amusement to expect any allusion to it to be followed by remark,—"I don't think I ever enjoyed an evening so much!" Said one, "There was something about it,—I can't tell what, but it was be-au-tiful!"

I have seen other kinds of entertainment—the *merely* entertaining and amusing, and the half-and-half affairs with a little of this world and a little of the next; but I undertake to say that none of them were pervaded with a tone of such downright happiness, such unflagging brightness of enjoyment, as this thorough-going *religious* one. There was an additional secret in the matter, which it will be no breach of confidence to tell. This remarkable and unmistakable tone of happiness was a special answer to special prayer. *This very thing* had been asked of the Lord, and *this very thing* He granted. It was by no human contrivance that this spirit of gladness and love and praise was poured out; but doubtless by that same loving kindness which sent such pleasant weather (for that too had been asked of God:) "*Thou hast put gladness in my heart.*"

The service, at 4 p.m., was well attended. The sermon, by the Rev. Samuel Thornton, Rector of St. George's, was on the beautiful harvest story of Ruth, which had been read as the first lesson. After services the bells had their say, and a right joyous say it was: for "Perry bells" (which rhyme so felicitously with "merry bells") are a sort of musical sunshine of sound, especially with Perry bell-ringers to wake their carol. Then came the tea-party, in Perry village schoolroom, which was very tastefully decorated by Miss and Mr. D. Cole. The inhabitants of Perry must all be on excellent terms with each other, to judge by the lively flow of chat all round. It must have been a sulky spirit indeed, that could not brighten up and be neighbourly at those cheery tables.

When the cup and saucer clatter of table-clearing was over, and grace had been sung, the Rev. C. B. Snepp opened, giving one verse of Scripture, Acts 14:17, as the key-note of the evening; after this the Rev. P. Browne offered prayer, and then all joined in Hymn 850; "Come, ye thankful people, come." Short addresses were then given, very varied, but all excellent and interesting, and all full of fervour and warmth. We hope that Perry memories proved faithful reporters, and that many stirring and helpful thoughts were carried away, which may prove good seed, springing up in new harvests of faith, hope, and love.

The Rev. Dr. Burgess, opening with the story of the ragged Italian girls and their gift, spoke of the debt of gratitude which we owe to Him who giveth us richly all things to enjoy, and who gave His own beloved Son for us; and of the glorious eternity throughout which His redeemed ones will be ever paying with joyful praises this never-to-be-paid debt of love and thankfulness.

The Rev. H. C. Thwaites followed with a few warm and loving words on the same happy theme.

The Rev. P. Browne said he would give a tune from his music book,—The Bible, a harvest tune founded on the seven notes of the scale. A, a note of admonition: "All things are of God." B, a note of assurance: "Blessèd shall be thy basket and thy store." C, a note of instruction: "Cast thy bread upon the waters." D, a note of encouragement: "Delight thyself in the Lord." E, a minor note, a note of warning: "Every tree is known by its fruit." F, a note of promise: "For as the rain cometh down . . . and watereth the earth, and maketh it bring forth and bud; so shall my word be." G, a note of praise: "Give glory to the Lord your God." Our readers will doubtless long recollect his striking story of the servant who sowed oats instead of wheat.

Mr. George Edwards gave some useful and interesting remarks on diligence and its results, especially with reference to agriculture, and on the blessings annexed to it.

Mr. James Atkins spoke on the practical lesson of economy give by our Savior in His command to "gather up the fragments;" and on liberality and kindness, illustrated by the story of the two five-shilling pieces and the two shoes.

The Rev. J. Meek spoke on the contrast between the so-called "good old times," when so many of our commonest fruits of garden and field were unknown, and the present. He desired the recurrence of harvest festivals to be a call to growth in grace and renewed life and zeal.

The Rev. S. Thornton spoke on the sweetest of all themes,—" the exceeding great love of our Master and only Savior;" dwelling on the breadth, length, depth, ad height of that "love which passeth knowledge." He vividly described his long and tiresome climb up a dark wall of rock in the Pyrenees, and the sudden coming upon a marvelously magnificent mountain view on reaching a cleft near the top, as an illustration of the first revelation to the heart of the love of God.

Between these addresses the promised hymns were sung,—and sung as they should be; not by a few voices only, but by the whole assembly, following the lead of the choir, and singing with a spirit and heartiness which would not easily be matched in any other parish. In fact, it was a perfect harvest of hymn singing, and must have been felt as such by him who had had such a long and laborious sowing time in preparing your "Songs of Grace and Glory." Who ever heard a more jubilant burst of unanimous voice than in Hymn 855: "O Nation, Christian nation," to the tune Zoan, which sets people singing, whether they intended to do so or not? "They *did* sing!" remarked one friend; "it was enough to blow the roof off!" Then the contrast of 839, "Lord, I hear of showers of blessing," with its tender and touching refrain, "Even me!" following upon an allusion to the coming Mission Week, could not but enter and stir hearts with hidden longings for blessing. But perhaps nothing was enjoyed more than the last hymn, No 653:—

> "Rejoice in the Lord! There is light in the dwelling,
> And peace in the spirit, where Christ is the guest;"

embodying both in its holy and joyous words, and its bright and melodious tune, the whole spirit of the evening.

Another challenge!—Did any one present ever find as much real enjoyment in singing or listening to any trifling or comic song, as in joining in these spirited and stirring hymns? The higher the standard, the more certain and pure and unmingled will the enjoyment be; and it really seems as if our gracious God gave us a practical lesson on the subject, by permitting us both to feel and to show what pleasure can be found in an evening where Christ Himself is the invited and honored and acknowledged Guest.

This feeling was expressed in the closing remarks of your pastor. After a warm recognition of the kind assistance of the speakers, and of the hearty goodwill as well as efficient services of the choir, whose pleasant and excellent singing is but the outward manifestation of a really model spirit of harmony and zeal;

he concluded with a fervently expressed hope that a harvest of blessing might indeed be reaped from this Harvest Thanksgiving Festival of 1872. *"They joy before Thee according to the joy in harvest"* (Isaiah 9:3).

THE HARVEST THANKSGIVING FESTIVAL.
SEPTEMBER 24.

THERE never was a more practical proof that—
> "Religion never was designed
> To make our pleasures less,"

than this Harvest Festival of 1872. "What is going to be done?" was asked. "We are going to have a *holy* and happy evening," replied your pastor; "looking up for God's blessing, and rejoicing in His goodness, and singing sweet and hearty hymns to His praise." "Dear me, how very slow it must have been!" some ignorant folks would say who were not "there to see!" Was it "slow"? Was it dismal? "Our own correspondent" challenges every one and *any* one present to say if they ever spent a happier and pleasanter evening in their lives! So many persons have said exactly the same words about it, that it has become quite an amusement to expect any allusion to it to be followed by the remark,—"I don't think I ever enjoyed an evening so much!" Said one, "There was something about it,—I can't tell what, but it was be-au-tiful!"

I have seen other kinds of entertainment—the *merely* entertaining and amusing, and the half-and-half affairs with a little of this world and a little of the next; but I undertake to say that none of them were pervaded with a tone of such downright happiness, such unflagging brightness of enjoyment, as this thorough-going *religious* one. There was an additional secret in the matter, which it will be no breach of confidence to tell. This remarkable and unmistakable tone of happiness was a special answer to special prayer. *This very thing* had been asked of the Lord, and *this very thing* He granted. It was by no human contrivance that this spirit of gladness and love and praise was poured out; but doubtless by that same loving-kindness which sent such pleasant weather (for that too had been asked of God:) *"Thou hast put gladness in my heart."*

The service, at 4 p.m., was well attended. The sermon, by the Rev. Samuel Thornton, Rector of St. George's, was on the beautiful harvest story of Ruth, which had been read as the first lesson. After service the bells had their say, and a right joyous say it was: for "Perry bells" (which rhyme so felicitously with "merry bells") are a sort of musical sunshine of sound, especially with Perry bell-ringers to wake their carol. Then came the tea-party, in Perry village schoolroom, which was very tastefully decorated by Miss and Mr. D. Cole. The inhabitants of Perry must all be on excellent terms with each other, to judge by the lively flow of chat all round. It must have been a sulky spirit indeed, that could not brighten up and be neighbourly at those cheery tables.

When the cup and saucer clatter of table-clearing was over, and grace had been sung, the Rev. C. B. Snepp opened, giving one verse of Scripture, Acts xiv. 17, as the key-note of the evening; after this the Rev. P. Browne offered prayer, and then all joined in Hymn 850: "Come, ye thankful people, come." Short addresses were then given, very varied, but all excellent and interesting, and all full of fervour and warmth. We hope that Perry memories proved faithful reporters, and that many stirring and helpful thoughts were carried away, which may prove good seed, springing up in new harvests of faith, hope, and love.

The Rev. Dr. Burgess, opening with the story of the ragged Italian girls and their gift, spoke of the debt of gratitude which we owe to Him who giveth us richly all things to enjoy, and who gave His own beloved Son for us; and of the glorious eternity throughout which His redeemed ones will be ever paying with joyful praises this never-to-be-paid debt of love and thankfulness.

The Rev. H. C. Thwaites followed with a few warm and loving words on the same happy theme.

The Rev. P. Browne said he would give a tune from his music-book,—the Bible, a harvest tune founded on the seven notes of the scale. A, a note of admonition: "All things are of God." B, a note of assurance: "Blessed shall be thy basket and thy store." C, a note of instruction: "Cast thy bread upon the waters." D, a note of encouragement: "Delight thyself in the Lord." E, a minor note, a note of warning: "Every tree is known by its fruit." F, a note of promise: "For as the rain cometh down . . . and watereth the earth, and maketh it bring forth and bud; so shall my word be." G, a note of praise:

"*Give glory to the Lord your God.*" Our readers will doubtless long recollect his striking story of the servant who sowed oats instead of wheat.

Mr. George Edwards gave some useful and interesting remarks on diligence and its results, especially with reference to agriculture, and on the blessings annexed to it.

Mr. James Atkins spoke on the practical lesson of economy given by our Saviour in His command to "gather up the fragments;" and on liberality and kindness, illustrated by the story of the two five-shilling pieces and the two shoes.

The Rev. J. Meek spoke on the contrast between the so-called "good old times," when so many of our commonest fruits of garden and field were unknown, and the present. He desired the recurrence of harvest festivals to be a call to growth in grace and renewed life and zeal.

The Rev. S. Thornton spoke on the sweetest of all themes,—"the exceeding great love of our Master and only Saviour;" dwelling on the breadth, length, depth, and height of that "love which passeth knowledge." He vividly described his long and toilsome climb up a dark wall of rock in the Pyrenees, and the sudden coming upon a marvellously magnificent mountain view on reaching a cleft near the top, as an illustration of the first revelation to the heart of the love of God.

Between these addresses the promised hymns were sung,—and sung as they should be; not by a few voices only, but by the whole assembly, following the lead of the choir, and singing with a spirit and heartiness which would not easily be matched in any other parish. In fact, it was a perfect harvest of hymn-singing, and must have been felt as such by him who had had such a long and laborious sowing-time in preparing your "Songs of Grace and Glory." Who ever heard a more jubilant burst of unanimous voice than in Hymn 855 : "O nation, Christian nation," to the tune Zoan, which sets people singing, whether they intended to do so or not? "They *did* sing!" remarked one friend; "it was enough to blow the roof off!" Then the contrast of 839, "Lord, I hear of showers of blessing," with its tender and touching refrain, "Even me!" following upon an allusion to the coming Mission Week, could not but enter and stir hearts with hidden longings for blessing. But perhaps nothing was enjoyed more than the last hymn, No. 653 :—

> "Rejoice in the Lord! there is light in the dwelling,
> And peace in the spirit, where Christ is the guest;"

embodying both in its holy and joyous words, and its bright and melodious tune, the whole spirit of the evening.

Another challenge!—Did any one present ever find as much real enjoyment in singing or listening to any trifling or comic song, as in joining in these spirited and stirring hymns? The higher the standard, the more certain and pure and unmingled will the enjoyment be; and it really seems as if our gracious God gave us a practical lesson on the subject, by permitting us both to feel and to show what pleasure can be found in an evening where Christ Himself is the invited and honoured and acknowledged Guest.

This feeling was expressed in the closing remarks of your pastor. After a warm recognition of the kind assistance of the speakers, and of the hearty goodwill as well as efficient services of the choir, whose pleasant and excellent singing is but the outward manifestation of a really model spirit of harmony and zeal ; he concluded with a fervently expressed hope that a harvest of blessing might indeed be reaped from this Harvest Thanksgiving Festival of 1872. "*They joy before Thee according to the joy in harvest.*" (Isa. ix. 3).

F. R. H.

MARRIAGES.

These two facsimile copies from the Perry Barr Magazine *are given in the newly typeset text on pages 1004–1007. The initials at the end look like Frances' handwriting.*

This manuscript letter in F.R.H.'s hand, found among Havergal manuscripts and papers, was apparently a rough draft by Frances of the letter published in The Christian Standard. *Apparently, she sent her final draft to the magazine editor and kept this rough draft. This manuscript letter has six pages, with two additions. Several changes were made after this rough draft, either by F.R.H. or by the Editor of* The Christian Standard.

Note: When the manuscript letter had only a blank sheet on the left side of her handwritten letter, the blank sheet was not shown here, and the page of the letter is given in portrait format to be larger; however, when the letter had an annotation by Frances to the left of the letter's text, both sides are shown, thus smaller copies, caused by the necessary landscape format.

intelligence [news] with a feeling of de=
pression & discouragement. When
if one-tenth as much in proportion
of had been reported of the good
& great things which are every week
being done & the evident tokens of
the Lord's blessing upon them, we
might have thanked God & taken
courage & gone on our way rejoicing
& praising, & longing to go & do like=
wise. though I could give scores.
I will give two instances only. Last
week a Mission was held in
Bristol, in which fourteen parishes united
the Churches & schoolrooms in each were, open, every
night, not for routine services, but
for heart to heart gospel work,
prayers, & addresses, and after meetings;
while many additional addresses &
prayermeetings took place at
other hours. X One of the Mission
Preachers says: "In churches & school
rooms & in the Gospel Tent there
were large gatherings every night.
The people seemed deeply impressed
& the Divine blessing manifestly vouch=
safed. The Spirit of God seemed moving

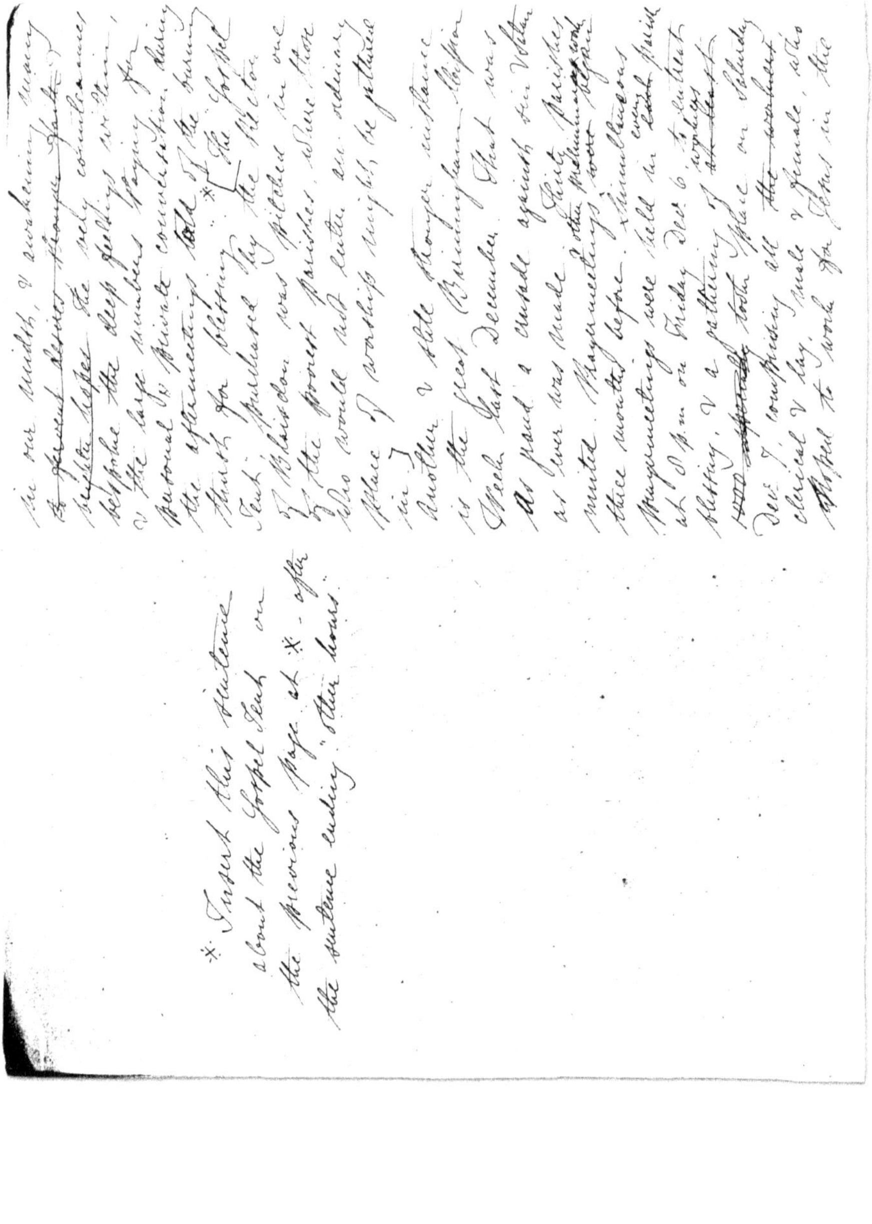

in our midst, & awakening many ~~to fervent desires stronger faith~~ & brighter hopes. The very countenances bespoke the deep feelings within, & the large numbers staying for personal & private conversation during the aftermeetings told of the burning thirst for blessing. * [The Gospel Tent, purchased by the Rector of Blaisdon was pitched in one of the poorest parishes, where those who would not enter an ordinary place of worship might be gathered in.]

Another & still stronger instance is the great Birmingham Mission Week last December. That was as grand a crusade against sin & Satan as ever was made. Thirty parishes united. Prayermeetings & other preliminary work ~~were~~ began three months before. Simultaneous prayermeetings were held in ~~each~~ every parish at 8 p.m on Friday Dec. 6, to entreat blessing, & a gathering of workers ~~at least 1000 specially~~ took place on Saturday Dec. 7, comprising all ~~the workers~~ clerical & lay, male & female, who hoped to work for Jesus in the

* Insert this sentence about the Gospel Tent on the previous page at * - after the sentence ending "other hours".

ensuing week. More than 1000 were assembled. The Bishop of the diocese was present, & a stirring address was delivered to the workers by Archdeacon Prest. More than 500 then gathered at the Lord's table. None who were present will ever forget that joyful yet solemn consecration service, for such it was felt to be. The work of the following week was tremendous. Arrangements had been made to reach all classes, by addresses at all hours & in all sorts of places. In the suburban parish in which I was staying, though among the smaller ones the week there were no less than thirty different services & meetings. The results, while showing God's sovereignty in sending His Spirit as & where He would, were such as to call for deep thankfulness, and in some parishes the blessing was Pentecostal indeed.

But, so far as I have been able to ascertain, not a single one but my own sent any commun

...ication whatever about this magnificent & most encouraging event, to any religious paper — whatever!

The different battalions in our great Captain's army would make better fight against the Enemy if they were told more of each other's (noble battles &) dauntless champions & glorious victories, & a little less of each other's traitors & deserters & their breaches of discipline. ~~& traitor~~ When Elijah was weary & depressed God did not tell him of the dark side of affairs but of the "seven thousand".

I am, dear Sir,

Yours cordially

Frances Ridley Havergal.

P.S. I will send you next week (D.V.) a short statistical account of the regular work going on in the parish from which I write, as a specimen of the quiet work of the Church of England ~~in a country place~~.

[This letter to the editor was published in the *The Christian Standard*. Only the cut-out clipping was found, and the date is not known.]

ONE-SIDED VIEWS OF CHURCH NEWS.

To the Editor of the "Christian Standard."

Sir,—In reading your valuable paper week by week, I have been struck with the one-sided character of the Church news supplied to you by correspondents. Every *fungus* on the brave old tree of the Church of England is spied and described, but rarely does any one take the trouble to tell of its *fruits*. Every traitor in our camp is taken to be a specimen soldier, while the faithful ones who are fighting tooth and nail against Romanism and Rationalism are unmentioned. All that discourages and disheartens is detailed, while almost all that would provoke unto love and to good works, promoting kindly feeling, stimulating by suggestive example, and cheering fellow workers on their way, is never heard of. It is easy to go home and write descriptions of ritualistic services, which the writers have been virtually encouraging by their presence, but no one cares to investigate and describe the splendid and faithful, but quiet work for God which may be going on in the very next parish. This noticeable fact does not apply to the Christian Standard alone, but more or less to every one of the Evangelical papers, whether denominational or undenominational. It is not the fault of the Editors, most of whom, like yourself, are "glad when they see the grace of God," but the default of correspondence. I have repeatedly spoken on the subject to clergymen whose labors of love abound exceedingly, and the reply always is—an easy smile,—and "Oh, that's not our way! How can we find time to write letters to newspapers? We don't care to make a fuss about our work. We leave all that sort of thing to others!" Or words to that effect. And so it comes to pass that one rises from reading any column of ecclesiastical news with a sense of depression and discouragement, when, if one-tenth as much in proportion had been reported of the good and great things which are being done every week, and the evident tokens of the Lord's blessing upon them, we might have thanked God and taken courage, and gone on our way rejoicing and praising, and stirred up to greater energy and zeal.

I will give two instances only, though I could give scores. Last week a Mission was held at Bristol in which fourteen parishes united. The churches and school-rooms in each were open every night, not for routine services, but for heart to heart gospel work—prayer, addresses, and after-meetings; while many additional addresses and prayer meetings took place at other hours. The "Gospel Tent," purchased by the Rector of Blaisdon, was pitched in one of the poorest parishes where those who would not enter any ordinary place of worship might be gathered in. One of the Mission preachers says—"In churches and school-rooms, and in the Gospel Tent there were large gatherings every night. The people seemed deeply impressed, and the Divine blessing manifestly vouchsafed. The Spirit of God seemed moving in our midst, and awakening many. The very countenances bespoke the deep feelings within, and the large numbers staying for personal and private conversation during the after-meetings told of the burning thirst for blessing."

But no one has sent you any account of this.

Another and still stronger instance of this is the great Birmingham Mission Week last December. That was as grand a crusade against sin and Satan as ever was made. Thirty parishes united. Prayer meetings and other preliminary work began three months before simultaneous prayer meetings were held in every parish at 8 p.m. on Friday, December 6, to entreat blessing. A gathering of workers took place on Saturday, December 7, comprising all, clerical and lay, male and female, who hoped to work for Jesus in the ensuing week. More than 1000 were assembled; the Bishop of the Diocese was present, and a striking and stirring address was delivered by Archdeacon Prest. More than 500 then gathered at the Lord's table. None who were there will ever forget that joyful and solemn *consecration* service, for such it was felt to be. The work of the following week was tremendous. Arrangements had been made to reach all classes, by addresses at all hours, and in all sorts of places. In the suburban parish in which I was staying at the time, there were no less than thirty different services and meetings. The results, while showing God's sovereignty in sending His spirit as and where He would, were such as to call for deep thankfulness, and in some parishes the blessing was Pentecostal indeed.

But, so far as I have been able to ascertain, *not a single pen but my own sent any communication whatever about this magnificent and most encouraging event to any religious paper.*

The different battalions in our Great Captain's army would make better fight against the enemy if they were told more of each other's dauntless champions, and noble battles, and glorious victories; and a little less of each other's traitors and deserters, and breaches of discipline. When Elijah was weary and depressed, God did not tell him of the dark side of affairs, but of the "seven thousand."—I am, Sir, yours cordially,

FRANCES RIDLEY HAVERGAL.

P.S.—I hope to send you next week, a short statistical account of the regular work going on in the parish from which I write, as a specimen of the quiet work of the Church of England.

[We have great pleasure in giving insertion to the above: and if Miss Havergal could only find time to do weekly for a season what she would like to do, as mentioned in her private letter to us, we will most gladly give her communications a prominent place in our paper, and they cannot fail to be productive of great good.—Ed., Christian Standard]

———— 🐾 ————

"THE QUIET WORK OF THE CHURCH OF ENGLAND."

To the Editor of "The Christian Standard."

Sir,—The quiet work of the Church of England in a country parish is rarely heard of beyond its boundaries. I purpose giving a very simple statement of such work in the parish from which I write. Though I here give only the initial, you are welcome to give the name to any who care to know it. P—— contains something over two thousand inhabitants; it is about three miles in extent each way; the population is agricultural and very scattered, except on one side, where the suburbs of a great town have overflowed into it; and in this part, which we will call B——, business men and artisans are increasing in numbers. The present Vicar was appointed to P—— Church in 1851.[1] In 1861 the district was made into a parish, and thenceforward his work for his Master and his flock was unfettered. *All* that follows is the result of the Divine blessing upon his energy and love.

---

[1] Though F.R.H. only gives the initials "P——" and "B——" (and later "O——"), this was very likely or almost certainly the parish of Perry Barr next to the great town of Birmingham in Warwickshire, England. "P——" would have referred to (St. John's Church,) Perry Barr, "B——" would have referred to (Christ Church,) Birchfield, and "O——" would have referred to (the) Oscott (Schoolroom). The Vicar, Rev. Charles Busbridge Snepp, was appointed to St. John's Church, Perry Barr, in 1851. This article and the following schedule of "Perry Privileges" was found on pages in the June, 1872 issue of the *Perry Barr Magazine*, Edition number 22. F.R.H. worked very extensively with Rev. Snepp at various times from 1870 to 1879 on the gold-mine—profoundly valuable—hymnbook *Songs of Grace and Glory*, visiting Perry Barr, also working with him in the church ministries there. See pages 111–112 of this book and pages 1075–1084 of Volume IV of the Havergal edition.

A second church was immediately built to anticipate the need or convenience of B——, with a schoolroom beneath it, seating three hundred, and commodious classrooms. Previous to this, another fine schoolroom had been built near the Parish Church; and there is a third licensed for Divine Service, at O——, a hamlet at the other end of the parish. Thus the means of grace were brought within easy reach of every inhabitant.

On Sundays there is a full service morning and afternoon at P——, morning and evening at B——, and afternoon or evening at O——. The Vicar opens P—— school; takes a Bible-class for men, which the eight bell-ringers are, by the rules of the belfry, required to attend; preaches in the morning at P——, and in the evening at B——; and when strength permits, visits the afternoon school or preaches at O——. The two excellent Curates divide the remaining services, the baptisms, marriages, and funerals, and the Sunday-schools. The Vicar's wife takes a large class of young women, besides the duties of Superintendent.

Monday has a Mothers' Meeting at 3 p.m.; and an open Bible meeting at 8 p.m.; where representatives of all classes, gentle and simple, meet the Vicar for the study of God's Word. Tuesday has a sewing-party for poor girls and women, with reading and prayer. Wednesday has an evening service. Thursday and Friday have night-schools conducted by the Curates. Saturday has a warm-hearted choir-practice, open to all members of the congregation, not for crotchet and quaver work, but for studying such thoughtful and expressive rendering of the hymns and canticles that they may indeed be "unto edification." In the winter this is preceded by a singing-class for those who wish to learn to read music from notes.

There are also weekly cottage readings in different parts of the parish, and gospel addresses by the Vicar during the dinner hour, at a cartridge manufactory.

The occasional parochial gatherings are frequent, varied, and profitable. "Always *something* for us!" said a grateful parishioner. Special seasons, Christmas, Easter, or harvest, are celebrated by social gatherings, often in all three schoorooms, because *one* cannot hold all. The tone of these is eminently that of *holy* gladness, the Lord Jesus Christ being the recognized and welcome guest, and the music of His name never absent. At other times, special Prayer-meetings, Evangelistic addresses, Bible Society, Church Missionary, or other religious meetings, interesting and instructive lectures and entertainments, intellectual or musical (but always pervaded by the really *spiritual* element), follow as opportunity can be found.

In the three Day-schools, supported entirely by private and *noble* liberality, Bible knowledge is in its right place, the *first*. And not *knowledge* merely, but intelligent *love* of that precious Word is the great lesson aimed at. The result of this "seeking first the kingdom of God" is, that while these schools have never failed to obtain excellent reports from the Inspectors for secular work, the number of intelligent and decided young Christian men and women who have come out of them is encouraging. These have formed material for much that is useful and influential around them, *e.g.*, a branch of the Young Women's Christian Association. That it is no forcing of religion upon the children, is shown by a number of them having for two years past regularly held a prayer-meeting among themselves.

There is a Clothing Club, a Shoe Club, a Provident Club, a Sick Club, and a Cottage Dispensary, where a doctor attends every week, and medicine is given gratis. But besides these important aids to the poor, it is well known that while the parish is in the present hands, no deserving or sick poor will apply at the Vicarage in vain for blankets, flannel, beef tea, or port wine; indeed, such applications are mostly forestalled, for the system of visiting makes it unlikely that any case of illness or distress could occur without coming under the cognisance of the Vicar within a few days.

Home work always tells upon Mission work; so you will not wonder that P—— has sent up no less than £1338 to the Church Missionary Society, since the formation of a parochial C.M.S. Associaton; and sums equally good in proportion, to the Bible Society, South American Missionary, Zenana Mission, Jews, and other branches of distant work; and also to the Church Pastoral-Aid and other Societies for Home Mission work. One little item in the annual list is £103 as the result of the Ladies' working party at the Vicarage, for the Mission Schools at Singapore. It would probably surprise some of our friends if they knew the number of different Societies which divide the money-collecting force of a good working parish. A parish which figures in, *e.g.*, The Church Missionary Report for £50 would probably figure for £500 or even £1000 per annum, if the sum total of its contributions to the work of God, local and distant, appeared under one head.

An important social influence in P—— is the Cottagers' Floral and Horticultural Society. The rules are so arranged that there is stimulus for all, and every fair effort, even of beginners, is sure of encouragement. In connection with this are numerous prizes for Cottage Neatness, which are greatly valued and sought, also for all sorts of miscellaneous performances involving home industry or care, *e.g.*, for the best honey, best knitted stockings, best *darned* ditto,[1] shirts, home-made loaves, patchwork quilts, etc., etc. The result of several years

[1] men's socks or ladies' stockings repaired by stitching usually with woolen thread (or yarn)

of this, is a strikingly high average of neatness and excellence in all that pertains to cottage home-life, both in house and garden. I may mention that it is from this parish that Cottage Window Gardening first emanated, an energetic Curate having transplanted the idea to London.

That excellent penny monthly, *Home Words*, is localized as the *P—— Magazine*, and in its extra pages of local matter the Vicar supplements his full and faithful pulpit teaching and pastoral visits, by words which may reach the hearts, improve the heads, or cheer the homes of his people. A further supply of good general literature is provided by a Parish Library.

"Of course the Vicar is well paid for his work, and therefore merely does his duty and renders what is due!" says my reader. On the contrary, his twenty-two years' work has been simply *gratis!* the income of the living being such, that when the curates' stipends and other parochial expenses are paid, the known charities of the Vicar (not to mention the manifold unknown ones, at which a few cottage visits enable us to guess) nearly swallow up the sum remaining. Such devotion of life and powers without earthly reward is far more frequent than people suppose. One of the above-mentioned curates lately told me that his venerated father worked a large and important town parish for 30 years (and it was noble and successful work), and reckoned that he was always out of pocket by his living. My own beloved father likewise spent more upon his successive parishes than the income received from them, during 41 out of the 54 years of his faithful ministry.[1] My object in writing this letter may be inferred from the following query—Would not those who "love the Lord Jesus Christ in sincerity," love, help, and sympathise with each other more, if they knew better *what* others are really doing, and *how* they are working for Him?

Perry Privileges.

SUNDAY.—St. John's Church, Perry Barr:—Divine Service, at 11 a.m. and 3.30 p.m. Christ Church—Divine Service, at 10.30 a.m. and 6.30 p.m. Oscott Schoolroom—Divine Service at 6.30 p.m.

THE TWO SACRAMENTS.—Baptisms: the second-Sunday in the month, at Perry Church, in the Afternoon; the third Sunday in the month at Oscott.

[1] Rev. William Henry Havergal first ministered as curate under Rev. Thomas Tregenna Biddulph (vicar of St. James's, Bristol, and rector of Durston and Lyng) in 1816. He last ministered as chaplain for English services in Pyrmont (a health resort in Northwest Germany, where he went in summers for the medicinal benefit of the mineral waters there), his last service there being on September 12, 1869. He died at his home in Leamington on April 19, 1870. See pages 589 and 665–668 of Volume IV of the Havergal edition.

The LORD'S SUPPER: the first Sunday in the month, at Perry Church, after morning service; the third Sunday in the month, at Christ Church evening service; and quarterly, at Oscott Schoolroom service.

SUNDAY SCHOOLS, at 9.20 a.m. and 3 p.m.

BIBLE CLASS FOR YOUNG MEN, by the Vicar, at Perry Schools, 9.20 a.m.

BIBLE CLASS FOR YOUNG WOMEN, by Mrs. Snepp, at Perry School, 9.20 a.m.

MONDAY.—MOTHERS' MEETING, at Christ Church Schoolroom, at 3 p.m. Bible Reading, at Christ Church Schoolroom, at 8 p.m.

TUESDAY.—SEWING CLASS and BIBLE READING, at the Lion Works, Aston Lane, at 6.30 p.m.

WEDNESDAY.—DIVINE SERVICE, at Christ Church, at 7 p.m. CHOIR PRACTICE at 8.15 p.m. Cottage Lectures, Bible and Prayer, at 7 p.m.

THURSDAY.—NIGHT SCHOOL for Boys and Young Men, at Christ Church, at 7.30 p.m.

FRIDAY.—NIGHT SCHOOL, at Christ Church, at 7.30 p.m.

SATURDAY.—SINGING CLASS, at Christ Church Schoolroom, at 6.30 p.m. Choir Practice at 7.30.

YOUNG WOMEN'S CHRISTIAN ASSOCIATION MEETINGS.—At Perry Schoolroom, on the second Thursday in the month, at 7.30 p.m.; at Perry Villa, on the third Friday in the month, at 3.30 p.m.

THE LIBRARY in Christ Church Rooms contains a large supply of valuable and interesting books.

THE SICK CLUB.—The medical officer is in attendance at the Dispensary, at Thomas Grimmett's Cottage, in Perry Village, from 3 to 4 p.m., every Wednesday. Many are availing themselves of it. It appears to be doing much good: there are about 130 members already.

CLOTHING AND SHOE CLUB.—Payments may be made the first Monday in the month, at Perry School, from 10 to 12 o'clock.

BOOKS from Perry Hall Library may be obtained on payment of 1*d*. a month.

Thus we see every day in the week presents some privilege before the parishioners of Perry Barr; some opportunity either of doing or getting good. And it is much hoped that the improved attendance, manifested of late, will still go on and increase.

[This was published in the newspaper *The Christian Standard.*]

THE GREAT MISSION WORK NOW GOING ON.

SOME months ago, Miss Frances Havergal wrote to us, expressing regret that, while deploring the prevalence of pernicious errors in the Church of England, as well as in other denominations, there was a tendency to overlook the great good which is being done by faithful and devoted Christian workers in various parts of the country.

We remarked at the time that, speaking for ourselves—and, we doubted not, we spoke for others also—it would give us immeasurably more pleasure to have to record the good that was then being done, than to have to denounce the awful errors, and expose the deadly delusions which are so fearfully rife in the present day.

Since then, we rejoice to say, a multitude of devoted servants of Christ have consecrated all their energies to the work of converting sinners; and their zealous, unwearied, and self-sacrificing labours have been blessed wth an amount of success which reminds us of the triumphs, in a measure, which the first missionaries of the Cross, achieved in the days of the Apostles. The accounts which reach us from all parts of the country, are truly marvellous. If they were not attested beyond all question, one could hardly be able to accord unqualified credence to them.

The number of conversions in Newcastle, and other northern towns, which have taken place in these parts, and the solemn feeling in relation to eternal things which seems to have taken possession of the minds of masses of the people, are, indeed, wondrous not only in the eyes of those Christian workers—laymen, as well as ministers of the Gospel—through whose instrumentality they have been accomplished, but of all who are acquainted with them.

But, perhaps, no more wonderful work in the way of conversion, has been lately accomplished, in the same space of time than that in Derby. It seemed for the last fortnight that a Divine influence had overshadowed myriads of the inhabitants of that town. Wherever special services were held, the places in which they were so, became crowded with those who felt themselves to be lost and undone sinners, and the prevailing individual cry—mentally, if not audibly—has been, "what must I do to be saved?"

On Thursday afternoon, Miss Beamish gave an account, at a meeting of Christians held at the house of Mr. D. Matheson, Queen's-gate, South Kensington, of what she had witnessed within the last fortnight, in relation to the wondrous work in Derby. Day and night the places of meeting were not only crowded, but a feeling of deep solemnity on the part of the assemblages brought together, manifestly pervaded every one present. All seemed as if they realized the power of God so overshadowing them, as if they were in another sphere than that of the world. The address of Miss Beamish, who not only described what she had seen, but that also in which she had been an active instrument, was listened to with the most profound attention throughout, and with no ordinary pleasure.

And yet, great and gratifying as are the accounts of the work of conversion in nearly all parts of the country, we regard them as but the earnest of far greater things which are to follow. We hope and believe that we are on the eve of many myriads of conversions, and of a great revival of true religion in the minds and hearts of the people of God. It is a remarkable fact, and one which ought to be mentioned, that the great majority of those who are most earnest and laborious in this great work of conversion, are clergymen of the Church of England. This great fact is one which, in some measure, compensates for the Romanism which so extensively prevails in the National Establishment.

———— ✥ ————

[The following article was found as a cut-out clipping. No date nor name of the periodical was given. The narrow column of the printed text looks like a newspaper item.]

MISSION-WEEK IN BIRMINGHAM IN DECEMBER.

Dear Sir,—Will your readers make earnest supplication during the next two months for a special and abundant blessing upon the great mission week to be held in Birmingham and its suburbs from December 8 to 15. There is, perhaps, no place where the opposing forces of good and evil are brought into sharper contrast. This great Midland Metropolis being, on the one hand, a stronghold of scepticism, and, on the other, a stronghold of evangelicalism. There is so much mental activity and energy, that we cannot but feel that any outpouring of blessing here would be likely to radiate in wide and influential circles, that, if blessed, this town would indeed *be* a blessing.

The proposed mission week claims, therefore, strong sympathy and earnest prayer from all who desire the extension of our Master's kingdom. Every possible means will be used in the thrity parishes which have united in this scheme. Twenty-two mission preachers, including many of the most eminent and powerful evangelical clergy, are already engaged for the week. Arrangements are being made to reach all classes, from the highest to the lowest, and to "go out," and "compel them to come in." And the already over-worked clergy are prepared to strain every nerve to bring these golden opportunities to bear upon the hearts of thousands. But we can only lay the wood in order. Now, will not the Lord's people unite with us in intense and continued prayer, that He may send the fire of the Holy Spirit upon it?

Already the spirit of grace and of supplication appears to be poured out, both upon individual Christians in private and upon special prayer meetings commenced in anticipation. As an instance, I may mention that in this parish the vicar, the Rev. C. B. Snepp, preached two fervent and heart-rousing sermons on Sunday last, from the text, "There shall be showers of blessing," stirring up his people to plead this promise, and exhorting them all to seek that preparation of heart which the Lord alone can give. At the conclusion of the morning sermon, he called upon choir and congregation to rise and join him in singing the hymn, "Showers of blessing, gracious promise," from his own rich and beautiful hymnal, "Songs of Grace and Glory," and this breaking of the usual routine appeared to have a singularly touching and solemnizing effect, deepening the impression of the burning words preceding it. He then invited his congregation to meet on the following evening for special prayer. This meeting was crowded, and was characterized by great solemnity. There was true wrestling with God for his great promised gifts, especially for the outpouring of the Holy Spirit, to convince, convert, and revive, for the manifestation of the Lord Jesus to many, many hearts.

Is not all this an earnest of coming blessing? And may it not stimulate to still greater faith and prayer and expectation? We ask your readers to join the prayer, that they may have the joy of joining in the praise, for which we trust there will, indeed, be new and glorious cause, —I remain, dear sir, yours faithfully,

FRANCES RIDLEY HAVERGAL.

———— ❧ ————

[This was a letter F.R.H. wrote on one of her trips to Switzerland, addressed to and published in a newspaper. In the cut-out clipping found among Havergal manuscripts and papers, no date nor name of the periodical was given, only the date and location of Frances' letter.]

BOOKS FOR CONTINENTAL HOTELS.

Dear Sir,—May I suggest to those of your readers who are planning a continental trip, the desirability of taking a little Sunday reading for the benefit of their fellow sojourners at Swiss hotels. Even where there is English service, there are several hours to spare, and those who are too conscientious to take up the novels which usually form the only hotel library, and yet have not learned the enjoyment of sweet hours with God's Word only, catch eagerly at any chance supply. If every Christian tourist took only one book for each hotel at which a Sunday is to be spent, it would be a very trifling addition to luggage, and would soon accumulate a fair supply for the want.

A good plan is to send forward a small parcel of books, etc., by post, immediately on reaching Switzerland, to about three or four principal points on the route; the parcel post being so very much cheaper than ours, that, supposing we have brought quite a large stock of books, tracts, and portions from England, two or three francs wll place them conveniently at our different headquarters, ready for use on arrival, without being encumbered with them as luggage.

Hotel keepers are always gratified at the gift of a book for their *salon*, and take care to keep them within sight or reach of visitors. At this pleasant little hotel, the friendly landlord, on recognizing me, ran at once into the *salon* to show me a book I had left with him three years ago, and which still lay with a few others on the table.

No one is much inclined for heavy reading after a week's mountaineering; therefore except in pensions, where longer halts are made, it is not much use leaving books which require close attention or consecutive reading. I have found nothing more practically useful than bound copies of *Woman's Work*, as a present to the landlord, and odd numbers of the same, and of THE CHRISTIAN, to strew about on the tables. These are too full of facts to be thought dry, and the articles are not too long to be alarming. Religious books or periodicals which contain no facts or narratives, do not answer the same purpose, as they offer no attraction to the very persons whom one wishes to interest. I find many young persons will read THE CHRISTIAN and *Woman's Work* with great interest who would not touch a book which they would at a glance pronounce " goody," however pleasingly written.

Such tiny books as " All for Jesus" (Partridge), are sure to be taken up and read, especially if several are strewn about so that one or two can be quietly carried away without notice.

This appears to me a valuable opportunity for quiet seed sowing. For some, who never see such things in their own homes, and would not read them if they did, will take them up for the sake of getting through a long Sunday afternoon with " nothing to do."

As the mass of novels in all the larger hotels is a great temptation where there is really nothing else to read, the gift of any better books which might compete with them in attractiveness, would be very useful, in addition to the " Sunday books," such as Emily Sarah Holt's " Ashcliffe Hall," Agnes Giberne's " Mists of the Valley," or Mrs. Prentiss's " Stepping Heavenward." Second hand copies will do just as well as new ones.—Yours cordially,

FRANCES RIDLEY HAVERGAL.

Hotel des Alpes, Zermatt, July 20.

["What Are the Bishops Doing?" was published by the newspaper *The Christian Standard*. In the cut-out clipping found among Havergal manuscripts and papers, there is no date, and the next item, "The Late Mission Week at Liverpool," was printed immediately below the article "What Are the Bishops Doing?", on the same page, same column.]

WHAT ARE THE BISHOPS DOING?

For the "Christian Standard."

THIS question has so often been asked of late in connection with leaving undone things which ought to be done, that it is pleasant to be able to vary it by appending a different answer. The following paragraphs are tokens for good in quarters where, it may be, little or nothing of this kind had been looked for:—

THE LONDON MISSION OF 1874.—There is to be a Mission in London in February, if God permit; a meeting preliminary to which was convened in St. Paul's Cathedral last week, by the Bishops of London, Winchester, and Rochester. A very large number of the London clergy responded to this appeal, and filled the whole space under the dome of St. Paul's. There were men of every doctrinal section in the English church; addresses were given by the three bishops, between which were two intervals of prayer, "perhaps," says one of the daily papers, "the most impressive of all forms of worship, especially in the center of a great city." "The service was," says the same report, "a very exceptional one indeed for the metropolitan cathedral." The addresses were of a most stirring and thoroughly missionary character, and in the afternoon a conference of incumbents took place at King's College for the purpose of arranging the details of the forthcoming Mission.

The Hereford Mission Week, between Nov. 1st and 8th, appears to have been remarkably successful. On Saturday, the 1st, the services were inaugurated by an address from the Bishop to the clergy, missioners, and workers, who were joined by a large congregation. The text taken by his Lordship was Exodus 12:26, "What mean ye by this service?" After the service, the Bishop met and prayed with the clergy and the Deanery, and the Rev. W. Haslam, incumbent of Curzon chapel, St. Peter's missioner, fully explains the manner in which it was thought advisable to conduct the after-meetings. The plans carried out were similar to those adopted in other missions, services being held in the churches at frequent intervals, together with prayer meetings, and other agencies for bringing the truth to bear on the people gathered together, the result of much previous prayerful effort.

The Bishop of Rochester will open a Mission Week at Rochester, on Sunday, the 16th inst., at St. John's Church. In the afternoon of that day he will deliver an address to men in St. Peter's Church. The volunteers and benefit societies have accepted an invitation to be present. During the Mission, the Bishop will preach in the garrison chapel and in the convict prison, besides addressing men in factories, and assisting in various ways at the different churches. Bishop Piers Claughton, Archdeacon of London (the Bishop of Rochester's brother) will also take part in the Mission. It is expected that he will visit the Union and give addresses to bargemen and others. It is proposed to close the Mission, in which the Bishop will be assisted by several London clergymen, and by Canon Miller, by a thanksgiving service, to be held in the Cathedral on the evening of Tuesday, Nov. 25th. Prior to the Mission, the Bishop and Canon Miller will deliver explanatory addresses to men in the Gymnasium, Brompton; the New Corn Exchange, Rochester; and the Lecture Hall, Chatham.

The Archbishop of Canterbury has quietly sanctioned after-meetings in churches.

The Archbishop of York did "the work of an Evangelist" during the Hull Mission Week, preaching fifteen times, and giving several open air addresses in the dockyards. He himself took part in the after meetings, and afterwards stated that he had learnt more from that week, and especially from those after-meetings, than in years of ordinary study and work.

The Bishop of Worcester met the workers, clerical and lay, to the number of more than 1000 at the Birmingham Mission Week, an exclusively Evangelical movement. On this occasion Archdeacon Prest gave a most interesting and stirring description of Mission Week work, and especially of its "revival" features, and the mode of conducting after-meetings in which he has been peculiarly blessed and successful.

The Bishop of Gloucester has issued the following simple, earnest and truly pastoral letter, with the appended comprehensive and spiritual prayer.

TO THE PARISHIONERS OF THE PARISH OF ST. MARY'S CHELTENHAM.

My Dear Christian Friends—I heartily commend to you all the Mission which, by God's grace, is about to be held in Cheltenham, and in which I hope to take a part.

I entreat you, as your friend and pastor, to avail yourselves in your different parishes of this great opportunity.

No influences are, I humbly believe, more calculated, on the one hand, to arouse the careless and unawakened, and, on the other, to deepen spiritual life and to produce an abiding effect in the soul, than those which are vouchsafed through the earnestly conducted Christian Mission.

Pray, then, that a blessing may rest on our labors; pray for us; and dear friend, pray with us.—Your faithful Friend and Bishop,

C. J. GLOUCESTER & BRISTOL.

Palace Gloucester, Nov. 3rd, 1873.

No better prayer than the following can be recommended, which may be used daily at private or family prayer:—

Almighty God, our Heavenly Father, who has given thine only Son to die for the sins of Thy people, we pray Thee to send abundant blessings upon the special effort which is now to be made in this place to spread the knowledge of the Gospel, and to win souls for Christ.

O Blessed Saviour, do Thou Thyself uphold and strengthen all those Thy Ministers and Stewards of Thy mysteries who have been called to take part in this blessed work. Fill them with a deep and earnest love for souls, and especially for the souls of those to whom they have been sent.

O Holy Spirit of God, without whom nothing is strong, nothing is holy, give them Thine own persuasive power, that they may preach with boldness and success the truth as it is in Jesus. Prepare the hearts of the sinful to hear the Message of Salvation, and to seek the only Savior. Strengthen with greater grace those who have already begun to seek Him.

Finally, O Holy, Blessed and Glorious Trinity, three Persons and One God, prosper, we beseech Thee, all our labors, and answer these our prayers, to the glory of Thy great name, and the salvation of immortal souls, through the merits and meditation of Jesus Christ, our Blessed Lord and Savior. Amen.

The glorious tide of blessing which seems setting in with the great Mission Week movement is evidently reaching the "high places," and no doubt many more similar testimonies will follow. Little has been written or said on the subject—"Still waters run deep,"—but there can be no doubt that many a shower of blessing has been, and even now is, falling, and that we have reason yet to look for "greater things than these." A clergyman much connected with the movement remarks that his conviction is that great revival in the Church of England has really begun, and that the tide is gathering strength week by week.

FRANCES RIDLEY HAVERGAL.

August 17.

THE LATE MISSION WEEK AT LIVERPOOL.

MOST willingly would we have inserted the report from the *Christian*, sent to us by Miss Havergal, of the proceedings of Mission Week at Liverpool, but its length, and the lateness of the hour at which it reached us, preclude the possibility of our doing so. But we subjoin what some of those who were present say on the subject:—

> Miss F. R. Havergal writes:—"It seems to me that it would be nearly impossible for any one worker in a large Mission Week to give any fair and comprehensive account. The work is chiefly so entirely parochial, so concentrated and absorbing in each parish, that there is no time to see what others are doing; it is too intense to be wide, and yet the means and modes, and the results too, are so varied, that the work in one parish by no means represents all."

> The Rev. W. F. Stubbs got a lady named Miss Boileau to preach in the very worst streets, accompanying her himself, with a little band of singers, in the most horrible alleys, and she was marvelously successful in winning miserable creatures out of their houses, which no one could do before, and getting them to listen to the story of peace, and then to promise to come to church, which numbers actually did, and then many of these poor creatures, with mere rags pinned on them, listened with tears to Mr. Snepp, and many found Jesus during his evening services.

> "The Rev. Mr. Robinson, vicar of St. Augustine's, had immense blessing amounting to a real revival in his parish, all his workers seeming to have quite a baptism of the Holy Ghost, and great numbers awakened and converted. Nearly two hundred communicants at his church on Sunday evening, and a wonderful spirit of joy. He himself was laid aside by illness the whole week, but is convinced that this great disappointment was overruled for good, as many came forward to speak to the Mission preacher (Mr. Richardson) who would not, he thinks, have done so if they thought they were being watched and noticed by their own pastor."

"A Page from Irish History" was found among Havergal manuscripts and papers. She wrote items anonymously, and she was called "Correspondent" elsewhere. This is almost certainly the "sketch" referred to by F.R.H. in a letter she wrote, dated June 6, 1859 (see page 113 of Volume IV of the Havergal edition). She is almost certainly the author of this.

A PAGE FROM IRISH HISTORY.

[The following sketch, which is supplied by a fair correspondent, will furnish an introduction to the deputation who will attend the meeting of the Irish Society to be held in this city in the week after next, particulars of which meetings will be duly announced by advertisement in our next *Journal*] :—

It may not be generally known that about one fourth of the population of Ireland, or rather more than a million and a half of our fellow subjects, are Irish speaking, that is, are either totally unacquainted with English, or use it with reluctance as a disliked foreign tongue. They regard whatever is presented to them in it with distrust and prejudice, but hail the sound of their own language with a singular confidence and affection. They are accustomed to say, the Irish is one of the only three tongues in the world of which the devil is not master, inasmuch as " St. Patrick wouldn't let him learn it." Hence it would follow whatever is spoken in it cannot proceed from him.

In years gone by, this much loved tongue was a means of influence neglected by the Protestant Church. But at length one earnest hearted clergyman, the Rev. John Gregg, now Archdeacon of Kildare, who had preached many an eloquent sermon in the city of Dublin, resolved that his own Irish fluency should no longer be a talent unemployed. He consequently determined on a tour to the West of Ireland, there to speak for his Master in their own tongue, to those who scarcely understood the Saxon speech, and to whom it was unwelcome. He came to Athlone, a town where an Irish Protestant sermon had never yet been delivered. After much opposition he obtained the use of the County Courts, every other door being closed against him. The news spread far and wide that a sermon in Irish would be preached on an appointed day by a gentleman from Dublin. Such a thing had never been heard of before. The ears of the priests tingled as the burst of wave after wave of the quickly awakened excitement fell upon them; and they began to bethink themselves how this dangerous move might be met.

They were not long in choosing an instrument well fitted for the purpose in view. A young man lived in the place, already distinguished by rare mental gifts, and also endowed with great physical strength. He was withal a zealous adherent of the Holy Roman Church, ready for anything or everything in her defiance, whether by tongue or by arm. To him the priest, in his fear, addressed himself. "Tom, my boy, you're a faithful son of the Holy Mother Church, I'm thinking!"

"Bad luck to the spalpeen[1] that denies the same, your reverence!"

"There's a small job, Tom, that wants to be done by a true hand at the County Courts to-morrow, and where will I find anyone, do you think!"

Tom, who was no ways dull of comprehension, "took" immediately, answering his Reverence's insinuation with an anticipatory grin of delight, and "I'm the boy, yer reverence!"

The details of the "small job" were speedily arranged to their mutual satisfaction.

The appointed day and hour came, and good Mr. Gregg, in default of a pulpit, took his post on a platform covered with green baize, in the midst of a throng of Irish excitables, whom no priestly admonitions had been able to deter from coming to hear this wonderful sermon. Denser and denser grew the crowd, pressing and pushing and packing, till retreat from any of the inner ranks became an impossibility, and the chance of obtaining silence apparently about as great as if it were requested from a beehive on the point of swarming! At length no more could enter, and Mr. Gregg stood up to face a congregation that would have astonished a sober Saxon. One spell alone could enchain the turbulent mass, and that one he was about to exercise. He spoke: and the tones of their own musical tongue, which never fail to reach the Irish heart, glided forth like oil on the waves. Every noisy tongue was hushed, every eye fixed, as the words of God's own Book, so sweet, so new, poured through the building. Suddenly— ere even the first sentence was complete—there arose a tremendous thundering beneath the very feet of the speaker. He stopped—the thundering stopped. He continued—the thundering continued louder than ever. But above it was heard Mr. Gregg's strong voice, "Ah, Satan, I always knew you would oppose me if you could, but I didn't expect you this way!" Then the hum of the great bee hive waxed louder. "Indeed, and it's the devil himself come to carry him off!" cried one. "Whisht there, sure an it's the blessed St. Patrick himself that's warning us not to hearken," shouted another. "Holy Virgin and St. Michael if ye'll help me out, I'll never come in again!" exclaimed a third. Getting out being out of the question, the ejaculators had to remain *nolens volens*,[2] to see the solution of the doubt as to whether the noise proceeded from the devil or St. Patrick! Mr. Gregg was not to be out-done by any inimical power, human or fiendish. So assuming an attitude of defiance of whatever might be beneath him, he cried

[1] spalpeen: Irish word for rascal   [2] *nolens, volens*: Latin, meaning perforce, forcibly

out with a stentorian voice, "You shall not be too much for me yet, Satan, we will see who can hold on the longest."

As the reader may conjecture, the deafening noise really proceeded from the devoted Tom, concealed under the platform; he was wielding with vigorous energy a large sledge hammer. Mr. Gregg, heedless of the uproar, perseveringly went on with his sermon, waging with his voice the contest of wind versus muscle. The assembly grew quiet out of sheer curiosity. Mr. Gregg's lungs were remarkably strong, and the sledge hammer was remarkably heavy; and ere long the strokes of the latter became less tremendous. Then occasional rests became necessary followed by spasmodic efforts to keep it up. Fainter and fainter grew the blows, for Tom's arm now ached terribly. Still grew the multitude, for Mr. Gregg held on his way triumphantly. At last, nothing was to be heard but the strange and glorious story of peace touching the hearts of those untaught hearers, sounding with trumpet clearness in their eager ears, entering with harp-like sweetness into their restless souls—and all in Erin's own beautiful language!

Three days after, the preacher was leaving Athlone, when a young man begged of an interview. "That wasn't all true, your honor," he exclaimed, "that you said three days ago!" "Indeed," replied Mr. Gregg; "It was true—blessed be God!" "And how will I know that it is, then?" asked the enquirer. Offering him a book, the preacher said, "Will you take this, and then you will know." The book was accepted. It was an Irish Bible.

*   *   *   *   *   *   *   *   *

Several years passed, and many more Irish sermons were preached, and many more eager listeners found in the Emerald Isle. But the sweet story of peace had not yet been heard in the stormy and mountainous peninsula of Ventry, in the far South-west. Through the twenty miles of its rock bound length, there was not one who knew the Word of God and its glad messages. But the word was coming. A young clergyman, full of love and zeal, stood there, at length, and preached for the first time of Redemption only through the Blood of Christ.

An uncouth congregation had assembled, rougher if anything than Mr. Gregg's. Still, Irish words could entrance even them, and they crowded round the minister with their ragged hats overshadowing their rugged brows. Ere long one took his hat off, then another and another followed the example, until, before the sermon ended, every head was reverently uncovered. When the last words were spoken, there was silence, and more than one tattered sleeve was seen brushing away a tear—for the speaker had spoken from heart to heart. In deep and earnest tones one poor fellow burst forth—"Thank ye, sir, ye've taken the hunger off us today!"

*   *   *   *   *   *   *   *   *

Year's again fled on, till the summer of 1856. A great change had passed over Ventry. The same clergyman, young no longer, stood now on his own pleasant lawn in the midst of that once benighted peninsula. Churches and schools gleamed cheerily amid its magnificent scenery, where nothing but dreary cabins had been built before. Few were the homes where the Irish Bible was not read and known, to the shaming of many an English dwelling,—might we not add, of many a Worcester one too?

But it is a "high day" in Ventry. Again the preacher is surrounded. But he does not now see before him a herd of wild looking, half clothed beings, like those who listened to him when he first set foot in beautiful sea-girt Ventry, when he might have said—

> "All creation pleases
> And only man is vile."

Now, two hundred of her sons and daughters have assembled. They are neatly appareled, books are in their hands, they are quiet and solemn in demeanor. The greater part are still young, and they are all Candidates for Confirmation—to the surprise and joy of the Bishop who is there to lay the hand of blessing upon them. Some are the children of converts, others have themselves passed through the struggle of giving up the mistaken faith of their youth; but all are freed from the galling fetters of Popery, and all are ready to bless God for him who has been His instrument in the wonderful work.

The enquiry cannot fall to interest us—Who is he?

Let the priest of Athlone recognize the broad forehead and powerful frame of his once willing tool! Let Mr. Gregg recognize his voice as that of the young man who strove not to believe what he heard, yet took the Irish Bible to "search and look!" It is even so. Tom Moriarty, the zealous and the bigoted, he of the strong arm and the sledge hammer, is now the Rev. Thomas Moriarty, the eloquent, the earnest, and the loving,—one who sees even now the fruit of his many years toil in the immense parish of which he is rector. Truly the two hundred confirmants around him are a noble harvest already, but he is still sowing and watering, and a yet richer ingathering may be vouchsafed to him.

Where shall we find him next? and when?

Among ourselves, in our own "ancient and faithful city of Worcester," it is hoped, ere many more days have passed, employing his gifted warmhearted-ness in the cause of the society which sent him to the scene of his present labors, striving to awaken the sympathy of many toward his beloved country. Who will not give him the *Cead mille failthe?*[1]

From "Berrow's Worcester Journal," of May 28, 1859.

[1] *Cead mille failthe* (Gaelic): a hundred thousand welcomes.

———— ✦ ————

[This next piece was found in a cut-out clipping, and the date and name of the periodical were not given.]

MUSICAL MARIOLATRY.

Sir,—It is noteworthy fact that while the Birmingham Festival of 1873 was on the whole, both numerically and financially, "the most successful on record," one morning of that festival should have shown a great and significant decrease, both as compared with the previous days of the same and with the correspond-ing morning of 1872. On that day an "Ave Maria" was conspicuously an-nounced as one of the special attractions. Every consistent Protestant was thus debarred from attending that performance. How could those who rejoice in the one glorious Mediator sanction the invocation of a mediatrix!

"Ave Marias" by different composers are creeping into our choral societies, and accustoming thoughtless minds and lips to the very Shibboleth of those who would have us worship the creature as well as the Creator. Why should not individual members of such societies make a brave stand, and refuse to lend their voices to such insidious idolatry? Are there none loyal enough in their allegiance to the one name to do this thing? A few years ago an "Ave Ma-ria" was sung at a practice night of an excellent provincial choral society. One young lady simply sat still, neither rising nor singiing with the rest. The con-ductor called her to account. She briefly gave her reason, and courteously stat-ed her decided refusal to join in what her conscience told her was wrong. The conductor hesitated for a moment, during which the young recusant sent up a swift prayer for help. He then quietly remarked to the choir, "I think we will not repeat this now; proceed at once to the other work for tonight, Handel's 'Jephtha.'" The experiment was never repeated, and thus that society was kept from touching the unclean thing. The "season" of many musical societies is about to commence; will it not be well if their Protestant members see to their duty in this matter?

FRANCES RIDLEY HAVERGAL.

———— ❧ ————

[This next piece was found in a cut-out clipping, and the name of the periodical was not given. The date October 15, 1870 was printed at the top of the article, very likely the date the periodical was published. Only the part of Curwen's paper that quotes F.R.H. was found. Rev. John Curwen (1816–1880) was the founder and leader of the Tonic Sol-fa system of music. His son, John Spencer Curwen, was also a leader and educator in this movement. This is an adaptation (with only slight changes) of a letter by F.R.H. to J. S. Curwen in 1869, published in *Letters by the Late Frances Ridley Havergal* (London: James Nisbet & Co., 1886), original book pages 68–69, page 165 of Volume IV of the Havergal edition.]

October 15, 1870.

THE PHILANTHROPIC ASPECT OF THE TONIC SOL-FA MOVEMENT.

A paper read, September 27th, 1870, before the Social Science Congress at Newcast-on-Tyne,

BY JOHN SPENCER CURWEN.

Of labour in another sphere the following lead from Miss Havergal speaks:

During the winter months we opened two nice rooms every evening, and gave free invitation to young dress-makers and girls of that class (especially those living in lodgings), hoping that it would prove a safe and pleasant retreat for them after work hours. Classes were arranged for each evening in the smaller room, in the other the girls read, wrote, worked and chatted. It was not as successful as to numbers as we expected, but the attendance on the evening on which I gave a Tonic Sol-fa lesson, was nearly double. I tell you frankly that it was not for the sake of Sol-fa that I began the class, but solely because I believed it was the greatest attraction I could contribute to our little scheme for bringing these poor girls within the range of loving Christian care and influence. My chief reason for adopting it with them instead of the established notation was that all the Sol-fa songs are sound and safe, and I knew I could not give them access to anything low or bad through it, while I had no such certainty had I taught the old notation. This weighed with me more than the obvious and indisputable advantages of greater facility, cheapness, etc., which the Tonic Sol-fa system has. There was no question as to the class being attractive, and great was the disappointment when, as frequently happened, the members were kept at work too late and "lost the singing." One evening two girls came in panting and flushed, about fifteen minutes before the close. "Why Lizzie and Jane what *is* the matter?" "We were kept overtime, but we thought half a loaf better than no bread, so we took to our heels the moment we could get out of the workroom, and we never stopped running till we got here." They had literally run a good mile to be in time for a few minutes' singing. One young girl who had just begun to form acquaintances which would have led to no good, and to saunter about the streets with them, was attracted to our rooms solely by the singing class, but soon became one of our most regular attendants at all the classes, and we have reason to hope that she is not only saved from the dangers into which she was rushing, but that good impressions have been made, and a good work begun in her heart. I have no musical results to show, for after about eight lessons I was interrupted by illness, but I believe that my Tonic Sol-fa class had been a grappling iron to draw many little drifting vessels close to our side, bringing them within hearing of loving and sympathising words, and of the One name which is sweeter than any music.

———⊛———

THE PHILANTHROPIC ASPECT (
THE TONIC SOL-FA MOVEMENT.

A paper read, September 27th, 1870, before '(
Social Science Congress at Newcastle-on-Tyne,
BY JOHN SPENCER CURWEN.*

Of labour in another sphere the following l(
from Miss Havergal speaks :—
"During the winter months we opened two
rooms every evening, and gave free invitatio1
young dress-makers and girls of that class (especi
those living in lodgings), hoping that it would p
a safe and pleasant retreat for them after work h(
Classes were arranged for each evening in the sm:
room, in the other the girls read, wrote, worke(
chatted. It was not as successful as to numbe1
we expected, but the attendance on the evenin;
which I gave a Tonic Sol-fa lesson was nearly do1
I tell you frankly that it was not for the sake of S(
that I began the class, but solely because I beli
it was the greatest attraction I could contribu
our little scheme for bringing these poor girls w
the range of loving Christian care and influ
My chief reason for adopting it with them inste
the established notation was that all the Sol-fa s
are sound and safe, and I knew I could not give
access to anything low or bad through it, while I
no such certainty had I taught the old nota
This weighed with me more than the obvious an
disputable advantages of greater facility, cheap
&c., which the Tonic Sol-fa system has. There
no question as to the class being attractive, and
was the disappointment when, as frequently happ(
the members were kept at work too late and '
the singing." One evening two girls came in pa1
and flushed, about fifteen minutes before the (
"Why Lizzie and Jane what *is* the matter?" '
were kept overtime, but we thought half a loaf b
than no bread, so we took to our heels the mo:
we could get out of the workroom, and we 1
stopped running till we got here." They had I
ally run a good mile to be in time for a few mi1
singing. One young girl who had just begun to
acquaintances which would have led to no good,
to saunter about the streets with them, was attr(
to our rooms solely by the singing class, but soo1
came one of our most regular attendants at al
classes, and we have reason to hope that she i:
only saved from the dangers into which she was 1
ing, but that good impressions have been made,
a good work begun in her heart. I have no mu
results to show, for after about eight lessons I
interrupted by illness; but I believe that my T
Sol-fa class had been a grappling iron to draw n
little drifting vessels close to our side, bringing t
within hearing of loving and sympathising w
and of the One name which is sweeter than
music."

The clipping, all that was found of this article, among Havergal manuscripts and papers. This is newly typeset on pages 181–182.

A PAGE FROM IRISH HISTORY.

[The following sketch, which is supplied by a fair correspondent, will furnish an introduction to the deputation who will attend the meeting of the Irish Society to be held in this city in the week after next, particulars of which meetings will be duly announced by advertisement in our next *Journal*] :—

It may not be generally known that about one fourth of the population of Ireland, or rather more than a million and a half of our fellow subjects, are Irish speaking, that is, are either totally unacquainted with English, or use it with reluctance as a disliked foreign tongue. They regard whatever is presented to them in it with distrust and prejudice, but hail the sound of their own language with a singular confidence and affection. They are accustomed to say, the Irish is one of the only three tongues in the world of which the devil is not master, inasmuch as "St. Patrick would'nt let him learn it." Hence it would follow whatever is spoken in it cannot proceed from *him*.

In years gone by, this much-loved tongue was a means of influence neglected by the Protestant Church. But at length one earnest-hearted clergyman, the Rev. John Gregg, now Archdeacon of Kildare, who had preached many an eloquent sermon in the city of Dublin, resolved that his own Irish fluency should no longer be a talent unemployed. He consequently determined on a tour to

parish of which he is rector. Truly the two hundred confirmants around him are a noble harvest already, but he is still sowing and watering, and a yet richer ingathering may be vouchsafed to him.

Where shall we find him next? and when?

Among ourselves, in our own "ancient and faithful city of Worcester," it is hoped, ere many more days have passed, employing his gifted warmheartedness in the cause of the society which sent him to the scene of his present labours, striving to awaken the sympathy of many towards his beloved country. Who will not give him the *Cead mille failthe?*

FROM "BERROW'S WORCESTER JOURNAL," OF MAY 28, 1859.

See pages 175–179 for the complete text of this essay (the published copy only partially shown here for lack of space), an essay almost certainly written by F.R.H.

MUSICAL MARIOLATRY.

SIR,—It is a noteworthy fact that while the Birmingham Festival of 1873 was, on the whole, both numerically and financially, "the most successful on record,' one morning of that festival should have shown a great and significant decrease, both as compared with the previous days of the same and with the corresponding morning of 1872. On that day an "Ave Maria" was conspicuously announced as one of the special attractions. Every consistent Protestant was thus debarred from attending that performance. How could those who rejoice in the one glorious Mediator sanction the invocation of a mediatrix?

"Ave Marias" by different composers are creeping into our choral societies, and accustoming thoughtless minds and lips to the very Shibboleth of those who would have us worship the creature as well as the Creator. Why should not individual members of such societies make a brave stand, and refuse to lend their voices to such insidious idolatry? Are there none loyal enough in their allegiance to the one name to do this thing? A few years ago an "Ave Maria" was sung at a practice-night of an excellent provincial choral society. One young lady simply sat still, neither rising nor singing with the rest. The conductor called her to account. She briefly gave her reason, and courteously stated her decided refusal to join in what her conscience told her was wrong. The conductor hesitated for a moment, during which the young recusant sent up a swift prayer for help. He then quietly remarked to the choir, "I think we will not repeat this now; proceed at once to the other work for to-night, Handel's 'Jephtha.'" The experiment was never repeated, and thus that society was kept from touching the unclean thing. The "season" of many musical societies is about to commence; will it not be well if their Protestant members see to their duty in this matter?

FRANCES RIDLEY HAVERGAL.

ADMIRAL KEMPENFELT'S GREAT HYMN.
TO THE EDITOR.

SIR,—You will find that Admiral Kempenfelt's grand hymn, "Hark, 'tis the trump of God," has not been overlooked by the Editor of "Songs of Grace and Glory." It stands in full as Hymn 990 in that comprehensive hymnal. May I suggest that the effect of alternating major and minor settings of the tune Moscow, for different verses of the hymn, is very fine. Moscow can easily be changed into the minor by any one with a slight knowledge of harmony.—Yours very truly, FRANCES R. HAVERGAL.
December 11.

See pages 179 and 186.

[These next three items were printed in a periodical, with no date nor name of the periodical given, only the cut-out clippings of the three pieces, found among Havergal manuscripts and papers. At the end of the first item, J.E.J. was a friend of Frances (the initials J.E.J. were found as the signature of an In Memoriam poem on F.R.H. after her death). At the end of the second item, "Choristers in Cathedrals," below the published, printed "S.M." the initials "F.R.H." were written by hand. At the end of the third item, the name Frances Ridley Havergal was printed below the letter, and then the date December 11 printed, in the newpaper clipping.]

QUESTIONS BY A LADY.

TO THE EDITOR.

Sir,—Can any of your readers give information as to whether the juveniles (paid singers) in cathedral, abbey, and church choirs have ever been known to derive spiritual blessing through that channel?

Do the unconverted ever become converted by this means?

And is there any *Scriptural* authority (Jewish apart) for this custom?

Does not the New Testament imply that "Psalms, and hymns, and spiritual songs" are only appropriate to *Christian* singers?—Yours, etc.,

J.E.J.

Nov. 26.

CHORISTERS IN CATHEDRALS.

TO THE EDITOR.

Sir,—In reply to the first of the "Questions by a Lady," in your number of November 28 it is a well known fact that the eminent and devoted missionary, George Duncan, of Metlahkatlah, was a chorister in York Minster, and considers that he received great blessing and spiritual enjoyment during his attendance at the services. I do not say that this may not be a very exceptional case. I only mention it as supplying the information requested, and as showing that the sovereign God of Grace may, and does, work by what may appear unlikely means.—Yours faithfully,

S.M.

ADMIRAL KEMPENFELT'S GREAT HYMN.

TO THE EDITOR.

SIR,—You will find that Admiral Kempenfelt's grand hymn, "Hark 'tis the trump of God," has not been overlooked by the Editor of "Songs of Grace and Glory." It stands in full as Hymn 990 in that comprehensive hymnal. May I suggest that the effect of alternating major and minor settings of the tune Moscow, for different verses of the hymn, is very fine. Moscow can easily be changed into the minor by any one with a slight knowledge of harmony.—Yours very truly,

FRANCES R. HAVERGAL.

December 11.

———⁂———

[This "Suggestion" was published in the January, 1876 edition of Charles Bullock's *Home Words* magazine. This may be the piece Frances included in a list of pieces she had written or planned to write ("'A Suggestion.' Short paper for *Home Words*."), listed in a letter she wrote at Ormont Dessus in September, 1874. This letter was published posthumously in *Swiss Letters and Alpine Poems* (Chapter IX, page 347 of Volume IV of the Havergal edition).]

HOW TO KEEP OURSELVES WARM.

By Frances Ridley Havergal.

Although the Swiss peasants are what we should consider very poor, working very hard and earning very little; doing without many little comforts which are almost necessaries in an English cottage, and dressing at less cost than our own cottagers; one hardly ever hears of any real poverty or suffering from want or cold, yet their winters are far longer and more severe than ours. In the valley from which I write this (September), the snow lies from November till April.

One of their contrivances for winter warmth is so very simple that it might surely add to the comfort of many an English cottage, where there are many little ones to be kept warm at night and not many warm blankets or counterpanes to cover them. It is *a hay quilt;* and as I have several times slept cosily under one of them, on cold nights among the mountains, I can tell from experience how comfortable they are.

They are nothing but a large square cotton bag, with a few good handfuls of hay, shaken lightly into it; but they are as warm as two or three thick blankets. They need cost almost nothing. The breadths of a very old cotton dress run together, or old curtains, or any other used-out or washed-out material will do for the large double squares, which should be quite as wide as the bed which it is intended to cover. Any farmer would give a few handfuls of hay to shake into it; and there is a coverlet which will keep out any amount of cold!

A Hay Quilt Working Party would in one afternoon provide almost as much comfort as an expensive Blanket Fund. Or poor mothers might themselves, with little trouble and less expense, make their little children or aged parents nice and warm at night, if they would only try this simple plan of the poor Swiss mountaineers.

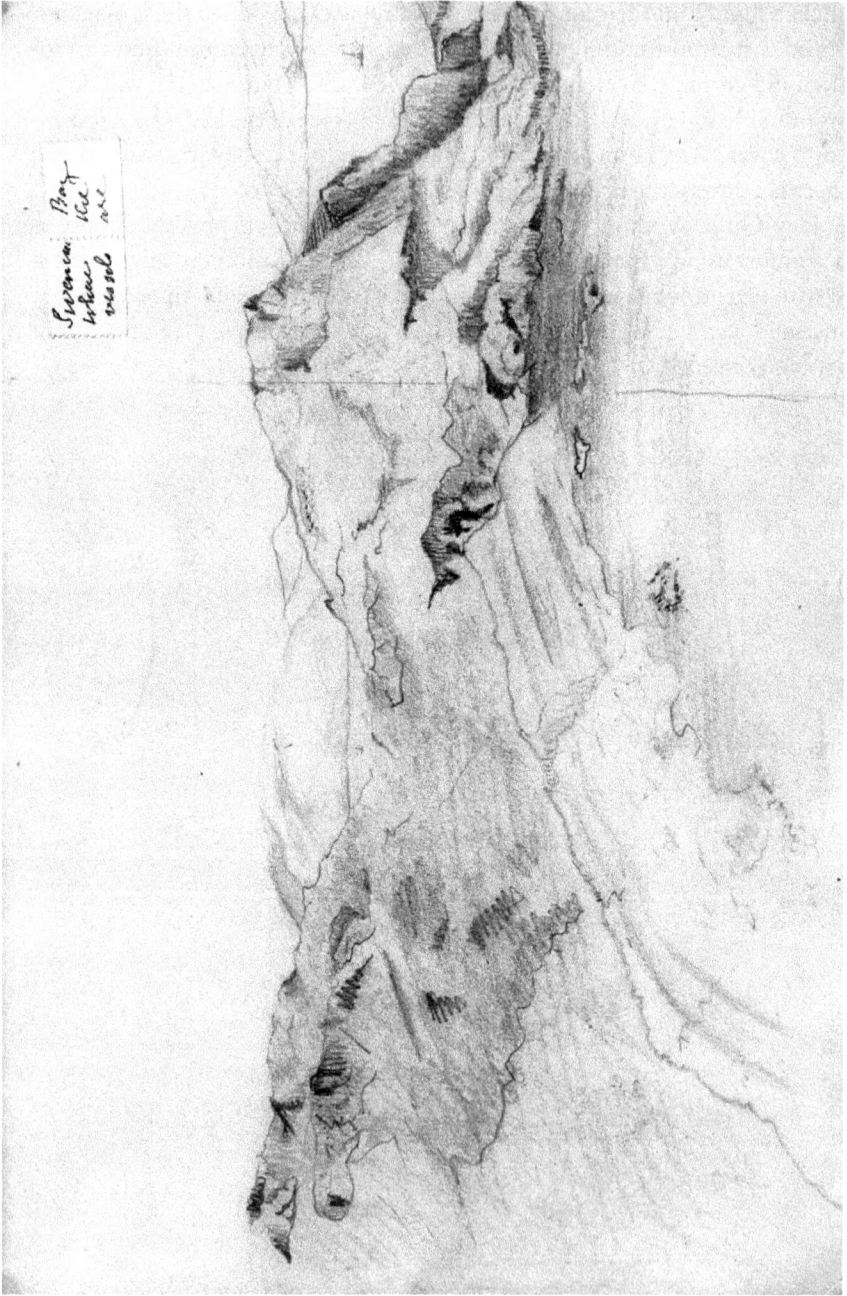

This landscape of Caswell Bay and the Mumbles lighthouse was drawn by F.R.H. in 1854 when she was 17. This was found in an album of several landscape drawings by her, in pencil or black chalk. The lighthouse warned ships of the Mumbles rocks, and Frances would have surely known the analogy of being a lighthouse to show the light of Christ and warn sinners of their danger.

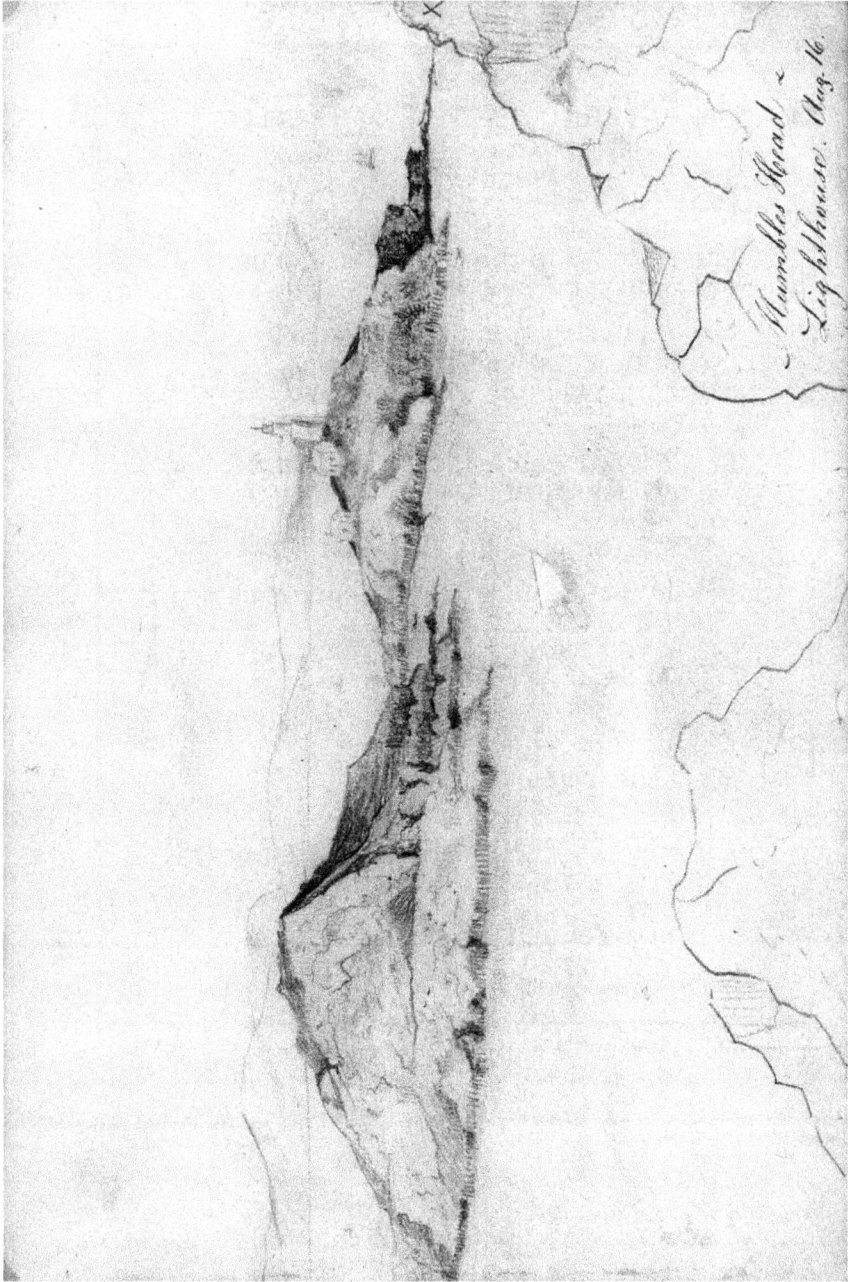

Mumbles Head ~
Lighthouse. Aug. 16.

Twenty-four years later, she moved to Caswell Bay to live with her sister Maria in 1878, having no idea that she would live her last eight months here. Maria wrote of her, "Delighting in all knowledge, she studied the 'Nautical Almanac,' and at the top of the Mumbles lighthouse learnt all that the keeper could tell her."

WHAT THOU WILT.

DO what thou wilt! yes, only do
   What seemeth good to Thee:
Thou art so loving, wise and true,
  It must be best for me.

Send what thou wilt; or beating shower,
  Soft dew, or brilliant sun;
Alike in still or stormy hour,
  My Lord, Thy will be done.

Teach what Thou wilt; and make me learn
  Each lesson full and sweet,
And deeper things of God discern
  While sitting at Thy feet.

Say what Thou wilt; and let each word
  My quick obedience win;
Let loyalty and love be stirred
  To deeper glow within.

Give what Thou wilt; for then I know
  I shall be rich indeed:
My King rejoices to bestow
  Supply for every need.

Take what Thou wilt, beloved Lord,
  For I have all in Thee;
My own exceeding great reward,
  Thou, Thou Thyself shalt be?

FRANCES RIDLEY HAVERGAL.

J. & R. PARLANE, PAISLEY.   Price 3d.   J. NISBET & CO., LONDON.

This was a stiff card-stock board, a placard, with two holes at the top for a ribbon or string, to hang this on a wall, approximately 9.75 inches by 12.25 inches. F.R.H. very nearly died a number of times before her final illness and searingly painful death at forty-two and a half. At different times she had been invalid or extremely ill. Frances wrote this poem November 29, 1878, after much severe illness and a little more than six months before her death.

Chapters learnt by F.R.H.

Genesis. 1. Learnt in Hebrew
        Sept. 1856.
Isaiah. 1. ditto. Aug. 1856
— 4 Learnt. March. 1852.
— 12. Learnt. 1846.
— 35 Learnt 1847.
— 40 Learnt 1849
— 53. Learnt 1846.
— 55. Learnt 1846.
— 63. Learnt 1852.

The Epistle to the Romans.
  Finished learning Dec. 1854
  Relearnt. Nov. 1857,
Galatians, Finished learning
    Feb'y 6th 1858.

Epistle to the Hebrews
  Finished learning Oct. 24. 1857.
Epistle of James
  Finished learning. Nov. 9. 1857.
1st Epistle of Peter
  Finished learning, Nov. 25. 1857.
2nd Epistle of Peter
  Finished learning Dec. 5. 1857.
1st Epistle of St John
  Finished learning Dec. 22. 1857.
2nd Epistle of St John
  Learnt Dec. 24. 1857.
3rd Epistle of John
  Learnt Dec 26 1857.

Epistle of Jude
  Learnt Dec. 30. 1857.

Revelation, chapters 1 — 6
  Learnt July 1852

Many other chapters are
scored with dates, but as it
is not stated that they were
learnt they have not been
added to this list.

This list was found among Havergal manuscripts and papers, likely gathered and written by one of her three sisters. We also know from her sister Maria that F.R.H. memorized all the New Testament except the Book of Acts, all the Minor Prophets, Isaiah, and all the Psalms.

"What things soever ye desire, when ye pray, believe that ye receive them, and ye shall have them."—*Mark xi., 24th ver.*

"But thou, when thou prayest, enter into thy closet, and when thou hast shut the door, pray to thy Father which is in secret; and thy Father which seeth in secret shall reward thee openly."—*Matt. vi. chap., 6th ver.*

Monday .... Pray for ———————
Tuesday ..... ,, ———————
Wednesday ... ,, ———————
Thursday .. ,, ———————
Friday ...... ,, ———————
Saturday .. ,, ———————
Sunday ..... ,, ———————

"It shall be well with them that fear God."—*Eccl. viii., 12th ver.*

"And they shall be Mine, saith the Lord of Hosts, in that day when I make up My jewels.—*Mal. iii, 17th ver.*

"I love them that love Me; and those that seek Me early shall find Me."—*Prov. viii., 17th ver.*

"O satisfy us early with Thy mercy, that we may rejoice and be glad all our days."—*Psal. cx., 14th ver.*

This card was found among Havergal manuscripts and papers.

ADDENDA: 2 BIBLE STUDIES PUBLISHED IN *LETTERS*

These two lessons were published in the volume of *Letters by the Late Frances Ridley Havergal* edited by her sister, Maria V. G. Havergal (London: James Nisbet & Co., 1886), original book pages 272–275, pages 223–224 of Volume IV of the Havergal edition. These are similar to items near the end of *Starlight Through the Shadows* (see pages 560–597 of Volume II of the Havergal edition).

Deuteronomy 28:12: "The Lord shall open unto thee His good treasure."

Lesson I.—*The Good Treasure—The Unsearchable Riches of Christ* (Ephesians 3:8).

I. The Treasure itself. His, not ours, we have nothing, we are "poor" (Revelation 3:17). Consider the Riches of—1. Goodness; 2. Forbearance; 3. Longsuffering (Revelation 2:3); 4. Wisdom; 5. Knowledge (Colossians 2:3); 6. Grace (Ephesians 2:7); 7. Glory (Philippians 4:19), corresponding to our— (1) Sinfulness; (2) Provocations; (3) Repeated waywardness; (4) Foolishness; (5) Ignorance; (6) Spiritual need and weakness; (7) Immortal spirit.

How this treasure is purchased? (2 Corinthians 8:9). For whom?—1. The needy and poor (Revelation 3:17); 2. See context of Deuteronomy 28:12; 3. Christ's (1 Corinthians 3:21–23).

If Christ's, then all are yours.

II. The Promise itself. 1. Our need of the promise "shall open"; we cannot open ourselves: it is the Holy Spirit's office (John 16:14, 15). Some of us can bear witness, "I was blind, now I see," but cannot say Song of Solomon 2:16. Some can say 1 Peter 2:7. Praise Him! 2. The certainty of the promise "*shall* open." Do not say, "I hope He will"; come boldly and claim. Do not say "perhaps" when He says "shall" (Numbers 23:19). Faith is the key to this treasure; God *gives* it, it fits the lock of any promise. The Lord always responds to the claim of faith. He meets you with Matthew 7:7. There is always a promise at the back of everything: Expect and watch for the opening of the lock. (1) If opened to you, it will never be shut again, "He openeth and no man shutteth" (Revelation 3:7); (2) If opened, you will never come to the bottom—the riches are "unsearchable," always "more and more," "incorruptible"; now and through eternity, they are "the fulness of the Godhead." 3. If opened, we shall not care for other things, *e.g.* as they were opened to St. Paul (Philippians 3:8). 4. If opened, draw from it, be spiritual millionaires, use it, trade with it, the responsibility is great (1 Peter 4:10). What will you do with these riches this week?

Dwell on each word "THE LORD"—no human promiser, but God that cannot lie; "*shall*," fling this in Satan's teeth when tempted to doubt or to be negligent in search; "*open*," it is never shut up from you; "*unto thee*," really, personally, not merely to somebody else, or folks in general; "*His*," not yours, all His very own, you had no right or claim to it; "*good*," recollect it is seven-fold, perfection; "*Treasure*" even Jesus Himself, the Treasure of treasures, in all His fulness as your own Saviour, Friend, and King.

Lesson II.—*The Good Treasure.*

I. His Word. *His*; the value of the gift is enhanced by the giver. It is Christ's gift (John 17:14), and the Father's gift to Him (verse 8). *Treasure*; the value is relative and actual. *Relative*, "MORE than gold" (Psalm 19:10; 119:72, 127). If we really find treasure, we are glad (Psalm 119:162; Jeremiah 15:16).

A *test* to apply to ourselves in Psalm 1:2, "delight," and in Jeremiah 6:10, no delight. If there is no rejoicing in it, the treasure is not yet opened to us; this is the work of the Holy Spirit (John 14:26). The answer to the prayer Psalm 119:18 is Jeremiah 33:3. See Christ's own double opening, Luke 24:32, 45.

II. *Actual.* The value of the treasure is proved by what it will do for us. "Do not My words *do good*," etc. What good?
1. We are born again by it (1 Peter 1:23).
2. Growth thereby (Psalm 1:2, 3) in grace and in knowledge (1 Peter 2:2; 2 Peter 3:18).
3. It gives light (Psalm 119:105).
4. It gives understanding.
5. It gives quickening (Psalm 119:50, 93).
6. It gives patience (Romans 15:4).
7. It gives comfort.
8. It gives hope.
9. It keeps from sin (outward) (Psalm 119:11).
10. It sanctifies (inward) (John 17:17).
11. It is profitable for, etc. (2 Timothy 3:15, 16).
12. It is able to save your souls (James 1:21).
13. The climax—by these ye become "partakers of the divine nature" (2 Peter 1:4).

Faith is the key of this treasure (1 Thessalonians 2:13); "worketh" all this "effectually in you that believe" (compare Hebrews 4:2: "Not mixed with faith").

Isaiah 55:11: "My word . . . shall prosper . . . whereto I sent it"—all this!

III. Responsibility attached to the Treasure. The command is Colossians 3:16 (connect 2 Corinthians 4:7). See the promise (Proverbs 8:21), "I will fill their treasures." They *bring forth* out of this good treasure things new and old (Matthew 12:35; 13:52).

ADDENDA: 7 BIBLE STUDY CARDS,
AND BIBLE STUDY OR OUTLINE

This Bible study card for December 30, first Sunday after Christmas, was likely written for December 30, 1877, and was found among Havergal manuscripts and papers, written in her handwriting. After this one, there are six more that were typewritten by her.

Dec 30. 1st Sunday after Xmas [Christmas]. Isa 42
Selected Text. 4th verse. He shall not fail [oe ? illegible] Isa 9.7 & I Cor 15.20. Connect with verse 16 "not forsake" and both with Joshua 1–5. Comp[are] Zeph 3.5. (Present Tense) with Psa[lm] 89.33. & Lam 3.22. Comp[are] Psa 38.10 & Psa 70.1 Josh 23.14 & I Kings 18 [? not sure of writing here] 18.56. Why? Thou art the same & Thy years shall not fail. Heb 1.12. Look out New Test. Fulfillment of the prophecies in verses 1.7 of Xt [Christ]
  Sev illust of the form [illegible] promises in v.16
  [illegible] 1 . John 9.35–38. 2 . Hosea 2–6.14
  3 . Mic 7–8 I Pet 2.9. 4 . Gen 42.36 – 48.11.

[Note: The Greek letter X (chi) is the first letter of the Greek name Χριστόσ, Christ. When F.R.H. (who was either fluent or at least very proficient in reading the Greek New Testament) wrote "Xmas," that was an obvious shorthand for Christmas, and similarly "Xt" meant Christ.]

DEC. 31. MONDAY. ISAIAH 43. SELECTED TEXT, VERSE 2. ''WHEN THOU
PASSEST THROUGH THE WATERS , I WILL BE WITH THEE''. PARALLEL
PROMISE, PSA. 91. 15; CONNECT MATT. 28. 20. & V. 5. LITERAL
FULFILMENTS, EX. 14. 29,30. ISA. 63. 13. JOSH. 3. 17. PSA. 107.
23---30. JONAH 2. 3---6. MATT. 14. 27. ACTS 27. 23. SPIRITUAL
FULFILMENTS, 2 SAM. 22. 5,17. PSA. 32. 6. PSA. 66. 12. COMPARE
PSA. 84. 6. PSA. ZEC. 13. 9. ACTS 14. 22. SEE PSA. 29. 3. &
CANT. 8. 7.

　　　NOTICE IN THIS CHAPTER 10 ~~THONS~~ THINGS THAT GOD HAS DONE FOR US,
& 10 PROMISES OF WHAT HE WILL DO. CONTRAST ALL THESE WITH VERSES
22--24. CONNECT VERSES 3,11, & 25. DEC. 31. MONDVA'
　　　EVENING READING, REVELATION 22. 10---21.

JANUARY 1. TUESDAY. ISAIAH 44.
　　　SELECTED TEXT, V. 23. ''SING , O YE HEAVENS; FOR THE LORD HATH
DONE IT.''I.E., HATH REDEEMED US. THUS WE BEGIN THE NEW YEAR WITH A
NOTE OF PRAISE. PSA. 52. 9. CONNECT JOHN 19.30.''FINISHED'' ;
DEUT. 32.4. ''PERFECT''; & PSA. 111. 3. ''HONOURABLE & GLORIOUS.''
SEE ECC. 3. 14. COMPARE PSA. 22.30,31. WITH ISA. 44. 3 & 17; ''SEE
''SEED'' & ''DONE.'' ''JEHOVAH HATH DONE IT.''SEE V. 6; PSA.
34.22; PSA. 111.9; ISA. 47.4; 63. 17. CHRIST FULFILLED IT; EPH.1.7;
HEB. 9.12; 1 COR. 1.30; 1 PET. 1.18,19.
　　　TAKE THE WORDS ''YET NOW HEAR'' IN V. 1, AS KEYNOTE OF THE CHAPTER,
& LET THE HEART-REPLY BE PSA. 85.8.
　　　CONTRAST ''MY'' & ''THEIR OWN'' IN VERSES 8, 9.
　　　OBSERVE IN THIS & TWO FOLLOWING CHAPTERS HOW OFTEN GOD DECLARES
THAT THERE IS ''NONE BESIDE HIM'' ''NONE ELSE;'' & NOTICE THE CONTEXT
IN EACH CASE.
　　　EVENING READING, MATTHEW 1.

The first two of six Bible study cards which F.R.H wrote with a typewriter.

These six typewritten cards with Bible studies (and also one handwritten card) were found among Havergal manuscripts and papers. Though we definitely do not know the time these were written, they likely were between December 31, 1877 and January 5, 1878, because the typewriter was used, and we have a typewritten manuscript of her poem "The Song of a Summer Stream" which was written February 18, 1879. There is also an extant letter from "The Typewriter Company" in London (dated October 24, 1878, addressed to "Miss Havergal [either Maria or Frances], the Mumbles, Swansea") concerning the typewriter sent to them to be repaired. We do not know the occasion for these six Bible studies, and these six were the only ones found. These cards were typed in all capital letters, and the words written in by hand very much look like F.R.H.'s handwriting. These were almost surely written and typed by Frances.

Dec. 31. Monday. Isaiah 43. Selected text, verses. "<u>When thou passest through the waters, I will be with thee</u>" Parallel promise, Psa. 91.15; connect Matt. 28.20. & v. 5. Literal fulfilments, Ex. 14.29,30. Isa. 63.13. Josh. 3.17. Psa. 107.23–30. Jonah 2.3–5. Matt. 14.27. Acts 27.23. Spiritual fulfilments, 2 Sam. 22.5,17. Psa. 32.6. Psa. 66.12. Compare Psa. 84.6. Psa. [No reference was typed here.] Zec. 13.9. Acts 14.22.   See Psa. 29.3. & Cant. 8.7.

Notice in this chapter [Isaiah 43] 10 things that God has done for us., & 10 promises of what He will do. Contrast all these with verses 23–24. Connect verses 3, 11, & 25.

Evening Reading, Revelation 22. 10–21.

January 1. Tuesday. Isaiah 44.

Selected text, v. 23. "Sing, O ye heavens; for the Lord hath done it." i.e., hath redeemed us. Thus we begin the new year with note of praise. Psa. 52.9. Connect John 19.30. "Finished", Deut. 32.4. "Perfect"; & Psa. 111.3. "Honourable & glorious." See Ecc. 3.14. Compare Psa. 22.30,31. with Isa. 44.3 & 17, "seed" & "done." "Jehovah hath done it." See v.6; Psa. 34.32; Psa. 111.9; Isa. 47.4; 63.17. Christ fulfilled it; Eph. 1.7; Heb. 9.18; I [sic as found typed] Gen. 1.30; I Pet. 1.18,19.

Take the words "Yet <u>now near</u>" in v.1, as keynote of the chapter and let the heart-reply be Psa. 85.8.

Contrast "my" & "their own" in verses 8,9.

Observe in this & the following chapters how often God declares that there is "none beside Him," "none else;" & notice the context in each case.

Evening Reading, Matthew 1.

JAN. 2. WEDNESDAY MORNING. ISAIH 45.
SELECTED TEXT, V.24. ''EVEN TO H IM'' SHALL MEN COME.'' LITERAL FUL-
FILMENT, JOHN 3. 26. TEN INSTANCES IN 8TH & 9TH CHAPTERS OF ST. MATT.
Present fulfilment. THOSE WHOM THE FATHER GIVES , JOHN 6. 37. THE SON DRAWS, JOHN 12.32.
RESULTS OF COMING; 1. ACCEPTANCE, JOHN 6. 37. 2. REST, MATE. 11.28.29.
3. BUILDING UP, 1. PET. 2 2.4. 4. SATISFACTION, JOHN 6. 35. LET US
REPLY WITH JER. 3. 22. FUTURE FULFILMENT. GEN. 49.18. JOHN 6.10,
JOHN 11.52. ISA. 66.6-8. COMPARE JOHN 6. 37.44.45, WITH JOHN 7.37.& REV.
22.17. CONTRAST VERSES 4 & 7. SEAL EACH PROPHECY WITH V.10, & EACH DECLA-
SEE IN THIS CHAPTER , HOW MANY THINGS ARE SAID ABOUT JEHOVAH, WHICH
ARE ELSEWHERE SAID OF JESUS CHRIST.

Evening Reading. Matt. 2.

JAN. 3. THURSDAY MORNING. ISAIAH 46.
SELECTED TEXT, V. 13. ''I BRING NEAR MY RIGHTEOUSNESS''. PARALLEL,
ISA.51. 5. HOW ? 2 COR.5.21. ''NEAR'' TO THOSE THAT ARE ''FAR'', V. 12.
SEE DAN.9.24, ''BRING IN''. ROM. 1.16,17. CONTRAST ISA. 64.6.
CONNECT ISA.45.24, ''HAVE I'', WITH ISA. 61.10, ''HATH CLOTHED'', &
ROM. 3. 22. SEE MATT.5.20, & PHIL. 3.9. CONNECT JER. 23.5. &
I COR. 1.30. OBSERVE ROM. 10.3.
   CONTRAST VERSES 4 & 7. SEAL EACH PROPHECY WITH V.10, & EACH DECLA-
RATION & PROMISE WITH LAST HALF OF V. 11.
   EVENING READING, MATT. 3.

Frances typed these cards, and the penned words are her handwriting. Apparently, when she was not ill and was not short on time, her handwriting was usually clear and beautiful.

Jan. 2. Wednesday morning. Isaiah 45.

Selected text, v.24. "Even to him shall men come." Literal fulfilment. John 3.26. Ten instances in 8th & 9th chapters of St. Matt.

Present Fulfilment. ["Present Fulfilment" was written in by hand, in F.R.H.'s handwriting.]

Those whom the Father gives, John 6.37. The Son draws, John 12.32. Results of coming; 1. acceptance, John 6.37. 2. rest, Matt. 11.28,29. 3. building up, I Pet. 2.3,4. 4. satisfaction, John 6.35. Let us reply with Jer. 3.22. Future fulfillment. Gen. 49.10. John 10.16. John 11.52. Isa. 60.6–8. Compare John 6.37,44,45, with John 7.37. & Rev. 22.17.

See in this chapter how many things are said about Jehovah, which are elsewhere said of Jesus Christ.

Evening Reading. Matt. 2. ["Evening Reading. Matt. 2." was written in hand by F.R.H.]

Jan. 3. Thursday morning. Isaiah 46.

Selected text, v.13. "I bring near my righteousness." Parallel, Isa. 51.5. Now [question mark typed and crossed out] 2 Cor. 5.21. "Near" to those that are "far", v.12. See Dan. 9.24, "bring in". Rom. 1.16,17. Contrast Isa. 64.6. Connect Isa. 45.24, "have I", with Isa. 61.10, "hath clothed", & Rom. 3.22. See Matt. 5.20, & Phil. 3.9. Connect Jer. 23.5 & I Cor. 1.30. Observe Rom. 10.3.

Contrast verses 4. & 7. Seal each prophecy with v.10, & each declaration & promise with last half of v.11.

Evening Reading, Matt. 3.

Jan. 4. Friday morning. Isaiah 47.

Selected text. "Thou that art given to pleasures, that dwellest carelessly." Compare 2 Tim. 3.4, "loving"; I Tim. 5.6, "living in"; Titus 3.3, "serving"; & Luke 8.14, "choked with". See I John 2.17. Contrast "thy pleasures", Psa. 36.8. Job 36.11. * Psa. 16.11. See Zeph. 2.15. Compare Ezek. 16.49. & Prov. 1.32, margin. See Isa. 32.9,10,11. Ezek. 39.6. Contrast "without carefulness", I Cor. 7.32. I Pet. 5.7.

Contrast the threats to Babylon with promises to Zion. E.G. v.1, with Isa. 52.2. v.5, "silent", with ch. 30.29; 35.10; &6. "Darkness", with ch. 60.19. "Shalt no more be called", with ch. 62.4. v.9, "loss of children" with ch. 54.1; 61.9. "widowhood" with ch. 64.4,5. And other contrasts.

Evening Reading, Matt. 4.

JAN. 4. FRIDAY MORNING. ISAIAH 47.

SELECTED TEXT. ''THOU THAT ART GIVEN TO PLEASURES, THAT DWELLEST CARE-
LESSLY.'' COMPARE 2 TIM. 3. 4,''LOVING''; I TIM. 5.6, ''LIVING IN'';
TITUS 3.3, ''SERVING''; & LUKE 8. 14, ''CHOKED WITH''. SEE I JOHN 2.
17. CONTRAST ''THY PLEASURES' , PSA. 36.8. JOB 36.11.& PSA.
16. 9II. SEE ZEPH. 2. 15. COMPARE EZEK. 16. 49. & PROV. 1.
32, MARGIN. SEE ISA. 32.9,10,11. EZEK. 39.6. CONTRAST
''WITHOUT CAREFULNESS'', I COR. 7.32. I PET. 5.7.

CONTRAST THE THREATS TO BABYLON WITH PROMISES TO ZION. E.G. V.1,
WITH ISA.52.2. V.5,''SILENT'', WITH CH.30-29; 35.10; &c. ''DARK-
NESS'', WITH CH.60.19. ''SHALT NO MOREBE CALLED'',WITH CH. 62.4.
V. 9, '''LOSS OF CHILDREN'' WITH CH.54.1; 61.9. ''WIDOWHOOD'' WITH
CH.54.4,5. AND OTHER CONTRASTS.

EVENING READING, MATT. 4.

JAN. 5. SATURDAY MORNING . ISAIAH 48.

SELECTED TEXT, V. 16. ''COME YE NEAR UNTO ME.'' CONTRAST EXOD. 19.
12,21. THEN SEE HEB. 12. 18--24,''YE ARE COME,'' ''TO JESUS.'' SEE
NUM. 16. 5; JER.30.21; & PSA. 65.4. THEN COMPARE NUM. 16.5,7, & LEV.
10.3.; & SEE 2 CHRON. 29.31. TYPES. GEN. 45.4,9,10,18,19. ESTHER
5.2. SEE EPH. 2.14; & PSA. 148.14. THEREFORE HEB. 10.22.

NOTICE GOD'S REASON FOR GIVING PROPHECIES, VS.3--7.

CONTRAST OUR CHARACTER IN V.8.WITH WHAT HE SAYS HE HAS DONE & WILL
DO THROUGH THE REST OF THE CHAPTER.

OBSERVE THE MENTION OF THE THREE PERSONS OF THE HOLY TRINITY IN ONE
CLAUSE OF V.16.

EVENING READING. MATT. 5. 1---16.

The final two of seven Bible study cards.

Jan. 5. Saturday morning. Isaiah 48.

Selected text, v.16. "Come ye near unto me." Contrast Exod. 10.12,21. Then see Heb. 12.18–24. "Ye are come," "to Jesus." See Num. 16.5; Jer. 30.21; & Psa. 65.4. Then compare Num. 16.5,7, & Lev. 10.3.; & see 2 Chron. 29.31. Types. Gen. 45.4,9,10,18,19. Esther 5.2. See Eph. 2.14; & Psa. 148.14. Therefore Heb. 10.22.

Notice God's reason for giving prophecies, vs. 3–7.

Contrast our character in v.8. with what He says He has done & will do through the rest of the chapter.

Observe the mention of the three persons of the holy trinity in one clause of v.16.

Evening Reading. Matt. 5.1–16.

These are comments on the two pages of notes written in F.R.H.'s handwriting, shown on pages 202 and 203 of this book. Frances wrote this in a letter dated October 23, 1878: "Just finishing reading Exodus—so strange and tantalizing that I never get the spiritual enjoyment out of that set of types that I really do out of the historical ones, though I know all the typical points. But Joseph! I am so sorry I touched that type in one or two chapters of *Royal Invitations,* for when reading Genesis four or five weeks back, I thought I should so like to do a little book like *My King or Our Brother,* and work that aspect of Christ with Joseph rather prominent, as David in *My King.*" (in *Letters by the Late Frances Ridley Havergal,* original book page 399, page 259 of Volume IV of the Havergal edition) After her death, a list was found in her desk, entitled "Work for 1879 'If the Lord will.' " (a facsimile copy of the list given on pages 208–209 of Volume III of the Havergal edition), and on the second page of that list she wrote "Our Brother; or Daily Thoughts for those who love Him." Apparently (we do not know with certainty) she was thinking of a 31-day book like the five Royal Books, and apparently (again, we do not know with certainty), these two pages written in Frances' handwriting may have been notes written in preparation for *Our Brother.* Faintly showing from the other side of the paper are typewritten words, so that apparently she wrote these notes on a used or scrap piece of paper. The first page of these notes is on page 202, and the second one is on page 203.

Gen. 27. 29. be lord over thy br.
Gen. 49. 8. Thou art he whom thy br. shall praise
Deu. 17. 15. king — from among br.
Deu. 18. 15 Prophets from among br
I Sam. 17. 17, 18. look how thy brethren fare

Joseph.

Gen. 37. 13. I will send thee unto them c. 45. 5.
— 16. I seek my brethren
— 23 When J. was come unto his b. they stripped J.
42. 7, 8, 23 saw — knew his br. they knew not him
— — they knew not him.
— 21 verily guilty concerning our brother
— 24 — wept & returned & communed
— 35 Thus did he unto them
43. 16 these men shall dine with me
— 30 J. made haste &c
44. 1. as much as they can carry.
45. 1 there stood no man with him while &c
— 3, 5 I am Joseph.
— 7. to save yr lives by a gt deliverance
— 15 after that, his br. talked with him
— 16 fame thereof was heard
— 24 see that ye fall not out
— 26 Jo. is yet alive & is governor
46. 31. I will go up & shew P.
47. 2. presented them unto P.
47. 11 placed his father & br. in the best of the land
& 12. nourished his br
50. 15 — they said, J. will peradventure hate us.
— 21 comforted them & spake kindly

Please read the paragraph at the bottom of page 201 for an explanation of this page
of notes in F.R.H.'s handwriting.

Prov. 17.17. a brother is born for adversity
Pr. 18.24. friend that's sticketh closer
Cant. 8.1 O that's thou wert as my brother
Math. 12.50. the same is my br. & sister
Gen. 4.10. the voice of thy brother's blood
Ex. 28.1. Lev. 21.10. Aaron thy brother (priesthood)
Lev. 25. 35-37. duties to a brother fulfilled
Deut. 15.11. ditto
Lev. 25. 25. redeem that w. thy b. sold.
Lev. 25. 47 — if be — sell himself
Ex. 2.11. Moses ... looked on their burdens
De. 33.24 acceptable to his brethren
Jud. 11.3. fled from his brethren
I Sam. 16.13. anointed him in the midst of br.
1 Sam. 22.1 br. went to him at Adullam
I Ch. 5.22 br. came to comfort him
Ob. 5.3. remnant of his br. shall return
Heb. 2.17 — made like his br.
Ex. 4.18. let me go & return to my br.
I Sam. 30. 23. Ye shall not do so, my br.
II Sam. 19.12 Ye are my br
Pr. 22.22 v Heb. 2.12 I will declare .. unto my br.
Ps. 69.8 I am become a stranger to my br.
Matt. 25.40 done it unto least of these my br.
Matt. 28.10 v John 20.17 — go tell my br.

Please read the paragraph at the bottom of page 201 for an explanation of this page of notes in F.R.H.'s handwriting.

REVELATION 1:7 BEHOLD, HE COMETH.

This manuscript, written in F.R.H.'s handwriting, was found among other Bible studies or outlines, a number of them given at the end of *Starlight Through the Shadows*. Almost certainly this one has never been published until now.

Though she never wanted nor approached any position as "clergy," she prepared studies both for herself and for others to learn and grow. I think that few have had her knowledge of Scripture (others have, but few), and not a head knowledge with pride but from the Lord a heart knowledge with love. Her notes that Maria included at the end of *Starlight Through the Shadows*, especially her notes on the author of Hebrews and on the unity in diversity of Scriptures (pages 593–597 of Volume II of the Havergal edition), are examples, not wholly but partly showing what I mean. Far beyond her memorization (all the New Testament except the Book of Acts, all the Minor Prophets, Isaiah, all the Psalms, and also many other individual chapters, including chapters memorized in Hebrew), I think that she was intimately familiar with every page of Scripture and had a deep, vast knowledge—full of love.

This is an example of what she meant when she wrote of "searching" (searching the Scriptures)—which she so loved to do, and encouraged others to do. Scores of big baskets full can be gathered from examining her personal Bagster study Bible. This Bible has been photographed with a very high quality of resolution, and if the Lord wills, this should be published in its entirety as a facsimile Addendum to the Havergal edition.

F.R.H. loved the Author, and the Scriptures, His own and very words to us. After and from Him, she loved others and wanted them to know Him and to study, search, know His Word.

David Chalkley

Re.1.7. Behold, He cometh. (Ex.14.20.)

I. *Who is coming?* Acts 1.11. John 14.3 - J.
Isa. 52.6. Job 19.27.

Who shall see Him?
Rev 1.7 } Isa. 35.5. } I Cor. 13.12. }
Zech 12.10 } — 33.17. } Isa. 52.8. }

II. *How is He coming?*
1 (With clouds. Rev. 1.7.
2 { — shout - voice of arch. 1 Th. 4.16
3 { — angels Mat. 25.31. "all" Dan 7.10.
4 (— them that sleep. I Thess. 4.14.
1 (In His glory. Ps. 102.16. Mat 25.31. Rev.1.
2 { beauty. Is. 33.17. II Thess 1.10.
beaut. v gt. Is. 4.2.

III. *Why is He coming?*
1 (For judgment Ps. 98.9. II Tim 4.1. II Th.1.7.8.
2 { — Salvation Heb. 9.28. I Pet 1.7-9.
3 (To receive His people I Jo. 14.3.
4 { — reward them Rev 22.13 3 crowns. II Tim 4.8,
Rev. 2.10. I Pet 5.3.

IV. *When is He coming?*
Mark 13.32, 36. I Th. 5.2. John 16.16.

Therefore. II Pet. 3.11. Lu. 12.36,37. I Jo. 2.28.
1 Watching 2 Looking 3 Waiting 4 Loving
Mark 13.35. Tit. 2.13. } I Co.1.7. } II Tim. 4.8.
Ph. 3.20. } II Th. 3.5 }

No difference to us whether Col. 3.4. or I Th. 4.17.
Then. 1 Joy 2 Reunion 3 Likeness
Jo. 16.22 I Th. 4.17 I Jo. 3.2.
Is. 66.5. II Th. 2.1. II Th. 1.10 "in" m.w.
Rev 22.20. Even so, come, Lord Jesus!

F.R.H.'s manuscript of this Bible study or outline.

Revelation 1:7 Behold, He cometh. (Exodus 14:20)

I. *Who* is coming? Acts 1:11 John 14:3 Isaiah 52:6 Job 19:27

> Who shall see Him?
> Revelation 1:7   Isaiah 35:5   1 Corinthians 13:12
> Zechariah 12:10   Isaiah 33:17   Isaiah 52:8

II. *How* is He coming?

> 1. With clouds Revelation 1:7
> 2. With shout, voice of archangel 1 Thessalonians 4:16
> 3. With angels Matthew 25:31 "all" Daniel 7:10
> 4. With them that sleep 1 Thessalonians 4:14
>
> 1. In His glory Psalm 102:16 Matthew 25:31 Revelation 1: [Here Frances did not write the verse. (Possibly verses 6 and 7.)]
> 2. In His beauty Isaiah 33:17 2 Thessalonians 1:10
>   beauty & glory Isaiah 4:2

III. *Why* is He coming?

> 1. For judgement Psalm 98:9 2 Timothy 4:1 2 Thessalonians 1:7, 8
> 2. For salvation Hebrews 9:28 1 Peter 1:7–9
> 3. To receive His people John 14:3
> 4. To reward them Revelation 22:12 — 3 crowns 2 Timothy 4:8
>   Revelation 2:10 1 Peter 5:3 [She meant 5:4.]

IV. *When* is He coming?

Mark 13:32, 36 1 Thessalonians 5:2 John 16:16

Therefore. 2 Peter 3:11 Luke 12:36, 37 1 John 2:28

1 Watching	2 Looking	3 Waiting	4 Loving
Mark 13:35	Titus 2:13	1 Cor. 1:7	2 Timothy 4:8
	Philippians 3:20	2 Thess. 3:5	

No difference to us whether Colossians 3:4 or 1 Thessalonians 4:17.

Then.	Joy	Reunion	Likeness
	John 16:22	1 Thessalonians 4:17	1 John 3:2
	Isaiah 66:5	2 Thessalonians 2:1	2 Thessalonians 1:10 "in "
			[illegible?
			"Greek word"?]

Revelation 22:20. Even so, come, Lord Jesus!

On the following pages is the identically same outline or study with the Scriptures quoted after the references.

Revelation 1:7 Behold, He cometh. (Exodus 14:20)

Exodus 14:20 "And it came between the camp of the Egyptians and the camp of Israel; and it was a cloud and darkness to them, but it gave light by night to these: so that the one came not near the other all the night."

I. *Who* is coming? Acts 1:11 John 14:3 Isaiah 52:6 Job 19:27

Acts 1:11 "Which also said, Ye men of Galilee, why stand ye gazing up into heaven? this same Jesus, which is taken up from you into heaven, shall so come in like manner as ye have seen him go into heaven."

John 14:3 "And if I go and prepare a place for you, I will come again, and receive you unto myself; that where I am, there ye may be also."

Isaiah 52:6 "Therefore my people shall know my name; therefore they shall know in that day that I am he that doth speak: behold it is I."

Job 19:27 "Whom I shall see for myself, and mine eyes shall behold, and not another; though my reins be consumed within me."

> Who shall see Him?
> Revelation 1:7   Isaiah 35:5   1 Corinthians 13:12
> Zechariah 12:10   Isaiah 33:17   Isaiah 52:8

Revelation 1:7 "Behold he cometh with clouds; and every eye shall see him, and they also which pierced him: and all kindreds of the earth shall wail because of him. Even so, Amen."

Zechariah 12:10 "And I will pour upon the house of David, and upon the house of Jerusalem, the spirit of grace and of supplications: and they shall look upon me whom they have pierced, and they shall mourn for him, as one mourneth for his only son, and shall be in bitterness for him, as one that is in bitterness for his firstborn."

Isaiah 35:5 "Then the eyes of the blind shall be opened, and the ears of the deaf shall be unstopped."

Isaiah 33:17 "Thine eyes shall see the King in his beauty: they shall behold the land that is very far off."

1 Corinthians 13:12 "For now we see through a glass, darkly; but then face to face: now I know in part; but then shall I know even as also I am known."

Isaiah 52:8 "Thy watchman shall lift up the voice; with the voice together they shall sing: for they shall see eye to eye, when the Lord shall bring again Zion."

II. *How* is He coming?

1. With clouds Revelation 1:7

Revelation 1:7 "Behold he cometh with clouds . . . ."

2. With shout, voice of archangel 1 Thessalonians 4:16

1 Thessalonians 4:16 "For the Lord himself shall descend from heaven with a shout, with the voice of the archangel, and with the trump of God: and the dead in Christ shall rise first."

3. With angels Matthew 25:31 "all" Daniel 7:10

Matthew 25:31 "When the Son of man shall come in his glory, and all the holy angels with him, then shall he sit upon the throne of his glory."

Daniel 7:10 "A fiery stream issued and came forth from before him: thousand thousands ministered unto him, and ten thousand times ten thousand stood before him: the judgment was set, and the books were opened."

4. With them that sleep 1 Thessalonians 4:14

1 Thessalonians 4:14 "For if we believe that Jesus died and rose again, even so them also which sleep in Jesus will God bring with him."

1. In His glory Psalm 102:16 Matthew 25:31 Revelation 1:

Psalm 102:16 "When the Lord shall build up Zion, he shall appear in his glory."

Matthew 25:31 "When the Son of man shall come in his glory, and all the holy angels with him, then shall he sit upon the throne of his glory."

Revelation 1:   Here Frances did not write the verse. (Possibly verses 6 and 7.)

2. In His beauty Isaiah 33:17 2 Thessalonians 1:10
     beauty & glory Isaiah 4:2

Isaiah 33:17 "Thine eyes shall see the King in his beauty: they shall behold the land that is very far off."

2 Thessalonians 1:10 "And to wait for his Son from heaven, whom he raised from the dead, even Jesus, which delivered us from the wrath to come."

Isaiah 4:2 "In that day shall the branch of the Lord be beautiful and glorious, and the fruit of the earth shall be excellent and comely for them that are escaped of Israel."

III. *Why* is He coming?

1. For judgement Psalm 98:9 2 Timothy 4:1 2 Thessalonians 1:7, 8

Psalm 98:9 "Before the Lord; for he cometh to judge the earth: with righteousness shall he judge the world, and the people with equity."

2 Timothy 4:1 "I charge thee therefore before God, and the Lord Jesus Christ, who shall judge the quick and the dead at his appearing and his kingdom."

2 Thessalonians 1:7, 8 "And to you who are troubled rest with us, when the Lord Jesus shall be revealed from heaven with his mighty angels, in flaming fire taking vengeance on them that know not God, and that obey not the gospel of our Lord Jesus Christ."

2. For salvation Hebrews 9:28 1 Peter 1:7–9

Hebrews 9:28 "So Christ was once offered to bear the sins of many; and unto them that look for him shall he appear the second time without sin unto salvation."

1 Peter 1:7–9 "That the trial of your faith, being much more precious than of gold that perisheth, though it be tried with fire, might be found unto praise and honour and glory at the appearing of Jesus Christ: whom having not seen, ye love; in whom, though now ye see him not, yet believing, ye rejoice with joy unspeakable and full of glory: receiving the end of your faith, even the salvation of your souls."

3. To receive His people John 14:3

John 14:3 "And if I go and prepare a place for you, I will come again, and re-ceive you unto myself: that where I am, there ye may be also."

    4. To reward them Revelation 22:12 — 3 crowns 2 Timothy 4:8
               Revelation 2:10 1 Peter 5:3 [She meant 5:4.]

Revelation 22:12 "And, behold I come quickly; and my reward is with me, to give every man according as his work shall be."

2 Timothy 4:8 "Henceforth there is laid up for me a crown of righteousness, which the Lord, the righteous judge, shall give me at that day: and not to me only, but unto all them also that love his appearing."

Revelation 2:10 "Fear none of those things which thou shalt suffer: behold, the devil shall cast some of you into prison, that ye may be tried; and ye shall have tribulation ten days: be thou faithful unto death, and I will give thee a crown of life."

1 Peter 5:4 "And when the chief Shepherd shall appear, ye shall receive a crown of glory that fadeth not away."

IV. *When* is He coming?

    Mark 13:32, 36 1 Thessalonians 5:2 John 16:16

Mark 13:32 "But of that day and that hour knoweth no man, no, not even the angels which are in heaven, neither the Son, but the Father." Mark 13:36 "Lest coming suddenly he find you sleeping."

1 Thessalonians 5:2 "For yourselves know perfectly that the day of the Lord so cometh as a thief in the night."

John 16:16 "A little while, and ye shall not see me: and again, a little while, and ye shall see me, because I go to the Father."

    Therefore. 2 Peter 3:11 Luke 12:36, 37 1 John 2:28

2 Peter 3:11 "Seeing then that all these things shall be dissolved, what manner of persons ought ye to be in all holy conversation and godliness."

Luke 12:36, 37 "And ye yourselves like unto men that wait for their lord, when he will return from the wedding; that when he cometh and knocketh, they may open unto him immediately. Blessed are those servants, whom the lord when he cometh shall find watching: verily I say unto you, that he shall gird himself, and make them to sit down to meat, and will come forth and serve them."

1 John 2:28 "And now, little children, abide in him; that, when he shall appear, we may have confidence, and not be ashamed before him at his coming."

1 Watching	2 Looking	3 Waiting	4 Loving
Mark 13:35	Titus 2:13	1 Cor. 1:7	2 Timothy 4:8
	Philippians 3:20	2 Thess. 3:5	

Mark 13:35 "Watch ye therefore: for ye know not when the master of the house cometh, at even, or at midnight, or at the cockcrowing, or in the morning."

Titus 2:13 "Looking for that blessed hope, and the glorious appearing of the great God and our Saviour Jesus Christ."

Philippians 3:20 "For our conversation is in heaven; from whence also we look for the Saviour, the Lord Jesus Christ."

1 Corinthians 1:7 "So that ye come behind in no gift; waiting for the coming of our Lord Jesus Christ."

2 Thessalonians 3:5 "And the Lord direct your hearts into the love of God, and into the patient waiting for Christ."

2 Timothy 4:8 "Henceforth there is laid up for me a crown of righteousness, which the Lord, the righteous judge, shall give me at that day: and not to me only, but unto all them also that love his appearing."

No difference to us whether Colossians 3:4 or 1 Thessalonians 4:17 [I infer that she means no difference for those who have died and those who are still living when He comes.]

Colossians 3:4 "When Christ, who is our life, shall appear, then shall ye also appear with him in glory."

1 Thessalonians 4:17 "Then we which are alive and remain shall be caught up together with them in the clouds, to meet the Lord in the air: and so shall we ever be with the Lord."

Then.	Joy	Reunion	Likeness
	John 16:22	1 Thessalonians 4:17	1 John 3:2
	Isaiah 66:5	2 Thessalonians 2:1	2 Thessalonians 1:10 "in"
			[illegible?
			"Greek word"?]

John 16:22 "And ye now therefore have sorrow: but I will see you again, and your heart shall rejoice, and your joy no man taketh from you."

1 Thessalonians 4:17 "Then we which are alive and remain shall be caught up together with them in the clouds, to meet the Lord in the air: and so shall we ever be with the Lord."

2 Thessalonians 2:1 "Now we beseech you brethren, by the coming of our Lord Jesus Christ, and by our gathering together unto him."

1 John 3:2 "Beloved, now are we the sons of God, and it doth not yet appear what we shall be: but we know that when he shall appear, we shall be like him; for we shall see him as he is."

2 Thessalonians 1:10 "And to wait for his Son from heaven, whom he raised from the dead, even Jesus, which delivered us from the wrath to come."

Revelation 22:20. Even so, come, Lord Jesus!

The Lord's Prayer.[1]
"Our Father."

"Our Father" – the Beautiful Gate of this temple. Only if we can say "Our Father," that the rest will be prayer. In one sense God is Father of all –Creation – Preservation. In another not – John 8:42. The former not enough for life or death. Heart craves personal caring, loving: Father. If not – we have made ourselves orphans – sinned – wandered – Luke 15.
The Return – God begins it – sovereignty of call to return. Ephesians 1:4
How? John 1:12. Jeremiah 3:19.
Christ has taken away all obstacles to adoption. Galatians 4:4–7. "that we might receive the adoption."
Holy Spirit seals the adoption. Galatians 4:6. Romans 8:15,17.
The Tokens of Adoption. Galatians 4:6. Hebrews 12:6,7.
Privileges of Adoption. Ephesians 2:18 Romans 8:17. Isaiah 63:16. John 20:17. I John 3:1,2. I Peter 5:7.
Duties of Adoption. I Peter 1:13. &ᶜ [etc.] obedience, love, submission.
Conditions of Adoption. II Corinthians 6:17.
Promise of Adoption. II Corinthians 6:18. Revelation 21:7.

[1] This is a transcription of an important manuscript—in F.R.H.'s handwriting—of her study or lesson on the Lord's teaching on prayer, "Our Father, Who art in heaven," found among her papers. Like all of the Havergal edition, diligent effort has been made here to be precisely faithful to the manuscript, but as this study was written with abbreviations, and apparently as notes primarily or only for Frances herself to use, not prepared for publication, minor changes have been added (such as abbreviated words spelled out fully, and missing periods added for uniformity among the outline points, the niceties that she clearly would have wanted in a published copy); withal, the handwritten text is copied very precisely here.

After years of wanting to include this manuscript study in the edition, but being unable understand the illegible parts of the manuscript (enough illegible to render the text inadequate or inappropriate to publish, though truly valuable to publish), and very near the end of the completion of the edition, Mrs. Trudy Kinloch looked at a copy of the manuscript and was able to understand what was previously indecipherable, graciously and quickly providing the missing parts. Sincere thanks are expressed to her, and also to a colleague who referred me to her, Dr. Digby L. James, whose decades-long research and preparation of *The Complete Works of George Whitefield* is so very valuable, and who has been genuinely kind and helpful to me in the Havergal work since we first met in 2002.

"Which art in heaven." Isaiah 57:15.

"Hallowed be Thy name." illustrate. <u>Follows</u> naturally from <u>Our</u> F. Test of love – gladness at "speaks good of name", pain at contrary. Promise – Malachi 1:11. in full

"Thy Kingdom come"

Three "kingdoms" referred to in various places – avoid confusion –

1. Inward – Luke 17:20,21..
2. Millennial – Jeremiah 23:5, 6.
3. Heavenly – II Timothy 4:18.

I. Inward. <u>What</u> is it? Romans 14:17.
This cannot be without a <u>King</u> – Jesus. Is He <u>our</u> King? Contrast Luke 19:14 with David, Psalm 84.3 "<u>my</u> King".
If King – obedience & subjection. John 14:15 & John 2:6. [F.R.H. likely meant John 2:5 here.] but then I John 5.3.   II Corinthians 10:5.
If King – power &^c all on our side. illus. Abyssinian War. [In 1868, a huge force was sent to rescue a captured missionary, etc.]
Seek – Matthew 6:33.
<u>Are</u> we in? make sure – if not, in kingdom of Satan.

II. Millennial. Psalm 72.4. Revelation 20:6
"Jesus shall reign" &^c [F.R.H. is likely referring to Isaac Watts' hymn "Jesus shall reign where 'man' er the sun doth his successive journeys run."]
Behold thy King cometh. [Zechariah 9:9; Matthew 21:5; John 12:15]
His people share it. Daniel 7:27. II Timothy 2:12.
If He reigns in us now, we reign with Him then.

III. Heavenly. Revelation 11:15. Isaiah 33:17. I Corinthians 15:25,28.

"Thy Will be done".

Generally only thought of in connection with suffering, e.g. I Peter 4:19.
Christ's example. Matthew 26:42.
But Ephesians 5:17. "understanding <u>what</u>".

I. God's will <u>for</u> us. His will as His nature – <u>love</u>. Ephesians 1:5, 6, 11, 12. John 6:39,40. John 17:23,24. Luke 12:32.

II. His will <u>in</u> us. I Thessalonians 4:3. & 5:18.
Sovereignty Daniel 4:35 – cf. [compare] I John 5:14.
Promises – John 17:17. Matthew 7:21.
What makes a † [symbol of cross, possibly or likely shorthand for Christian]
What is His <u>will</u> that we shd [should] <u>do</u>? Ephesians 6:6. I Peter 2:15
Example of doing [His] will. John 4:34. Hebrews 10:7
Hebrews 10:36.   Psalm 103:20-21.
Psalm 143:10.
Hebrews 13:20. [F.R.H. likely also meant Hebrews 13:21.]

"Give us this day"

I. Literal bread. At the Fall curse linked with bread Genesis 3:19 Xt [Christ (from Greek Χριστόσ)] "turned it into blessing". He gave prayer & promises abt [about] it.
<u>Has</u> fulfilled it. Psalm 37.25.
He never taught prayer for riches, bec. [because] not true happiness — Xt's [Christ's] teaching always for our happ. [happiness]. I Timothy 6:9–10. Proverbs 30:8. I Timothy 6:8.
Promises Isaiah 33:16. I Peter 5:7. Matthew 6:25-34. Philippians 4:19.
Crowns all with Exodus 23:25.
Jesus <u>hungered</u>. [Matthew 4:2]

II. Spiritual bread. 1. The Word. Deuteronomy 8:3. Matthew 4:4. Jeremiah 15:16.
    2. Christ. John 6.33-35.
Bread – sustains life – gives strength.
Whatever can be done without, bread can't [bread can't be done without].
Must be <u>eaten</u> & become part of ourselves. Canticles [Song of Solomon] 5:1.
Hunger. Luke 15:17. Matthew 5:6.
Promises Joel 2:26. Isaiah 65:13. Luke 2:53. [This was a mistake, and F.R.H. almost certainly meant Luke 1:53.] Revelation 7:16,17.

"Forgive us" &ˢ

Exodus 34:6–7. Psalm 130:4.
Psalm 32:1.

Psalm 103:3,12. Micah 7:18–19.
Isaiah 1:18. & 44:22. & 55:7.
Jerermiah 31:34 & Hebrews 8:12.   Daniel 9:9.
Acts 5:31. 10:43. 13:38.   Colossians 1:14.
Mark 2:5. I John 2:12.
    Proverbs 28:13. Mark 1:4.
       Hosea 14:1–4.

Proverbs 19:16. Matthew 18:21–35. Mark 11:25.
Luke 6:37. & 17:4.   Ephesians 4:32.
Colossians 3:13.

"Lead us not" &^c

Temptation – 1. Different for each.
    2. Repeated (Hebrews 12:1) or Varied.
    3. Open or Subtle.

I. From Satan for ill. James 1:13. I Chronicles 1:21. [This looks like Chr., especially when compared with reference to Chr on the next manuscript page, but contextually I Chronicles 1:21 does not mention temptation; neither does I Corinthians 1:21. This was likely a slip of the pen. F.R.H. may possibly or likely have meant II Chronicles 21:1.] Matthew 26:41. I Corinthians 10:13. James 4:7. I Peter 5:8. Ephesians 6:11–15.

II. From God for good (trial.) II Chronicles 32:33. [This is another human mistake in F.R.H.'s notes. The Scripture that she was thinking of has not yet been found.] Genesis.22:1. [surely referring to all of Genesis 22:1–19] & Hebrews 11:17. Deuteronomy 8:2. Job 23:10. Zechariah 9:13. I Peter 1:6,7. I Peter 4:12.
Christ tempted – 1. – By Satan Matthew 4 & Luke 4.   2.– By wicked men. Matthew 16:1 & 22:35 &^c &^c.   Manifold – Luke 22:28. Hebrews 2:18. & 4:15.
Promise James 1:12. Rom. 8:35–37.

[The manuscript was left incomplete, ending with Romans 8:35–37. This is an example—a glimpse—of F.R.H.'s "searching the Scriptures." Her poem "Thine Is the Power" is given on the next two pages, 218–219.]

Thine is the Power.

Our Father, our Father, who dwellest in light,
We lean on Thy love, and we rest on Thy might;
In weakness and weariness joy shall abound,
For strength everlasting in Thee shall be found:
Our Refuge, our Helper in conflict and woe,
Our mighty Defender, how blessed to know
        That Thine is the Power!

Our Father, Thy promise we earnestly claim,
The sanctified heart that shall hallow Thy name,
In ourselves, in our dear ones, throughout the wide world,
Be Thy name as a banner of glory unfurled;
Let it triumph o'er evil and darkness and guilt,
We know Thou canst do it, we know that Thou wilt,
        For Thine is the Power!

Our Father, we long for the glorious day
When all shall adore Thee, and all shall obey.
Oh hasten Thy kingdom, oh show forth Thy might,
And wave o'er the nations Thy scepter of right.
Oh make up Thy jewels, the crown of Thy love,
And reign in our hearts as Thou reignest above,
        For Thine is the Power!

Our Father, we pray that Thy will may be done,
For full acquiescence is heaven begun;—
Both in us and by us Thy purpose be wrought,
In word and in action, in spirit and thought;
And Thou canst enable us thus to fulfil,
With holy rejoicing, Thy glorious will,
        For Thine is the Power!

Our Father, Thou carest; Thou knowest indeed
Our inmost desires, our manifold need;
The fount of Thy mercies shall never be dry,
For Thy riches in glory shall mete the supply;

Our bread shall be given, our water be sure,
And nothing shall fail, for Thy word shall endure,
        And Thine is the Power!

Our Father, forgive us, for we have transgressed,
Have wounded Thy love, and forsaken Thy breast;
In the peace of Thy pardon henceforth let us live,
That through Thy forgiveness we too may forgive;
The Son of Thy love, who hath taught us to pray,
For Thy treasures of mercies hath opened the way,
        And Thine is the Power!

Thou knowest our dangers, Thou knowest our frame,
But a tower of strength is Thy glorious name;
Oh, lead us not into temptation, we pray,
But keep us, and let us not stumble or stray;
Thy children shall under Thy shadow abide;
In Thee as our Guide and our Shield we confide,
        For Thine is the Power!

Our Father, deliver Thy children from sin,
From evil without and from evil within,
From this world, with its manifold evil and wrong,
From the wiles of the Evil One, subtle and strong;
Till, as Christ overcame, we, too, conquer and sing,
All glory to Thee, our victorious King,
        For Thine is the Power!

Our Father, Thy children rejoice in Thy reign,
Rejoice in Thy highness, and praise Thee again!
Yea, Thine is the kingdom, and Thine is the might,
And Thine is the glory transcendently bright;
For ever and ever that glory shall shine,
For ever and ever that kingdom be Thine,
        For Thine is the Power!

                          F.R.H. May 14, 1872

These are the title pages of the original small book Treasure Trove.

First Morning.

How extremely beautiful the context is in 2 Peter i.4, "Whereby are given unto us exceeding great and precious promises; that by these ye might be partakers of the divine nature." One often hears the "exceeding great and precious promises" quoted, but I am so delighted with what follows, "that *by these* ye might be partakers of the divine nature." As I take it, that dwelling on God's promises is not merely to be *enjoyment*, but that by their inherent power, the very dwelling on and accepting them shall make us partakers of the divine nature, of that holiness for which one longs afar off. It is virtually the same idea as "purifying their hearts by faith", (Acts xv. 9; also 1 John iii. 3), only it is so clearly and magnificently expressed by St. Peter. Oh that His promises were always present with us!

8

First Evening.

St. Paul's Seven Desires in Phil. iii. 8-10.

That I may—

1. Win Christ.
2. Be found in Him.
3. Have God's righteousness.
4. Know Him.
5. Know the power of His resurrection.
6. Know the fellowship of His sufferings.
7. Be made conformable to His death.

9

Similar, fine artwork was done throughout the original volume Treasure Trove.

Treasure Trove.

Extracts
From Unpublished Letters
And Bible Notes.

by
F. R. HAVERGAL.

Compiled by
FRANCES A. SHAW.

LONDON:
JAMES NISBET & CO.

O JESUS CHRIST, my Master,
   I come to Thee to-day;
I ask Thee to direct me
   In all I do or say.
I want to keep my promise,
   To be Thy servant true;
I come to Thee for orders,
   Dear Lord, what shall I do?
I want a heart not heeding
   What others think or say;
I want an humble spirit
   To listen and obey.
To serve Thee without ceasing,
   'Tis but a little while,
My strength, the Master's promise;
   My joy, the Master's smile.
O precious Lord and Master,
   I want to hear Thy voice,
Enduing me with power
   And bidding me rejoice;
That while Thou still dost tarry,
   I faithful may be found;
With lamp all trimmed and burning,
   I wait the trumpet's sound.

Preface.

WHAT glad surprise or gleams of joy are experienced as we recover lost jewels, or unearth some buried glories of the past; or as some new truth or thought bursts upon the mind, and we exclaim, "Treasure Trove!" And how fondly sometimes do the words pass our lips as we light upon some treasured memorials or words of a departed friend. Is there not a type of this last pleasure to be found when, as we stroll "among familiar things, and watch their lowly guise," we see the bright, tender leaves of the wood-sorrel springing from the surrounding sere[1], funereal leaves, gladdening us as life from among the dead?

> "The white-robed Alleluia[2] flowers
> Which spring from 'neath the sod
> Are voiceless—yet each leaflet gives
> Glory and praise to God."

Believing that my dear Sister's (F.R.H.) wealth of thought, and words of wisdom, which many have found to be "as choice silver," were given to her by Him who "gives to the righteous much treasure," and "fills the treasuries of those that love Him" (Proverbs 8:21, R.V.), it has been felt right to accede to the request to gather up some fragments that remain. They have been collected by my daughter Frances. May these rescued fragments give glory to God by yielding gladness and refreshment to some of His children; and if they should lead some to seek "treasure in Heaven," it will accord with some of her prayers, who "being dead, yet speaketh" by them:

> "O brother,
> Save by the rainbow arch of prayer to One
> Who draws our dewdrop longings up, to pour

---

[1] sere: dried, withered   [2] The wood-sorrel is called "Alleluia" by the Italians.

Their sparklets with His own rich blessing shower,
My voice may never reach thee."

(Unpublished fragment by F. R. H.)

Those who rejoice in the Word will be interested to know that the Evening portions in this little book are chiefly taken from F. R. H.'s own Bible.

Ellen P. Shaw.

Winterdyne, 1886.

First Morning.

How extremely beautiful the context is in 2 Peter 1:4, "Whereby are given unto us exceeding great and precious promises; that by these ye might be partakers of the divine nature." One often hears the "exceeding great and precious promises" quoted, but I am so delighted with what follows, "that *by these* ye might be partakers of the divine nature." As I take it, that dwelling on God's promises is not merely to be *enjoyment,* but that by their inherent power, the very dwelling on and accepting them shall make us partakers of the divine nature, of that holiness for which one longs afar off. It is virtually the same idea as "purifying their hearts by faith" (Acts 15:9; also 1 John 3:3), only it is so clearly and magnificently expressed by St. Peter. Oh that His promises were always present with us!

First Evening.

St. Paul's Seven Desires in Philippians 3:8–10.

That I may—
1. Win Christ.
2. Be found in Him.
3. Have God's righteousness.
4. Know Him.
5. Know the power of His resurrection.
6. Know the fellowship of His sufferings.
7. Be made conformable to His death.

Second Morning.

I have been dwelling on the *six* beautiful promises contained in Jeremiah 17:8, the developments of the "Blessed" in verse 7. Each is so full of significance—do you happen ever to have dwelt on them specially? The last "shall *not cease* from yielding fruit," carries it on into the endless fruit-bearing to the Master's praise in eternity, when "His servants shall serve Him," as they never can here.

Second Evening.

We would see Jesus! now by faith we may "see the Son" (John 6:40) yet only "through a glass darkly." Do not dwell on this to-day, but on the absolute certainty that we *shall* see Him, and the joy that this will be to those who love Him. Of the certainty of this let the Creed every Sunday remind you. His coming will not be the same to all. Look at Zechariah 12:10, Revelation 1:7, Matthew 25:41, and Numbers 24:17, also Isaiah 66:5, and 2 Thessalonians 1:7–10.

Third Morning.

I must tell you how glad it makes me to know that you have given yourselves to Jesus, or rather that He has *taken* you for Himself. You don't half know yet what a treasure you have, but you will find out day by day how sweet it is to trust Jesus, and how much He is able to do for you. When we find a new friend we don't know all about him at once, but as we find him loving us, saying beautiful things to us, doing us all sorts of kindnesses, helping us in all sorts of difficulties, then, as time goes on, we prove his value. So, only lean, and cling, and trust, and you will find out day by day *what* a friend you have found in Jesus.

Third Evening.

{ "Put on the whole armour of God."—Ephesians 6:11.
{ "Put on the Lord Jesus Christ."—Romans 13:14.
Ephesians 6:14. "Truth." John 14:6.
Ephesians 6:14. "Righteousness." Jeremiah 23:6.
Ephesians 6:15. "Peace." Ephesians 2:6.
Ephesians 6:16. "Faith." Hebrews 12:2.
Ephesians 6:17. "Word of God." John 1:1.
Thus to put on the armour is to put on Christ.

Fourth Morning.

It is Jesus, our Saviour, who is the ever fresh glory within us. It is the Holy Spirit, our Comforter, who shall pour His fresh oil upon us. With such resources ought we not to refresh those around us? Ought they not to take knowledge of us that we have such a well of water within us, springing up into eternal life? Ought there not to be a dewy fragrance in our lives, in our words and ways, that may silently witness to the reality of the source of our freshness? It is one of our special privileges to do this.

Fourth Evening.

"*My* sheep hear *My* voice, and I give unto them—" John 10:27, 28.

"My peace." John 14:27.
"My love." John 15:10.
"My joy." John 15:11.
"My grace." 2 Corinthians 12:9.
"My strength." 2 Corinthians 12:9.
"My rest." Hebrews 4:3.
"My glory." John 17:22–24.
"All are yours."

Fifth Morning.

"We will remember Thy love more than wine" (Song of Solomon 1:4), has always been my special favourite, taken with "Thou meetest them that remember Thee" (Isaiah 64:5), and illustrated by 2 Samuel 1:26, "Thy love to me was wonderful." Connect with this, "The desire of our soul is to Thy name and to the remembrance of Thee" (Isaiah 26:8), and compare Song of Solomon 1:6, "Look not upon me" with "Look upon the face of Thine anointed" (Psalm 84:9). Also compare Song of Solomon 1:2, 4 with ch. 4:10, which is the wonderful response of the Bridegroom. But the whole chapter is a constellation!

Fifth Evening.

Two fears about consecration.
1st. That we shall not be able to keep it up.
2nd. That we don't know what it may involve, are met by—
1st. "Thou shalt abide," and
2nd. "*I* also for thee."
Two motives for consecration.
1st. That He commands "Thou shalt abide *for Me.*"
2nd. That He has been, is, and shall be for us, "I—also—*for—thee.*" Hosea 3:3.

Sixth Morning.

Exodus 3:7 is a verse of intensest comfort. The climax in it has struck me as corresponding to three degrees of sorrow. That which can be *seen* is the lightest form really, however apparently heavy. That which is not seen, secret, private sorrow, which yet can be put into words, and told to near friends as well as poured out to God, comes next. But there are sorrows beyond these, which are not told to any one, which cannot be expressed in words, but only wordlessly laid before God—these are the deepest. Now comes the "supply" for each. "I have *seen*" that which is patent and external; "I have *heard* their cry," which is the expression of this and of as much of the internal as is expressible ; but this would not go deep enough, so God adds : " I *know* their sorrows " down be the very depths of all.

Sixth Evening.

"Touched with the feeling of our infirmities." Hebrews 4:15. John 4:6. "Wearied." Matthew 11:28. " Come to me—rest." John 4:7. "Thirsty." John 7:37. " Come to me—drink." John 4:8. "Hungry." John 6:35. "Cometh to me—never hunger." " Moved with compassion." Matthew 9:36.

Seventh Morning.

I must pass on to you the last specially "sent" text I have been enjoying : Exodus 15:13. What can one want more ?—" Led forth—in Thy mercy," and "guided—in Thy strength," and " Thou " hast done it, and it is "*Thy*" mercy and strength all along. " Sweet is Thy mercy," " Great is Thy mercy." And then the " hast redeemed " as to the past and perfect, and the " holy habitation " of the present (Psalm 91:1) and the future, from both of which we shall " go no more out." It is a very *chime* to me.

Seventh Evening.

"The sheep follow him." John 10:4.
" Immediately." Matthew 4:22.
" Hard." Psalm 63:8.
" Wholly." Joshua 14:8, 9.
" Whithersoever." Revelation 14:4. Matthew 8:19, 23.
" Continue." 1 Samuel 12:14.
" His steps." 1 Peter 2:21.
" Fully." Numbers 14:24.
" Follow thou me." John 21:22. Matthew 16:24.
Contrast " afar off." Luke 22:54.

EIGHTH MORNING.

PHILIPPIANS 2:12, 13, seems to me clearly to imply that those to whom St. Paul wrote had got salvation as an actual possession, "*your own,*" and, having got it, they are to work it out, carry out all the details and consequences of it, act up to it. Give a man a great gold mine, he has not got to work for it, it is his very own, he only has to work out the gold, to draw upon it, and enjoy it. I think the figure holds good, for enjoyment seems to hold an almost invariable proportion to work for Christ. I never knew any idle Christian really a rejoicing one (I do not speak of invalids), and conversely, if you see any one doing *all* they can, giving up time to work for Christ, you may be almost certain that they are happy in Christ.

EIGHTH EVENING.

I *know* this rest of faith to be a blessed life beyond what I thought possible on earth—the Master has astonished me with what I have proved Him willing and able to do for me, and so I long for all hindrances to be removed from others, so that more and more may " taste and see."

NINTH MORNING.

I DO think that these Mission weeks are just the counteractive needed for all the worldly tendencies of the day—so few are really living as if there really were eternal things *certainly* before them. "The things which are seen "—"temporal" though they are—fill up the whole foreground, and hide the tremendous background of eternity. And as for "amusing" folks in order to get good influence, it is worse than going to London round by Land's End. Sweet words about Jesus, clear and direct and fervent, will make more glad hearts than all the entertainments in the world.

Ninth Evening.

O come to Me, ye weary,
    And lean upon My breast!
O come, ye heavy laden,
    And I will give you rest!
Take but My yoke upon you,
    And learn of Me, your Lord,
For I am meek and lowly
    In heart, as well as word.
And then your souls shall surely
    Find rest from every care,
For My yoke is very easy,
    And My burden light to bear.

1854.

Tenth Morning.

If we believe, let us therefore speak much to our God for every one to whom we would speak of Him. Does He anywhere set any limit to expectant prayer except His will? And "He willeth not the death of a sinner." What unknown blessings we may have lost by restraining prayer! What unknown blessings may be granted us only for the asking! Pray especially that God would pour "the spirit of grace and of supplication" on us. Then how many prayers will be transmuted into praise! Let us look forward not merely with hope, but with expectation, believing that not we alone, and not the angels only, but our beloved Master Himself, will rejoice and be very glad over those, for whom we pray.

Tenth Evening.

Lists of names (1 Chronicles 1) suggest God's intimate knowledge of individual men and women; no member of any one's family forgotten by Him. Genealogies *not* recorded are still known to Him. These lists also prompt inquiry as to the history of those mentioned elsewhere—recollections arise at the mention of a single name.

ELEVENTH MORNING.

THE feather that wings our arrow must be LOVE, and if love be real it will be seen and felt. It flows spontaneously to some, but how shall we command it for all whom we would reach? Only believe the Word—"He died for all." Realise that Jesus so loved them that He died for them, and you will catch your Master's spirit, and speak with that winningness which love alone can give.

ELEVENTH EVENING.

"MY GOD shall supply all your need." Philippians 4:19.

Need of	Felt	Supplied
Pardon.	Psalm 130:3.	Psalm 130:4.
Cleansing.	Job 9:30, 31.	1 John 1:7.
Faith.	Mark 9:24.	Hebrews 12:2.
Grace.	Romans 7:18, 19.	2 Corinthians 12:9.
Guidance.	Jeremiah 10:23.	Psalm 32:8.
Temporals.	Matthew 6:32.	Matthew 6:33.
Strength.	Psalm 38:10.	Isaiah 26:4.
Patience.	Hebrews 10:36.	Romans 5:3.
Comfort.	Psalm 88:3.	Isaiah 66:13.
Love.	Song of Solomon 5:6.	John 15:9.
The Spirit.	John 3:8.	Luke 11:13.
Christ.	John 15:5.	John 14:23.
God Himself.	Job 23:3.	Hebrews 13:5.

Psalm 23:1 and Psalm 84:11.

TWELFTH MORNING.

WHAT do we believe? "The glorious Gospel of Christ!" A true belief in this is no light thing. Could we sever it from our hearts, what would be left but a very death in life? However feeble, it is *precious* faith. What is the practical result for others? We meet with those who have not "like precious faith," and we are content to speak only of what is nothing worth. Yet each is in the danger from which we have fled, each has the same soul needs.

TWELFTH EVENING.

LUKE 24:10, "Told these things unto the Apostles." Compare 2 Kings 7:9 (The lepers "said one to another ... now therefore come, that we may go and tell the king's household"); and then Luke 24:31, "Their eyes were opened," the first illustration of John 16:7. They had the joy of telling *others,* and *then* that of the re-appearance of Jesus.

THIRTEENTH MORNING.

CONSCIENCE will tell us that we do not want more opportunities so much as grace to see and use those which are continually given. Can we count the lost ones? Yet our Master noted each as it passed. It may be that a sense of coldness and sin is heavy upon us, and we hardly dare to speak of truths which have so little power over ourselves. Yet it does not say "we *feel,* and therefore speak," but "we believe." Could we say we do *not* believe? or quietly endure to hear our Saviour's name and work denied? Even in our suffering we may tell a fellow-sufferer of a cure; and while laying their case before the great Physician, we shall find He is nearer than we thought, and that His healing hand is laid upon us. "The Lord turned the captivity of Job when he prayed for his friends."

THIRTEENTH EVENING.

CHRIST'S CALL.
"Come and see." John 1:39.
"Come unto me." Matthew 11:28.
"Come holy." Isaiah 1:18.
"Come out." 2 Corinthians 6:17.
"Come apart." Mark 6:31.
"Come with me." Song of Solomon 4:8.
"Come, ye blessed." Matthew 25:34.

OUR ECHO.
"Come and see." John 1:46.
"Come and let us return." Hosea 6:1.
"Come speedily." Zechariah 8:21.
"Come into His courts." Psalm 96:8.
"Come, let us join." Jeremiah 50:5.
"Come with us." Numbers 10:29.
"Come, Lord Jesus." Revelation 22:20.

FOURTEENTH MORNING.

How nice the last verse of 2 Chronicles 2:18 is,—connected with Mark 13:34. "To every man his work,"—the three great divisions—"bearers of burdens," "hewers," and "overseers to set the people to work." Are you not glad of the *first?* You see they were just as much workers as the others!

FOURTEENTH EVENING.

"AARON and his sons shall go in, and appoint them every one to his service and to his burden."

Numbers 4:19.	Acts 9:6, 16.
Ephesians 2:10.	Revelation 2:10.
Mark 13:34.	1 Corinthians 12:18.
1 Thessalonians 4:11.	Matthew 25:15.
2 Chronicles 2:18.	1 Corinthians 3:8.
Nehemiah 3:28.	Galatians 6:5.

FIFTEENTH MORNING.

GOD prepares the worker for his work, and vice versa, see Luke 1:15, 17, 41, 67; he is not sent to work alone. John was sent "in the spirit and power of Elias," we "in the strength of the Lord GOD." Psalm 71:16.

The whole life of Christ was in the power of the Holy Ghost. Matthew 1:20, Hebrews 9:14. *Every* gift, grace, and power in Him,—in His members one has this, another that. Luke 2:25–27, gives us a glimpse of the Holy Spirit's work, Simeon "taught" and "led" by the Spirit.

Lake is the only Evangelist who connects prayer with the outpouring of the Spirit; see Luke 3:21, 22 and Luke 11:13. There was *indwelling* before. Perhaps we may see the shadow of this double work of the Spirit in the meat offering.

Fifteenth Evening.

References to Isaiah 22:21–24.

Verse 21.—See Revelation 1:13. John 5:22. Isaiah 9:6.

Verse 22.—Revelation 3:7, 8. Job 12:14. Matthew 25:10, "open,"
1 Corinthians 16:9. Ephesians 2:18. 2 Corinthians 2:12. Colossians 4:3, "Thou hast opened the kingdom of heaven," etc.

Verse 23.—Ezra 9:8. Zechariah 10:4. Acts 5:31. Luke 1:32. Luke
22:29. Revelation 3:20.

Verse 24.—Ezekiel 15:3. John 17:22. Revelation 5:12, 13. 2
Timothy 2:20.

For parallel to Shebna (Isaiah 22:15) and Eliakim see Jeremiah
22:28, Coniah "the Branch."

Sixteenth Morning.

"And the King shall answer and say unto them, Verily I say
unto you, Inasmuch as ye have done it unto one of the least of
these My brethren, ye have done it unto Me." I send you this, and
I want you to let it brighten all your work. Perhaps you do already
work in the light of it, but one can never come to the end of the
graciousness of "Inasmuch."

Sixteenth Evening.

"The things which are Jesus Christ's." Philippians 2:21.

"Above."	"On the earth."
Colossians 3:1, 2.	Colossians 3:2.
"Of the Spirit."	"Of the flesh."
Romans 8:5.	Romans 8:5.
"Heavenly."	"Earthly."
John 3:12.	Philippians 3:19.
"Before."	"Behind."
Philippians 3:13.	Philippians 3:13.
"That are God's."	"That are of the world."
Mark 12:17.	1 John 2:15.

"Seen and not seen."   2 Corinthians 4:18.
"Own and others."   Philippians 2:4.
"That please Me."   Isaiah 56:4.
"That belong to the Lord."   1 Corinthians 7:32.
"Old and new."   2 Corinthians 5:17.

SEVENTEENTH MORNING.

DESPISED, rejected, wounded now,
Bowed 'neath a cross of shame,
With visage marred, with bleeding brow,
Know ye the sufferer's name?

O Man of Sorrows!—Is this He
Who human form should wear,
And with transgressors numbered be,
Our mighty sins to bear?

O Son of God, who unto death
Hast loved, so lovèd me,
Henceforth be all my life and breath
Devoted unto Thee.

SEVENTEENTH EVENING.

REFERENCES to Isaiah 53:1–6.
Verse 1.—Matthew 11:25.
Verse 2.—Zechariah 6:12, Luke 2:52. Isaiah 4:2. John 9:29.
Verse 3.—1 Peter 2:4. Isaiah 49:7. John 1:11. Hebrews 12:2. Psalm 69:8.
Verse 4.—Exodus 3:7. Isaiah 63:9. 2 Samuel 17:2.
Verse 5.—Galatians 2:20. Genesis 3:15. Colossians 1:20. 1 Chronicles 21:17. Exodus 15:26. Jeremiah 17:14.
Verse 6.—Isaiah 57:17, 18. Isaiah 63:3. Jeremiah 8:6. Jeremiah 50:6. Ezekiel 33:11. Ezekiel 4:5. Proverbs 14:12.

EIGHTEENTH MORNING.

YOUR present prospects are sombre. Only, are you not anticipating God's providence in what you say about looking forward to anything but a *happy life?* Life is a long thing; you must not think, because a cloud rests upon your present years, that your life *taken as a whole* may not be a happy one. We do not know what pleasant things God may have in store for you. You are not called on to submit to *future dispensations,* only to present ones. Leave coming years with Him. He knows them, you do not. And as the future gradually becomes the present, God will be an ever-present God. We have not grace enough for any more than "to-day," and the particular sort of grace which we fancy we shall need to-morrow, may not be called for, not put to any strain.

Eighteenth Evening.

Isaiah 41:10, 13. "Yea, I will uphold thee with *the right hand* of my righteousness." "I the LORD thy God will hold *thy* right hand,"—this implies being face to face!
Isaiah 41:17, "promises to the needy." See also
Isaiah 14:30. "Safety."
Isaiah 25:4. "Strength."
Psalm 40:17. "God thinks upon them."
Philippians 4:19. "God supplies all need."

Nineteenth Morning.

I know well enough by experience that one cannot help oneself, but I do know also what power our Lord has over our thoughts when committed to Him, and how wonderfully He can make a way of escape for us. So I want you to lay the matter very simply before the Lord. Tell Him all that is in your heart, every bit of it. Then ask Him to "undertake" for you. Ask Him just to order everything, if it is His will (if it is His will at all), and to keep you very calm till His will *is* clearly shown, and very willing that He should take His own way with you and your life.

Nineteenth Evening.

The Great Temptations.
"Great temptations." Deuteronomy 29:3.
"Great terrors." Deuteronomy 4:34.
"Great troubles." Psalm 71:20.
"Great waters." Psalm 144:7.

Contrast.
"Great power." Exodus 32:11.
"Great mercies." Isaiah 54:7.
"Great deliverance." Genesis 45:7.
"Great love." Ephesians 2:4. Song of Solomon 8:7.

Twentieth Morning.

You speak of being "tempted to rebel at the answers to your prayers." I know that so well, having found how true in some such things it is that "ye know not what ye ask." Yet it is, I think, only temptation, for still one's heart, though sorely shaken, is fixed, and one is quite sure that we would not unsay or recall those prayers if we could, though their fulfilment prove to be at the time not joyous but grievous.—That is, one would not deliberately do so; the reed may be shaken in the wind of trouble, but that is a very different thing from uprooting it.

Twentieth Evening.

"Behold, upon the face of the wilderness there lay a small round thing." Exodus 16:14. "Round," Hebrew divested of its covering. Query, is this a type of Christ? Philippians 2:7, 8, compare John 13:3, where Jesus, the true manna, feeds His disciples, lays aside His garments, and teaches them humility.

Twenty-first Morning.

Sometimes the very fact of trial being sent for which one cannot appeal for general sympathy, and which one must bear alone, seems to give one all the stronger claim upon Christ's sympathy. May I send you a text from which I have found comfort and rest, when there seemed nothing else to comfort? "Be still, and know that I am God." That seems to go to the very root of everything, hushing down questioning, quieting forebodings, stilling vain efforts, bringing patience and strength as we listen to that solemn "Be still"—*His* word to the troubled heart, and *therefore* full of power. Again, only because we know Him in Christ Jesus, our sympathising High Priest, it is comforting: It is as if He laid His silencing hand upon us, and the very touch gives us strength and peace.

Twenty-first Evening.

I send you a little three-fold cord.

1. His promise, Isaiah 66:13. "As one whom his mother comforteth, so will I comfort you."

2. His *present* fulfilment of it. Isaiah 51:12. "I, even I, am He that comforteth you."

3. Our realisation of it. Isaiah 12:1. "Thou comfortedst me." Oh, how sweet His words are!

Twenty-second Morning.

I have appropriated "Whom having not seen ye love"; also, "blessed are they that have not seen, and yet have believed," in a way of my own—having not *spiritually* "seen" Him—not being able to say, as so many can, "I have seen Jesus." The notion has been a great comfort to me. Oh, to see Him as He is! Truly one cannot imagine the joy. But "Thine eyes shall see the King in His beauty."

Twenty-Second Evening.

References to Psalm 91:1.

"Dwelleth." 1 John 4:13, 16. Psalm 90:1. Isaiah 32:18. Psalm 71:3.

"Secret place." Song of Solomon 1:4.

"Abide." Psalm 61:4.

"Shadow of" Hand. Isaiah 49:2; Isaiah 51:16.

"Shadow of" Wings. Psalm 57:1; Psalm 63:7.

"Shadow of" Tree. Song of Solomon 2:3; Hosea 14:7.

"Shadow of" Rock. Isaiah 32:2; Isaiah 25:4.

TWENTY-THIRD MORNING.

"OUR Father" is the Beautiful Gate of *this* temple. (The Lord's Prayer.) It is only if we can say "Our Father" that the rest will be *prayer*. In one sense God is Father of all—"Creation, preservation," etc. In another sense, *not*. "If God were your Father, ye would love Me." The former is not enough for life or death. The heart craves a personal, caring, loving, Father. If He is *not*, we have made ourselves orphans, we have sinned and wandered. Luke 15:11–32,—the return—*God* begins it. Think of the sovereignty of the call to return. Christ has taken away all the obstacles to our adoption. Galatians 4:4–7, "that we might receive the adoption of sons," which is "sealed" to us by the Holy Spirit.

TWENTY-THIRD EVENING.

I HAVE been enjoying the words in our chapter to-day, Genesis 2:22, "taken from," "made" (margin builded), and "*brought* her unto the man," with Ephesians 1:4, "chosen in." Ephesians 2:22, "Ye also are builded," and John 6:44, the drawing of the Father to Christ. It is very complete and beautiful.

TWENTY-FOURTH MORNING.

SOME of our subjects bear on glorifying God in service. Realise the responsibility of the *eye*—it is for *direct* praise—it is our means for *admiration* of God. I use the "eye" for this. Romans 1:20, *observant* of His works, which, if "sought out," are full of teaching for ourselves and others. There is food for gladness here—"rejoice in the operations of Thy hands." Psalm 92:14 (P. B.V.[1]), compare Psalm 104:31, "My Father made them all!" and "*this* God is our God." Let the "eye" be for the Lord while we have it, before it is "darkened," Ecclesiastes 12:3. "Why should I keep my eyelids closed," etc.—a practical hindrance to Christianity, Proverbs 6:4, Isaiah 14:16. When we pray "Thy will be done," we are praying for this—"I will ... that they may *behold* My glory."

[1] P. B.V. : Prayer Book Version

Twenty-fourth Evening.

"That they may *rest,* from their labours,"—this is the *last* "rest"; the *first* "rest" is Matthew 11:28.

First in Old Testament, "Jehovah," see Genesis 8:21 (margin, "savour of rest").

First in New Testament, "Son." Matthew 11:28.

Last in whole. "Spirit." Revelation 14:13.

Twenty-fifth Morning.

I did not think I was actually *sinning* in thus giving way to strong and hasty expressions. "Fools make a mock at sin"; and I see that I come under *that* condemnation, for I have written and spoken "savagely," *in fun, i.e.,* lightly, thoughtlessly, smilingly. God helping me, I hope this may be a turning point, and that I may not thus sin again with either lip or pen, which I wanted to consecrate, but which are yet so unconsecrated practically. Then the feeling has come—if I have been for years committing sin which I have not recognised as such, and which is consequently unconfessed and unforgiven, in how many more ways may I be sinning against God which I have never yet thought of! I may well pray, "Cleanse Thou me from my *secret* faults."

Twenty-fifth Evening.

"The companions hearken to Thy voice; cause me to hear it." Song of Solomon 8:13.

"The companions," compare John 3:29.

"Cause me to hear it," compare Song of Solomon 2:14. Answer, Acts 22:14.

"Cause me to hear Thy lovingkindness." Psalm 143:8.

"Cause me to understand." Job 6:24.

"Cause me to know the way." Psalm 143:8.

"Cause Thy face to shine." Daniel 9:17.

Twenty-sixth Morning.

I should like to send you a text which I have enjoyed dwelling on, "I will purely purge away thy dross, and take away all thy tin." Isaiah 1:25. The *tin* seems to me so significant, it is not only the dross which shall be purged, away, but the *tin* too, *i.e.*, that which may glitter almost like silver, and yet it is not really so, the *seemingly* fair in us as well as the manifestly evil, so that we may become only and entirely that pure metal which may reflect the Refiner's image and bear His superscription.

Twenty-sixth Evening.

References to Exodus 29:4–9. (Fulfilment of this chapter in Leviticus 8).

Exodus 29:4. "Thou shalt bring." 1 Peter 3:18.

Exodus 29:4. "Wash them with water." Ephesians 5:26; John 13:10.

Exodus 29:6. "Put the mitre and holy crown." Revelation 1:5, 6 (kings and priests).

Exodus 29:7. "Anoint." Isaiah 61:1, 3; Psalm 92:10.

Exodus 29:8. "Bring his sons." Hebrews 2:10.

Exodus 29:8. "Put coats on them." Isaiah 61:10.

Exodus 29:9. "Gird them with girdles, Aaron *and* his sons."

Girded with {
"Strength." Psalm 18:32, 39.
"Gladness." Psalm 30:11.
"Fine Linen." Ezekiel 16:10.
"Truth." Ephesians 6:14.
} Christ. Isaiah 11:5. Christ. John 13:4. Christ. c.t. Rev. 1:13. Christ. Isaiah 45:5.

Twenty-seventh Morning.

I HAVE been thinking it all over again and again, and I would not have been without all this suffering. It has been a happy time, and I have learned a great deal. It is well to realise eternity—eternity—Heaven or Hell—no middle state. And then the thought, What is Heaven? What is Hell? Oh the contrast! If through grace—grace only—we escape the one and enter the other, how "light" will all these afflictions seem!

Twenty-seventh Evening.

"YE see your calling." 1 Corinthians 1:26; 1 Thessalonians 5:24.

1. "Called unto the grace of Christ." Galatians 1:6.
2. "Called unto liberty." Galatians 5:13.
3. "Called to inherit a blessing." 1 Peter 3:9.
4. "Called unto the fellowship of His Son." 1 Corinthians 1:9.
5. "Called to patient endurance." 1 Peter 2:21.
6. "Called unto holiness." 1 Thessalonians 4:7.
7. "Called to be saints." Romans 1:6; 1 Corinthians 1:2.
8. "Called to glory and virtue." 2 Peter 1:3.
9. "Called to the obtaining of the glory of our Lord Jesus Christ." 2 Thessalonians 2:14.
10. "Called unto His kingdom and glory." 1 Thessalonians 2:12.
11. "Called unto the peace of God." Colossians 3:15.
12. "Called unto His eternal glory." 1 Peter 5:10.

Twenty-eighth Morning.

WHAT could one do without Him in this lonely world of shadows? Well, we do not *need* to fancy it, for He will not let us do without Him. And I wonder whether we may not wonderingly and reverently say, "neither can He do without us!" I think so. His people are so entwined with His heart that it must be so, for, "the Lord's portion is His people."

Twenty-eighth Evening.

CHRIST SAYS:—
Luke 7:40. "I have to say," etc.
John 16:12. "I have," etc.
John 6:63. "The words," etc.
Isaiah 50:4. "The Lord," etc.
Hosea 2:14. "I will speak," etc.
Matthew 10:27. "What I tell," etc.
Isaiah 52:6. "They shall," etc.
HIS PEOPLE SAY:—
Luke 7:40. "Master," etc.
1 Samuel 3:10. "Speak," etc.
Habakkuk 2:1. "I will watch," etc.
Psalm 85:8. "I will hear," etc.
Psalm 35:3. "Say," etc.
Daniel 10:19. "When He," etc.
Job 13:22. "Then call," etc.

Twenty-ninth Morning.

I AM very sorry that the waves of this troublesome world should be surging round you. Still, how often is good brought out of evil, even as to temporal things ... The undisturbed course which your love would tenderly choose might be the very worst thing for that spiritual life which only a Heavenly Father can water and develop by His own perfectly wise trainings. Don't you think that He is really just as able to keep that which you have committed to Him, as your own soul? Only it often requires greater strength of faith to trust Him for a very dear one, than to trust

Him for one's self. This sort of trial would not be sent if your faith were not very precious in His sight.

Twenty-ninth Evening.

With Christ.
"Crucified." Galatians 2:20.
"Dead." Romans 6:8.
"Buried." Romans 6:4.
"Quickened." Colossians 2:13.
"Raised." Ephesians 2:6.
"In Heavenly places." Ephesians 2:6.
"Live." 2 Corinthians 13:14.

Thirtieth Morning.

He heareth prayer, and it may be that He is preparing answers which will make you praise and wonder. See how fully He has answered all your prayers for guidance as to your way; this has been so fully given that it may well encourage you for the other. But He is *Sovereign*, and will have us "be still, and know that I am God," and it may be just that His sovereignty may stand out in its awful glory before us that He sometimes "waits to be gracious." Still, even if He waits, it is "to be gracious," of that we may rest assured, for He says "therefore."

Thirtieth Evening.

"A more excellent name." Hebrews 1:4.
"And this is His name, whereby He shall be called." Isaiah 9:6.
"Wonderful," ⎫
             ⎬ compare Isaiah 25:1.
"Counsellor," ⎭
"The mighty God." Titus 2:13. Revelation 1:8. John 5:23. 1 Timothy 3:16. John 10:30. Jeremiah 32:18, 19. John 1:1. Isaiah 10:21.
"Everlasting Father." Hebrews 2:10. John 14:18 (margin). Isaiah 44:3.

Thirty-first Morning.

I was thinking of faith being "gold." For I think the antithesis in 1 Peter 1:7 lies in the words "that perisheth." So is *faith* the imperishable gold of Revelation 3:18? And is it not *gold,* because gold procures everything? "Whatsoever ye shall ask, *believing,* ye shall receive." Yet of Him only is the gold obtained,—"Buy of Me." It is fanciful, perhaps, but it bears carrying out further: gold is increased by trading with it, so increase of faith, I think, by exercise of what we have, rather than by direct and sudden additional gifts of it.

Thirty-first Evening.

"That ye may stand perfect and complete." Colossians 4:12.
"In grace." Romans 5:2; 1 Peter 5:12.
"In liberty." Galatians 5:1.
"In will of God." Colossians 4:12.
"In one spirit." Philippians 1:27.
"In the Lord." Philippians 4:1.
"By faith." Romans 11:20; 2 Corinthians 1:24.
"Before me." 1 Kings 10:8; Jeremiah 15:19.
"Upon rock." Exodus 33:21.
"Up and bless." Nehemiah 9:5.
"Against wiles." Ephesians 6:11, 13.
"At His right hand." Psalm 45:9.

Precious things from the heavenly store,
Filling thy casket more and more;
Golden love in divinest chain,
That can never be untwined again;
Silvery carols of joy that swell
Sweetest of all in the heart's lone cell;
Pearls of peace that were sought for thee
In the terrible depths of a fiery sea;
Diamond promises sparkling bright,
Flashing in farthest reaching light.

*   *   *   *   *

Brought to thee in the far-off land,
Brought to thee by His own dear hand.
Promises held out by Christ for thee,
Peace as a river flowing free,
Joy that in His own joy must live,
And love that Infinite Love can give.

*   *   *   *   *

OH what shining revelation of His treasures God hath given!
Precious things of grace and glory, precious things of earth and heaven.
Holy Spirit, now unlock them with Thy mighty golden key,
Royal jewels of the kingdom let us now adoring see!

*   *   *   *   *

Who shall paint the flash of splendour from the opened casket bright,
When His precious lovingkindness beams upon the quickened sight!
Priceless jewel ever gleaming with imperishable ray,
God will never take it from us, though the mountains pass away.

From " UNDER HIS SHADOW."

www.ingramcontent.com/pod-product-compliance
Lightning Source LLC
Chambersburg PA
CBHW071523040426
42452CB00008B/863

9 7 8 1 9 3 7 2 3 6 1 9 9